COLUMBIA COLLEGE CHICAGO

3 2711 00215 7141

DATE DUE

NOV 0 8 2012

Death of the Moguls

TMI TECHNIQUES of the MOVING IMAGE

Volumes in the Techniques of the Moving Image series explore the relationship between what we see onscreen and the technical achievements undertaken in filmmaking to make this possible. Books explore some defined aspect of cinema—work from a particular era, work in a particular genre, work by a particular filmmaker or team, work from a particular studio, or work on a particular theme—in light of some technique and/or technical achievement, such as cinematography, direction, acting, lighting, costuming, set design, legal arrangements, agenting, scripting, sound design and recording, and sound or picture editing. Historical and social backgrounds contextualize the subject of each volume.

Murray Pomerance
Series Editor

Wheeler Winston Dixon, *Death of the Moguls: The End of Classical Hollywood*

Joshua Yumibe, *Moving Color: Early Film, Mass Culture, Modernism*

Columbia College Library
600 South Michigan
Chicago, IL 60605

Death of the Moguls

The End of Classical Hollywood

WHEELER WINSTON DIXON

RUTGERS UNIVERSITY PRESS

NEW BRUNSWICK, NEW JERSEY, AND LONDON

Library of Congress Cataloging-in-Publication Data

Dixon, Wheeler W., 1950–
    Death of the moguls : the end of classical Hollywood / Wheeler Winston Dixon.
       p. cm. — (Techniques of the moving image)
    Includes bibliographical references and index.
    ISBN 978–0–8135–5376–4 (hardcover : alk. paper) — ISBN 978–0–8135–5377–1
(pbk. : alk. paper) — ISBN 978–0–8135–5378–8 (e-book)
    1. Motion picture studios—California—Los Angeles—History—20th century.
    2. Motion picture industry—California—Los Angeles—History—20th century.
    3. Motion pictures—California—Los Angeles—History—20th century.
    4. Hollywood (Los Angeles, Calif.)—History—20th century.   I. Title.
    PN1993.5.U65D59   2012
    384'.80979494—dc23
                                                                    2011046940

A British Cataloging-in-Publication record for this book is available from the British
Library.

Copyright © 2012 by Wheeler Winston Dixon

All rights reserved

No part of this book may be reproduced or utilized in any form or by any means,
electronic or mechanical, or by any information storage and retrieval system, without
written permission from the publisher. Please contact Rutgers University Press,
106 Somerset Street, New Brunswick, NJ 08901. The only exception to this
prohibition is "fair use" as defined by U.S. copyright law.

Visit our website: http://rutgerspress.rutgers.edu

Manufactured in the United States of America

For Gwendolyn

"There is only one word to describe Hollywood—fear."
—Grace Metalious

Contents

Acknowledgments

My thanks to Leslie Mitchner for initiating this project; to Dana Miller, for her excellent typing of my handwritten manuscript; to Mikita Brottman, David Sterritt, Patrice Petro, Lucy Fischer, Frank Tomasulo, Christopher Sharrett, Valérie Orlando, and many other colleagues for their advice and counsel; to Eric Schramm, for his superb job in editing the book; and of course to Gwendolyn Foster, who remains my best advisor and critic. The author also wishes to extend special thanks to Richard Graham, reference librarian at Love Library, the University of Nebraska, Lincoln, for his unstinting research assistance, and to Barry Keith Grant and Murray Pomerance for their useful comments on various drafts of this manuscript. Brief portions of chapter 6 first appeared as part of the article "Fast Worker: The Films of Sam Newfield," in *Senses of Cinema*; my thanks to Rolando Caputo, editor, for permission to reprint these materials here. This text also incorporates brief sections of *A Short History of Film* by Wheeler Winston Dixon and Gwendolyn Audrey Foster, reprinted through the courtesy of Rutgers University Press. The photos in this volume appear through the courtesy of the Jerry Ohlinger Archives; all box office figures come from the Box Office Mojo website.

Death of the Moguls

Prologue

Are you planning to visit Los Angeles in the near future? Then you should take a Hollywood studio tour. At Paramount, located at 5555 Melrose Avenue in Hollywood, you get a two-hour walk-through confined mostly to the exterior of various soundstages, as well as a stop at Lucy Park, a small section of the studio lot that at one time belonged to Desilu Studios, which in turn bought out most of the old RKO Radio Studio facilities. You'll probably also see some Foley artists plodding through reels of sound effects for forthcoming films and television shows; the famous "Blue Sky" cyclorama, which has been used as a backdrop for Leonard Nimoy's *Star Trek IV: The Voyage Home* (1986) and Cecil B. DeMille's *The Ten Commandments* (1956); the basement apartment shared by the lead characters of television's *Laverne and Shirley* (1976–1983); and some exterior locations used in the series *Seinfeld* (1989–1998). But the back lot itself is almost entirely gone; it's nothing like Warner Bros. or Universal, where faux New York City streets, European villages, and dusty western cow towns still exist side by side, ready for instantaneous use.

Sony Pictures, at 10202 West Washington Boulevard, the home of MGM for nearly a century, also offers a walking tour; here, too, as on the Paramount tour, ghosts predominate. The major phantom, of course, is MGM itself; while Sony may now own the studio facilities, it was MGM's home base from the studio's inception until 1990, and yet most of the contemporary tour focuses on Columbia's history. Columbia, originally located at 1438 North Gower Street, was one of the most down-at-the-heels studios in Hollywood until Harry Cohn's ruthlessly astute management propelled it into the majors with Frank Capra's *It Happened One Night* (1934). The film was originally designed as a "punishment picture" for Clark Gable, on loan from MGM in order to force him to accept studio dictates. Instead, the tactic backfired, Gable became a major star, and he returned to MGM in glory rather than as a chastened prodigal son.

But since the former MGM is now the home of Sony/Columbia/TriStar, you'll get a glimpse of the Thalberg Building, named after the "boy wonder" who ran MGM in the early 1930s and married star Norma Shearer. His reign ended with his untimely death at age thirty-seven in 1936, somewhat to studio head Louis B. Mayer's unspoken satisfaction, given that Thalberg was becoming too powerful and gradually eclipsing the patriarchal mogul. So you'll get a bit of MGM history, but not too much. The past is the past, and MGM moved out long ago—well, twelve years ago at this writing—and with all eyes fixed firmly on the present, who has time for history?

Universal Studios, on the other hand, at 100 Universal City Plaza, is a mini-empire unto itself, with its own post office and zip code. It functions not only as a working film studio but also as a "destination" amusement park. Along with Warner Bros., it is one of the two surviving studios to boast an extensive back lot, with standing sets going all the way back to the early 1930s. When I first visited Universal in 1960, the studio had long given up the idea of studio tours and wouldn't catch on to the idea of reviving them for additional profit, much less adding an amusement park to its facilities, for several more years. Instead, the Universal back lot tour was part of a Grey Line bus tour that roamed over all of Hollywood, spending the early afternoon at Universal, where we got to see a section of a TV western being shot.

The whole visit was low key, no pressure, and we were one of only two or three tour groups that day, comprising about sixty visitors in all.

So, to a degree, we were a novelty to the crew, a moment's distraction from a hard day's work. Dismounting from the bus, we were allowed to wander around the various exterior sets at will, snapping pictures, exchanging anecdotes, while the bus driver offered us an abbreviated history of Universal's output. Although we were no doubt a nuisance, the crews and stars we met tolerated us with a friendly diffidence, and I got to chat with an old grip who had been working there since the 1940s. Then, in a relaxed fashion, we got back on the tour bus, waved goodbye, and set off to see the Hollywood Bowl.

It was, of course, too good to last. By 1965, Universal had started running trams through the back lot in a rigidly organized forty-five-minute tour jammed with passengers, with almost no stops to explore the back lot. Today the trams also feature small video screens, as on airplanes, running a sanitized history of the studio with Ron Howard as a sort of host for a mélange of clips highlighting Universal's past. There's also, of course, plenty of time to purchase souvenirs in the gift shop. The tour isn't cheap; it costs $69 per person and doesn't include a lot of frills found on the $239 "VIP Tour," which, as described by online travel writer Gary Wayne, gives the visitor a more "immersive" studio experience, including

a behind-the-scenes guided tour with access to previously "off-limits" areas of the studio. The tours are limited to no more than 15 people at a time (aboard private trolleys and on foot), and include such extra perks as a continental breakfast at their VIP Lounge and tours of the studio's production areas. VIP guests get to visit sound stage sets from current TV productions such as *Desperate Housewives* [2004–2011], where *Leave It to Beaver* [1957–1963] was shot a half-century ago, as well as the studio's huge prop department, the sound department, a house built especially to accommodate cameras for interior shots, etc. The six-hour tour gives guests the chance to see how sets are built, how lighting is designed, how sound is added after filming, etc. Perhaps best of all, unlike the standard Universal tour, where guests are stuck on the giant

tram for the whole tour, the *VIP* tour allows guests to get off their small
trolley and walk among the sets, such as *War of the Worlds* [2005] and
Psycho [1960], and along the streets where movies such as *Back to the
Future* [1985], *Spartacus* [1960], and *Frankenstein* [1931] were filmed. . . .
Back in the theme park area, the VIP tour also gives you escorted front
of the line privileges, that lets you go straight to the head of the line
for all of the park's rides (such as *Jurassic Park* [based on the 1993 film]
and the *Mummy* roller coaster [based on the 1999 film]), and gives you
reserved seating at all the shows such as *Waterworld* [based on the 1995
film] and *Terminator 2: 3-D* ([based on the 1991 film *Terminator 2:
Judgment Day*] including behind-stage meet & greet with the shows'
performers). You also get unlimited food service at the park's cafes.
They even let you see an Oscar statuette up-close.

The real money spinner is Universal's City Walk, a tacky hodgepodge of
restaurants and souvenir shops to which one is afforded "free" admission
(aside from valet parking), where overpriced memorabilia and greasy
fast food combine to create an ersatz Coney Island atmosphere without
the charm.

You'll look in vain for a bookstore or DVD shop on the City Walk;
that's just outdated technology, and all that matters here is the present and
whatever cash one can wring out of it. There is, however, a comic book
store, where one can buy graphic novels of soon-to-be Universal franchise
releases, and a clothing store featuring a Universal logo windbreaker for
$59.95 that can't be washed by hand or machine or even dry cleaned; the
only thing one can do is "sponge dry" it from time to time, and then very
carefully. It's all appearance; utility is secondary. But the *Psycho* house is
still standing; you can always check that out for a photo op and get your
picture taken where Tony Perkins once acted out a homicidal fantasy.

At Warner Bros., they also have a VIP tour, which takes two hours and
covers much of the studio grounds, but again, if you'd like a more detailed
look at the facilities, the $249 Deluxe Tour is indicated. During six hours

of "insider" reconnaissance you actually get to pose with a real Academy Award in your hand (after donning protective white gloves), eat lunch in the Warner Bros. executive dining room, and visit the sets of the various sitcoms that now occupy the vast majority of the soundstages. They still have the set for the coffee shop in the television series *Friends* (1994–2004) in mothballs, and you can take turns posing with your significant other on the large sofa that dominates the cramped soundstage.

While the soundstages all carry plaques proudly listing the many classic films shot there, the tour guides are much more interested in telling you about Chuck Lorre's new sitcom *Mike and Molly* (2010–present) and taking you for a tour of the standing set; you also get to see the rather rundown production offices of the various independent production companies headquartered on the lot (such as Clint Eastwood's Malpaso Productions); the block of offices is often used as an exterior set for a scene requiring a rundown hotel. While references abound in the tour guide's patter to Bogart, Davis, and other luminaries of Warners' golden age, you'll see almost nothing of them in terms of memorabilia, and the studio museum (the last stop on the tour) is almost exclusively devoted (two whole floors worth) to *Harry Potter* costumes, props, and scripts.

If you look hard enough, you can find a few remnants of the past that still exist; the corner wall where James Cagney was nearly shot down (by real bullets) in William Wellman's *The Public Enemy* (1931) still stands, as well as the studio's New York street, constructed in 1930. The bulk of back lot production today is confined to television shows and commercials; on the day I visited Warner Bros. in the summer of 2011, an Old Navy ad was being shot on one of the ersatz city streets, which rent (apart from camera equipment, lights, actors, and technicians) for $10,000 a day.

The overwhelming impression I came away with was a sense of willfully manufactured nostalgia; this was a facility that belonged to the past, trying to eke out a living in the digital twenty-first century, where physical props and locations have been replaced by green screen/CGI technology. Despite all the visitors tromping through, one got the distinct feeling that both Universal and Warners were hanging on to their respective facilities by the skin of their collective teeth, although in Universal's case the move toward a Disneyfied theme park approach seems to have been paying off handsomely. The days when either of these studios boasted a roster of actors, writers, and directors ready at a moment's notice to undertake a production are long gone; now, "packages," put together by agents, stars, producers, and/or directors, or their representatives, constitute the main source of theatrical films. The studios are merely production facilities for hire, in addition to offering financing, distribution, and back lot facilities to those who still wish to work within the studio system.

There are other studio locations one can visit; Melody Ranch, for example, in Newhall, California, where most of Gene Autry's singing westerns were shot, along with scenes from John Ford's *Stagecoach* (1939) and Fred Zinnemann's *High Noon* (1952), still exists, as it has since 1915, and is now open to the public; Monogram Studios, one of the industry's smallest operations in the 1940s, often shot western programmers here as well. As with the other studios, some contemporary productions still use Melody Ranch for filming. But the giant Hollywood studios today are primarily a repository of merchandisable memories, where an image of the "glamorous past" can be conjured up at a moment's notice ("Imagine Humphrey Bogart walking up and down this studio street between takes of *Casablanca* [1942]," our Warner Bros. tour guide encouraged us, or "Here's where the Yellow Brick Road from *The Wizard of Oz* [1939] used to be" at MGM, only it's not there anymore either), to no real effect. The past is still dead.

The reminiscences are for the most part forced, synthetic, and largely prepackaged; at Warners, the most revealing exhibits I found were tucked away in the studio museum's back corner ("photography strictly prohibited"), our last stop on the tour, particularly some rather blunt memos documenting Jack Warner's displeasure with Arthur Penn's *Bonnie and Clyde* (1967) in no uncertain terms, addressed to the film's star, Warren Beatty. "Who wants to see the rise and fall of a couple of rats?" Warner queried in one note, apparently forgetting that *The Public Enemy* and Mervyn LeRoy's *Little Caesar* (1931) helped to put the studio on the map with just such a formula. Also intriguing was a memo regarding editor Dede Allen's participation in the project. Beatty insisted on using her, but at $650 a week she was seen as too expensive—certainly a reliable studio cutter could handle the project. Of course, Beatty prevailed over Warner on that decision, but with *Bonnie and Clyde*, as well as Alfred Hitchcock's *Psycho* (1960), Mike Nichols's *Who's Afraid of Virginia Woolf?* (1966), and other productions of that era, one could see the hold of the old moguls on the filmmaking process slipping.

I mentioned this to our tour guide, who smiled and used the opportunity to launch into yet another oft-repeated piece of studio lore. Jack Warner, it seems, used to "settle" arguments by pointing to the huge water tower that still dominates the studio lot, emblazoned with the WB logo, and demanding, "What do you think that stands for?" But when he tried this tactic on the star of *Bonnie and Clyde*, all he got was the laconic response "Warren Beatty." No love was lost between these two men; in an earlier era, Jack Warner would have simply fired him, or put him on unpaid suspension for an indefinite period. Now, that power was gone. Warner needed Beatty, and both Beatty and Warner knew it. The age of the great studio bosses was a thing of the past.

That said, there is a great deal of legitimate disputation as to exactly when the studio era ended; some say the 1970s, when the conglomerates began to take hold; some say the 1950s, when television first began to transform the studio landscape. But I would argue that what prefigured the end of the classical studio era was the death of the men—and they were all men—who ran the various production companies. All but Darryl F. Zanuck were Jewish, and they rose, for the most part, from very humble origins. The uncouth Harry Cohn, better known as "White Fang" or "King Cohn" at Columbia; Louis B. Mayer, purveyor of small-town pieties at MGM; Darryl F. Zanuck, absolute ruler of 20th Century Fox; David O. Selznick of Selznick International Pictures, or SIP; Jack Warner, ruthless overlord of the studio that bore his name; "Uncle" Carl Laemmle at Universal; Adolph Zukor at Paramount. RKO Radio, as we will see, is a special case and never really had one boss. The studio went through quite a number of regime shifts; perhaps this is one of the reasons the studio ceased production in 1957, leaving only a holding company behind.

These larger-than-life figures—the movie moguls—dominated the cinematic marketplace in the 1930s through the 1950s and early 1960s, and in their story one can find the rise and fall of a series of dynasties, based on fear, artifice, marketing, and absolute ruthlessness. More than that, what united these men was a feeling of absolute immortality; none of them could conceive of a world without them in it, and none of them really cared, I think, what would happen after they were gone. Deep down, of course, they were acutely aware of their mortality; like the pharaohs, fear of death was one of the reasons the moguls were so determined to leave something tangible behind as evidence of their existence. Their respective studios were monuments to their industry and stamina; when they died, the company would die with them—or at least it wouldn't be the same company. Warner Bros. without Jack Warner? In name only. Columbia without Harry Cohn? Just a corporate holdover. What would 20th Century Fox be without Darryl F. Zanuck? A business for lawyers and pencil pushers. Without the moguls, the real essence of their studios would die.

Some, like Adolph Zukor, spoke of company loyalty, but in the last analysis, none could really imagine a world in which they didn't play an important part. Their ends were varied: some sold out and had a few years of retirement; others died in harness; some were fired by their former protégés or squeezed out by the financial arms of their companies. But in all cases, their rule, during the classical studio era, was absolute and utterly dictatorial; these men controlled their empire with ruthlessness, cunning, and determination. It is their story that I tell in this volume. It is the story of Hollywood's golden era, the story of a world that existed only so long as the need for its services and physical production facilities existed; and when it collapsed it left but a corporate shell behind.

I start off with a brief chapter that introduces the studios and the moguls just before the collapse. Then I discuss how the studio bosses dealt with their fading empire in the era of television and the end of the conventional studio assembly line, in which producers had rosters of directors, writers, actors, and others under their command and could put together films quickly and cheaply. The demise of the assembly line led to the shift to today's reliance on "packaged" feature films. As Ethan Mordden succinctly put it,

> By about 1965, the studio system . . . was history. Aside from the major economic and social factors, a crisis of leadership had developed. The generation that succeeded the Golden Age moguls lacked the experience and instincts that guided the lots in the good old days. Not only was there no new Thalberg, no Zanuck, no Selznick, there was scarcely even a new Carl Laemmle. Once, a studio was a place governed by a budget set by a mogul who believed he could market certain kinds of stars who were presented by a staff of experts who held certain social, artistic, and political aperçus in common. As Adolph Zukor, the founder of [Paramount] looked on, the studio[s] dwindled into . . . firm[s] governed by various crass jerks who [held] nothing in common but a contempt for everything but money. (370)

"Crass jerks" may be putting it rather bluntly, but it's obvious that in Hollywood today, only the bottom line rules. Of course, one could just as easily argue that it was ever so. And yet, before movies were made by committees and cost so much that a single high-profile flop could bankrupt a studio (as happened with Michael Cimino's *Heaven's Gate* [1980], which sent United Artists into a financial tailspin), the average "A" feature film, as late as the 1970s, cost about $1–7 million to make, and about as much more for prints and advertising. Thus, one could afford to take chances, to produce an occasional loss leader, as Irving Thalberg urged during his meteoric tenure at MGM, simply to enhance the studio's image. Then, too, without the splintering of the marketplace effected by streaming video, video on demand, DVDs, cell phone videos, and other distribution methods (especially Netflix, Amazon, and the ubiquitous Red Box DVD machines that dispense "top 40" hits at your local mall), each film produced had only one primary marketplace: theatrical distribution. Every film had to play in a theater to make its money back.

Thus, there was a certain egalitarianism inherent in classical studio era film production; the lowest "B" could theoretically compete with the most prestigious "A" film for the public's affections and dollars, and, provided that the smaller film was sold by the studio on a percentage basis rather than a flat rental fee, even a modest film could potentially become an unexpected hit if properly marketed. But now, only the big-budget films make it into the multiplexes; the rest open only in "selected cities" (New York, Los Angeles, and a few other large metropolitan markets), or wind up going straight to DVD or streaming video.

Without a theatrical release, for all intents and purposes movies become invisible to the general public; only genre fans and film buffs will seek these smaller films out and take the time to see them. So where once smaller films occupied the numerous soundstages at the majors and minors in Hollywood, now sitcoms that cost $2–3 million *an episode* and hour-long dramas that cost much more predominate. The plaques on the studio walls commemorating past glories are thus ironic reminders of an era in which, despite almost tyrannical control from the top down, many of the greatest films were produced by cadres of dedicated men and women who labored in the dream factories for minimal pay, and even less glory.

It was a tough system, but in the end individual decisions, bolstered by audience research and test marketing, along with a desire to make films of lasting value, drove the rulers of the studios to create films that both entertained and enlightened. As this book opens, however, that era is coming to an end. This is the story of the decline, fall, and ultimate collapse of the studio system, a systemic failure so catastrophic that in the end only fragments of the majors were left, to be shuffled from one conglomerate to another. Their vast libraries of films were cast off in one direction while their facilities were pressed into service for new owners. This was the case with MGM; Ted Turner bought the MGM film library for television use and then sold off the studio itself through a series of complex negotiations (see Dixon and Foster 378–79), so that all that's left of the former MGM Studios are some repurposed buildings and a few tattered mementos. When the moguls of the old Hollywood studio system died, in the 1950s and 1960s, no one came along to take their place, because their kingdom itself had vanished.

CHAPTER 1

The Postwar Collapse

In 1946, the movies—as an industry—had their biggest year, reflecting Americans' desire for escapism from the events just concluded. The war had been a long one, truly global and on a scale hitherto unimaginable, with more than sixty million deaths. The development of the atomic bomb and its use on Hiroshima and Nagasaki had brought the war to a brutal end the year before; now, for the first time in history, humankind could destroy an entire city with the push of a button. With the end of the war in Europe came revelations of the German concentration camps, leading to the Nuremburg tribunals. Our former ally, the Soviet Union, was in the midst of enslaving Eastern Europe; no one, it seemed, could be trusted. During the war, a nonstop succession of flag-waving war films and escapist musicals and comedies had kept the public entertained during the long, wearying hours of the day. Now, everyone wanted to forget the war and get on with their lives.

Women, newly accustomed to being part of the workforce in defense plants and disinclined to return to kitchen duty, rebelled against a resumption of prewar patriarchal values. Men, confused by this new threat to their familial dominion, sought escape at the movies, in pool halls, in sports venues, and in VFW lodges as divorce rates reached record levels. The old order had been turned upside down, and things would never be the same in the little white house with the picket fence. As a female factory worker in one World War II poster had declared, "Now I can buy the things I love," brandishing a paycheck to prove her point. The tagline underscores this new order of things, as if to bluntly state, "Here's my passport to independence." Indeed: Why should women give this up just because their husbands had returned? Who needed husbands, anyway, or kids, or the home with the gingham curtains and the picture-perfect backyard? "Independence" was the new slogan, and it seemed there was no going back.

Returning veterans were blindsided by these changes. During the war, pin-up images of stars like Betty Grable had circulated on the battlefront as totemic objects of desire—"What we're fighting for"—alternating with pictures of faithful wives and children waiting at home: the classic "madonna/whore" paradigm. Sex, lust, and domesticity collided in these images, designed to both reassure and excite soldiers at the front. But as one woman noted, "When my husband finally came home we discovered we were two different people, so much had happened in those years apart. . . . After a while we settled to some sort of married life, but there were times I thought that if there was a hell on earth, I was living it" (qtd. in Costello 262–63).

Thus, audiences for movies had changed, the family structure had changed, and nothing was as it seemed. Film noir rose in popularity as a genre, reflecting the uncertainties of the era. The old Universal horror films no longer struck terror into the hearts of audiences; now, the fear was all around us. The atomic bomb, a surprise development at the end of the war, made life seem even more transient and quixotic; if a city could nearly be wiped off the map with a single bomb, how could anything be certain? The Andy Hardy films churned out by MGM seemed utterly out of place, almost ridiculously so; how could anyone believe in the small-town verities of the mythical city of Carvel when society itself was in such flux?

Just as men didn't foresee the shifts in social norms, so, too, the movie moguls didn't anticipate the rise of the unions within the studio system, a development they did everything they could to stop. The issue went back to labor disputes at the Disney studio in 1941. Walt Disney himself was bitterly opposed to unionization of his studio, portraying himself as a sort of benevolent father figure who was perfectly capable of equitably running the Disney lot without outside interference. The Cartoonists Guild, however, spearheaded by Disney animator Art Babbitt, brought about an end to Disney's unquestioned domain. Herb Sorrell had been attempting to organize the studio's animators since the late 1930s, and in January 1941 he met with Roy and Walt Disney to demand the unionization of Disney's animators, most of whom had signed a card requesting Guild representation for their services (Eliot 138). Animators were furious at the low pay and uncertain working conditions at the studio, as union representative George Bodle quickly found out: "There was just no negotiating with them. I had to deal mostly with Roy, because Walt simply refused to see me, who just told me what they [the studio] wanted, and that was it. . . . [Inkers and painters] were making $18.50 a week [and could] get fired at Walt's discretion, without reason or explanation" (Eliot 140).

During the week of May 17, 1941, the National Labor Relations Board shot down the legality of Disney's proposed "in house union," the Animator's Federation, but Disney responded by simply renaming the federation the American Society of Screen Cartoonists, which was also eventually ruled illegal (Eliot 140). Disney remained opposed to any real attempt at unionizing—just as Walmart, now America's largest single employer, does today—and fired Art Babbitt and several others who pressed for Guild recognition. Events then moved rapidly. On May 27, Richard Storey, a representative of Kidder, Peabody—underwriters of the Disney company's public stock offering—and Joseph Rosenberg of the Bank of America, one of the studio's main supply lines of production capital, met with Disney in an all-night, all-out effort to avoid a strike and recognize the Guild, but even these even-handed, pragmatic individuals could not sway Disney from his course.

The next day, May 28, 1941, Sorrell called the studio workers out on strike, an action that Disney predicted would soon backfire (Eliot 141–42). But it didn't. The strikers' resolve only strengthened in the coming days and weeks, despite a plethora of diversionary and divisive tactics from Disney. On July 2, Walt Disney took out a full-page ad in *Variety* offering his version of a settlement, but it was too little, too late. Public sentiment was moving, amazingly, against Disney, and by mid-July even the mainstream Technicolor Corporation sided with the strikers, refusing to process any film from the studio until the Guild was legitimized (Eliot 147). Disney remained intransigent.

Seeing the writing on the wall, however, his more practical brother Roy arranged for Walt to travel to South America as an "ambassador of good will" for the United States so that Roy and studio negotiator Gunther Lessing could hammer out an agreement with the Guild. Private, public, and business sentiment was now firmly with the strikers, and even that bastion of capitalism, Nelson Rockefeller, took a stand, advising Roy Disney by phone that capitulation was inevitable; on September 9, 1941, Roy reluctantly agreed to binding arbitration, to recognize the Cartoonists Guild, to rehire all employees fired because of union work, to offer better pay, severance guarantees, paid vacations, and a "closed shop," and to prevent freelancers from poaching studio jobs (Eliot 150). Walt Disney, predictably, was furious, and wrote an open letter that he paid to be published in numerous newspapers, stating, among other things, that "to me, the entire [strike] situation is a catastrophe. . . . I am convinced that this entire mess was Communistically inspired and led. . . . I am thoroughly disgusted and would gladly quit and establish myself in another business. . . . I have a case of the D.D.s—disillusionment and discouragement" (Eliot 151).

The episode served as a wakeup call to the industry as a whole, on both sides of the fence. Studio bosses saw their power, hitherto unquestioned, now in jeopardy; studio workers saw that they would have to fight for whatever rights they felt they deserved, and that management would use all possible means—up to and including strong-arm tactics—to prevent all-out unionization from happening. All this happened before December 7, 1941, and the United States' entry into World War II, meaning that management/worker hostilities were temporarily put aside for the duration of the war.

During the war, a "no strike" pledge was in effect at the studios, ensuring an all-out effort to achieve victory, but in 1944 the Motion Picture Alliance for the Preservation of American Ideals sprang up, an ultra-right organization dedicated to stamping out leftist influence within the studio system (Davis 343). When Franklin Delano Roosevelt died in April 1945, the right and left began to battle each other hammer and tongs for control of the system. Labor organizer Herb Sorrell coordinated a strike of the members of Hollywood's craft unions, starting with Warner Bros. on October 5, 1949, which led to violence on the picket line from both sheriff's deputies and the strikers themselves.

Actor Rosemary De Camp was working at Warner Bros. during the strike and later recalled that "you went in with an armed guard in the car in the morning, about six o'clock. It was rather grim to look out and see those guys [the LAPD strike squad] with rifles" (Davis 343). The Warner Bros. studio was an excellent target for Sorrell's efforts, as both Harry and Jack Warner saw the coming of the unions—or any threat to their complete dominion of the lot—as absolutely intolerable. Pickets were also seen at MGM, and at RKO Radio the studio employees simply stayed inside the lot rather than coping with getting in and out of the grounds each day. As a whole, the studios decided they would have to break the unions no matter what and dug in their heels for a protracted fight (Davis 344).

Labor issues were now merging with Cold War politics. On October 20, 1947, the House Un-American Activities Committee (HUAC) opened the first public hearing into supposed communist influence or infiltration in the motion picture industry. The first "friendly witnesses" included Walt Disney, Jack Warner, actors Robert Taylor, Gary Cooper, and Adolphe Menjou, director Leo McCarey (who would go on to direct the hysterical anticommunist screed *My Son John* in 1952), and writer Ayn Rand

(Vaughn 76). Disney, for his part, identified Sorrell as a communist and averred that the 1941 strike was a direct result of communist infiltration into the industry:

> I believe it is an Un-American thing. The thing that I resent the most is that they are able to get into these unions, take them over, and represent to the world that a group of people that are in my plant, that I know are good, 100-percent Americans, are trapped by this group. . . . I feel that they really ought to be smoked out and shown up for what they are, so that all of the good, free causes in this country, all the liberalisms that really are American, can go on without the taint of Communism. (Vaughn 85)

So much for organized labor. When Disney spoke, he shaped public perceptions; after all, the Disney organization was a "family studio," and the public and press followed his early lead. The unions were now aligned in the public mind with communism, and the social landscape had changed a great deal since 1941. By 1947, the Soviet interventions in most of Eastern Europe had made clear that Stalin was a totalitarian dictator of the first order. Then, when the Soviets got the atomic and later the hydrogen bomb, East and West became locked in a genuinely deadly power struggle with no end in sight. Movies were, of course, the most pervasive social media of the era; communications were confined to radio and television broadcasts, letters, commercial or clandestine shortwave broadcasts (which the Soviets often jammed within their sphere of influence), phonograph records, wire and tape recordings, and motion pictures.

Of all these media, film was the most immersive, because it could incorporate all the other methods of disseminating information and largely used images that transported the viewer into another world. In short, film was potentially dangerous. It needed to be watched closely. Even the president was under scrutiny. As Michael Mills notes,

> In 1946, for the first time since the Hoover administration, the Republican Party had won control of Congress. Political events in Europe and the rest of the world bewildered most Americans. Early polls indicated

official U.S. foreign policy at odds with that of the average citizen. As a
result, President Truman came to be regarded by many as being soft
towards Communism, especially *domestic* Communism. Because of the
newly empowered Republican majority and to combat these increasing
uncertainties, Truman put into effect the first of many of the so-called
anti-Communist loyalty acts. However, rather than shoring up a per-
ceived weakness within his administration, these executive mandates
lent credence to Truman'[s] detractors, and fueled his own self-doubts.

But even as the HUAC conducted its hearings, some in Hollywood
objected to the reckless manner in which anyone could be tagged as a
"pinko" by insinuation alone, creating an atmosphere of paranoia and
distrust in which anyone could be denounced by anyone else for whatever
reason—political persuasion (right versus left), race, creed, color,
religion, or simply professional jealousy. At first it seemed that the
hearings might be counteracted by those willing to speak out against the
proceedings, and in Hollywood the Committee for the First Amendment
(CFA) was formed. Among its principal figures were Humphrey Bogart,
Lauren Bacall, William Wyler, John Huston, and Gene Kelly.

As HUAC went through its list of whom to subpoena and finally came
down to eleven "unfriendly" witnesses, the CFA group flew to Washington
on a plane ironically lent to them by Howard Hughes, who would soon
become one of the most outspoken, eccentric, and malign supporters of
HUAC's efforts. The first of the eleven was the playwright Bertolt Brecht,
who, through equivocation and the translation barriers between German
and English, managed to dodge the brunt of HUAC's questions; nevertheless, Brecht left the United States the day after his appearance, leaving ten
"unfriendly" witnesses who became forever known as the Hollywood Ten:
screenwriter and director Herbert J. Biberman, director Edward Dmytryk,
screenwriters Lester Cole, Ring Lardner Jr., John Howard Lawson,
Albert Maltz, Samuel Ornitz, Alvah Bessie, and Dalton Trumbo, and
producer Adrian Scott.

It soon became apparent to Bogart, Bacall, Huston, and the others that they were overmatched by the atmosphere of distrust and fear engendered by HUAC. The CFA quickly folded their tents, returned to Hollywood, and successfully (through the efforts of their publicists and handlers) managed to avoid being blacklisted. Still, Bogart was forced to sign a ghostwritten piece for the March 1948 issue of *Photoplay* magazine, "I'm No Communist," and actors Edward G. Robinson and John Garfield soon did the same (Mills). As the hearings ground on, with the implicit support of the Truman administration, more than 300 people were barred from working in the motion picture industry, including director Joseph Losey (who fled to England, where he launched a successful career), John Garfield (who died of a heart attack at the age of thirty-nine as a result of the stress of the ordeal), and Larry Parks, who had just begun his career as an actor, rising to stardom impersonating entertainer Al Jolson in two tepid biopics for Columbia.

The Hollywood Ten went to jail for contempt of Congress. But Edward Dmytryk found that he couldn't face prison life and appeared again before the HUAC committee, this time naming names. Almost immediately, Dmytryk was allowed to return to the director's chair with one of his most vicious films, *The Sniper* (1952), with HUAC supporter Adolphe Menjou as its nominal star—perhaps to keep an eye on Dmytryk. The hysteria surrounding the HUAC hearings led to the Blacklist, an organized effort by the Hollywood studios to bar those suspected of communist sympathies from employment within the industry. Effectively, once you were on the Blacklist—since all the studios cooperated with each other—you couldn't work at any studio at all. The industry was cut into two warring factions, with a large group of quivering, uncertain, apolitical workers in the middle buffeted by both sides until the Blacklist finally eroded in the early 1960s, bit by agonizing bit. The impact on personal lives and public careers was incalculable, with the climate of fear destroying any faith that employees had in the system. Thus the anticommunist, right-wing purge of the late 1940s and early 1950s, in reality an attack on organized labor and the politics of the left, dealt a blow to the studio system in a curiously circuitous fashion by making employees realize it was time to become free agents rather than deal with capricious, dictatorial, and ultimately cowardly overlords who would capitulate to political pressure. So long as the moguls themselves remained above the political fray, all was well, at least as far as they themselves were concerned. But the cracks were beginning to show.

A number of important legal decisions also hastened the demise of the studio system. In 1944, the U.S. Supreme Court handed down what became known as the de Havilland decision, ruling that the standard seven-year contract then given to most actors could not be indefinitely lengthened by suspensions caused when an actor balked at appearing in a particular project. Olivia de Havilland, best remembered for playing the sweet and gentle Melanie in Victor Fleming's *Gone with the Wind* (1939), brought the suit against Warner Bros. Bette Davis had tried the same tactic in the early 1930s to no avail. Now, under the de Havilland decision, actors would know exactly when their contract was up, and key players within the industry, no longer indentured servants to their home studios, began to look around for better scripts, directors, and projects.

Thus in 1947 Humphrey Bogart left Warner Bros., his cinematic home of more than twenty years, to found his own independent production company, Santana, which released its films through Columbia Pictures. Maverick independent director Ida Lupino struck out on her own after a long career as an actor at Warners and launched the Filmakers, making films about social issues no other studio would touch. James Stewart, a conservative who was untouched by the Blacklist, made Hollywood business history when he appeared in Anthony Mann's *Winchester '73* (1953) for a percentage of the film's profits rather than on a straight salary, under the astute guidance of his agent, Lew Wasserman of MCA. He became a millionaire overnight (McDougal 152–55).

Then there were people like Stanley Kubrick, whose 1955 film *Killer's Kiss*, which he wrote, directed, photographed, and edited, proved that one could work entirely outside the system on minimal budgets and still get sufficient distribution. The list goes on, but if the late 1940s and early 1950s were a time of fear, they were also an era of liberation as actors, directors, and writers found their true market value and were no longer cogs in the studio machine, assigned to projects by administrative fiat.

Then came another ruling: in 1947, the Supreme Court declared that the long-approved practice of block booking, in which a studio could force an exhibitor to take an entire slate of films, many of them inferior, in order to get more desired films, violated federal antitrust laws. Again, the studios reeled. As a result, each film had to be sold solely on its individual merits. Similarly, blind bidding—in which exhibitors were forced to bid for a film without even seeing it, based on its stars or the story (usually a hit novel) alone—was also ruled illegal. The distribution strong-arm tactics that had served the studios so well for nearly half a century were suddenly outlawed, and thus the studios cut back on production, making fewer films but with higher budgets and production values, signaling the beginning of the end for "B" movies, or second features.

This was followed by yet another ruling: the government filed antitrust suits against Technicolor and Eastman Kodak, alleging that the companies held an effective monopoly on the production of color motion pictures. For years, Technicolor had held Hollywood in a stranglehold with its proprietary three-strip color additive process, which required the use of Technicolor's own cameras and cameramen. Meanwhile, Kodak quietly developed a single-strip color film that could be used in any camera. The industry had gradually begun to shift from three-strip Technicolor to Eastman's monopack system, using a single strand of film to record the full spectrum of color—it was cheaper, simpler, and much more convenient. But Kodak refused to license the single-strip technology to others. By late 1948, however, Kodak agreed to make its color film patents available to competitors, thus ending Kodak's lock on raw stock production and color processing. Now, anyone could easily make a film in full, rich color.

The same year, RKO Radio Pictures decided to sell its theaters, anticipating that the other studios would soon be forced by the government to take the same action. Owning production, distribution, and exhibition facilities clearly constituted an unfair business advantage that the studios had been taking for years. In May 1948, the Supreme Court ordered a district court to look into the possibility of forcing the other studios to sell their theaters, thus signaling an end (for the time being) to Adolph Zukor's master plan of "vertical integration," in which a studio controlled the production, distribution, and exhibition of all their films. (Today's cable systems, controlled by various media conglomerates, actually mark a return to Zukor's principal strategy, although in a much more complex and devious fashion.) Paramount, which had fought the government the hardest on this decision, finally signed a consent decree in 1949 that required it to sell its theaters and distribution exchanges, wisely choosing to hang onto the studio end of the business and get rid of the theaters. Soon 20th Century Fox, MGM, and Warners were forced to sell their theaters as well. No longer did the majors have a guaranteed market for their films. Now, theaters could play whatever films they wanted, and the majors had to compete in an open marketplace. The studios were being backed into a corner by a combination of rising costs, shrinking markets, and new legal restrictions on their methods of doing business. To compete, the studios cut production costs to the bone, recycling scripts, sets, costumes, and musical scores to create cost-conscious films. Theater owners, with their new freedom to book whatever they wanted, began to turn to independent producers, who offered more favorable terms and reacted swiftly to fill the power vacuum left by the studios' loss of power.

Upstart production companies, in particular American International Pictures (AIP), entered the arena in April 1956, correctly identifying teenagers as the new, primary postwar audience, and creating a series of low-budget but highly exploitable films directed specifically at that demographic. Further, AIP gave distributors a much better percentage break than the majors on their films, often taking as little as 50 percent of the profits from some bookings, just so long as they controlled both the top and bottom halves of the double bill: an "A" film backed up by a rerelease or a "B" picture—a practice that was still in force but waning fast.

Then as now, most big-budget films are inherently "front loading," meaning that they make the majority of their earnings in the first weeks of their release, gradually trailing off in profitability as new films enter the marketplace. Today, of course, with the window between theatrical and home video/on-demand/streaming release relentlessly narrowing, so that many smaller films now open in theaters and in home markets on the same day, the front-loading aspect of contemporary box-office jugger-nauts is more pronounced than ever.

Even in the 1950s and 1960s, before nontheatrical playoff markets (to say nothing of international distribution) were truly lucrative, films made most of their money when first released and by the fourth week or so were playing to significantly diminished returns. Thus, studios would demand onerous "splits" on box office returns for the first week of a film's theatri-cal engagement, usually as high as a 90/10 cut in favor of the studio. After all, the studio would argue, we took all the financial risk—you're the beneficiary of our largesse. This worked until AIP came along; AIP was also, amazingly, the first studio to recognize the potential profitability of the summertime market. In the early 1950s, studios assumed that families would be on vacation in the great outdoors and uninterested in the movies. AIP, with its relentlessly teen-oriented films, such as Gene Fowler Jr.'s *I Was Teenage Werewolf* and Herbert L. Strock's *I Was a Teenage Frankenstein* (both 1957), and later its "sand-and-surf" *Beach Party* series (1963–1966), proved this axiom wrong.

Thus the studios found themselves competing with maverick produc-ers and distribution networks for theater space they had once literally owned; Paramount theaters (once the largest theatrical chain in the United States) had played only Paramount pictures, and the other majors had followed suit. Universal, however, didn't own any theaters, and so it had learned long ago to compete in an unregulated marketplace; significantly, Universal was also the studio that adapted most efficiently to television by becoming a virtual factory of small-screen fare, something it remains to this day.

It was the advent of television, in the midst of this atmosphere of distrust and paranoia, that now loomed as the newest threat to the industry. Back in 1939, television was a novelty in the United States, featured as a scientific wonder at the World's Fair in New York, but hardly a household item. When the National Broadcasting Corporation began regular daily television broadcasts the same year, there were fewer than a million television sets in use nationwide. Thus it seemed that the new medium posed no serious threat to Hollywood dominance. In only ten years, however, the number of sets rose fivefold, and the studios were scrambling to lure back to the theater those viewers who were staying home to watch Milton Berle for free. This meant a reversal of Hollywood's early strategy of simply ignoring television, in which networks were forbidden to employ studios' contract stars or to broadcast their older films. A new industry sprang up, however, providing viewers with such classic television series as *I Love Lucy* (1951–1957), *The Honeymooners* (1953–1956), and *Dragnet* (initial run, 1951–1959; the series was rebooted in 1967 and lasted until 1970), as well as an array of variety shows and sports programming that were cheap to produce.

With the rise of television and the decline of the proprietary lure of the theatrical experience, Hollywood fought back with a host of technological advances, such as CinemaScope, Panavision, Cinerama, and 3D, all designed to deliver spectacle that could not be enjoyed at home. Television, of course, had the advantage of being free. I remember vividly when this magic box suddenly appeared in my room, capable of pulling in no fewer than seven stations, operating on a nearly twenty-four-hour basis with programming that consisted almost entirely of filmed entertainment.

In the early 1950s, of course, most of this was non-Hollywood programming, as the studios tried to fight back against the television juggernaut by forbidding broadcast of their classic films, but gradually the ban was done away with and home viewers gained access to a nearly inexhaustible library of films, with the minor annoyance of an occasional commercial. At that time, you bought a television, put an aerial on the roof, and that was it; no monthly cable bills, premium channels, or on-demand services—just free, albeit sponsored programming. How could Hollywood compete with that? As we will see, both Warner Bros. and Universal quickly redesigned their studios into purveyors of made-for-television programming, while other studios, such as Columbia, made a fortune releasing their old short films, especially The Three Stooges' twenty-minute comedies, to television.

Walt Disney embraced the medium early on, with a Sunday night hour-long show that served as a promotional device for forthcoming Disney product while allowing the studio to carefully showcase and repackage older material. Alone among the studios, Disney managed—as it still does to this day—to rerelease again and again their older theatrical films to new generations of viewers, controlling the flow of product so that the market never becomes saturated. Disney also created an hour-long, five-day-a-week "strip" series, The Mickey Mouse Club (1955–1958), which was an excellent way to introduce children of the 1950s to cartoon characters from the 1930s and 1940s as if they were contemporary creations, and also to market the Disney brand.

There was another factor to consider beyond the emergence of television: the collapse of the star system and identifiable studio signatures as part of the moviegoing experience. "If it's a Paramount picture, it's the best show in town," went one studio slogan, and at the peak of the studio system, audiences were lured by stars, studios, and carefully targeted marketing to venture out of their homes at least once a week to see the latest major studio release. Just as the studios had battalions of directors, cinematographers, editors, grips, set designers, and other technicians to help them churn out films in an unceasing torrent of images, so too did they cultivate a studio farm system of actors, who became dependable commodities in film after film. As Serge Rocco notes,

Studios were self-sufficient dream factories with their own back lot (for the exteriors), soundstages, their own crews of decorators, set designers,

lighting technicians, cinematographers, editors and most of all, stars . . .
who kept the dream alive. . . . . Films were the product of a very organized process, where everything was achieved within the studios' gates
by studios' employees. Actors were bound to only appear in movies
produced by their contracting studio (under the threat of suspension).
On one hand, those stars were limited and could only be 'loaned'
to other companies (when offered the occasional good script). On the
other hand, though, they had everything at the tip of their fingers:
horseback riding, fencing, bodybuilding, speech lessons, etc.

But that entire system is gone. The studios have instead become the
repositories of dreams of the distant past, a past they relentlessly fetishize
and merchandise, even as they rent out their facilities to anyone who has
the money, in order to make ends meet. What the studios lost in the 1948
Paramount decision was a guaranteed outlet for all their wares, and now
they found themselves competing not only with each other but with anyone else who had the money, and the chutzpah, to break into the business.
Gone were the days when the so-called "Big Five"—20th Century Fox,
Paramount Pictures, Warner Bros., RKO Radio, and Loew's Incorporated
(owner of MGM)—controlled the nationwide box office. Universal and
Columbia were production facilities only, never owning more than a few
theaters, and United Artists, the last of the major production companies,
was basically a forerunner of the current system, functioning as a funding
source and distribution outlet for independent (albeit studio-connected)
producers.

The Big Five, as noted, were fully integrated operations, controlling
the creation of films from initial concept through distribution and exhibition, a hegemonic monopoly that allowed the classical studio system to
function so effectively. Yes, the studios had rosters of skilled technicians,
actors, and producers adept at creating entertainment news the public
demanded and keeping abreast of current audience trends, but most
important they had—through block booking, blind bidding, and in many

cases their own chain of theaters—a guaranteed outlet for their films, which meant that a torrent of films had to be created on an annual basis; some "A" films, some "B" films, and some even more modestly budgeted. The pipeline was always there—exhibitors could depend on MGM, Paramount, 20th Century Fox, RKO, and Warners each churning out at least one film a week, and then something new would always be playing. Without television as competition, and radio functioning primarily as advance publicity for their efforts, the studios engaged in an almost limitless control over the public's moviegoing habits.

Howard Hughes, who had in the late 1940s acquired a controlling interest in RKO, shrewdly realized that since RKO owned the fewest theaters of the Big Five, agreeing with the government's demand that the studios divest themselves of theaters might work to RKO's advantage. On November 8, 1948, Hughes agreed to split RKO Radio Pictures into two separate companies, RKO Pictures Corporation and RKO Theaters Corporation. Hughes then consented to sell either the studio or his theaters—deciding, of course, to keep the studio facilities—and soon the rest of the Big Five were forced to follow suit. Paramount was next, forced to agree to divestiture on December 31, 1949, and with that the rest of the studios fell in line. Vertical integration was finished. The exhibition business was now an open market, and independent producers rushed in to serve the newly liberated theater chains, momentarily forcing the studios to renegotiate distribution terms for the product. Soon, however, it became apparent that the independents lacked both the capitalization and the organizational skills to keep theaters reliably supplied with exploitable product, and so rapidly, through the use of star power, spectacle, and new exhibition processes, the studios regained the upper hand.

———

MGM, the studio with "more stars than there are in heaven," was also the most conservative of the Hollywood majors, both politically and in its filmmaking philosophy. Although MGM created many smaller films, most notably the Andy Hardy series starring Mickey Rooney and Lewis Stone, as well as a raft of short films, such as the Pete Smith novelty one-reelers or John Nesbitt's Passing Parade series, the studio never acknowledged that these more modest productions could in any way be considered "B" films. MGM, or simply Metro as studio boss Louis B. Mayer often referred to the company, was considered a class act, seemingly above the rest of the industry through a combination of nearly overwhelming star power and sheer volume of production, as well as market penetration. MGM's directors, with the exception of the cheerfully slapdash W. S. "One Take Woody" Van Dyke, were methodical and reliable studio craftsmen, such as Vincente Minnelli, George Cukor, Victor Fleming, King Vidor, and others, but the MGM look was first and foremost the major selling point of an MGM production—their films were glossy, safe, resolutely mainstream, and cloth-coat Republican in every respect.

The studio's sets seemed as if they were museum pieces rather than actual locations, and its stars—both male and female—were groomed to shimmering perfection, with makeup and lighting to fully enhance their phantom desirability. Alone among the majors, MGM was profitable in each year of the 1930s, the most perilous financial landscape this country has ever known. In 1939, MGM pulled in roughly $9.5 million in profits, or about what all the other studios combined realized in that year. Top MGM stars included Clark Gable ("The King"), Spencer Tracy, Robert Taylor, Katharine Hepburn, Hedy Lamarr, Judy Garland, William Powell, Myrna Loy, Mickey Rooney, and many others; all were under long-term contracts that could be extended at will through suspension, until the de Havilland decision put an end to perpetual indentured servitude. The studio facility, a 187-acre plant that encompassed numerous sound stages and standing sets, was one of the most impressive and stable in Hollywood. MGM also made considerable revenue by loaning out their stars to rival companies for individual projects, as when independent producer David O. Selznick absolutely had to have Gable for the role of

Rhett Butler in *Gone with the Wind (1939)*. MGM brokered a deal that not only gave the studio a handsome profit on the actor's services but also included distribution rights to the film itself.

Created in 1935 with the merger of Fox Film and 20th Century Pictures under the leadership of Darryl F. Zanuck, 20th Century Fox was much more thinly capitalized in terms of star power than MGM, but it hit pay dirt with a long line of Shirley Temple films from 1934 to 1940, which effectively kept the studio out of bankruptcy. Other 20th Century Fox stars included Don Ameche, Tyrone Power (perhaps the studio's biggest box-office draw), Dana Andrews, Henry Fonda, Gene Tierney, and the "exotic" Carmen Miranda. Since the studio's whole library was minuscule compared to that of the other majors, Zanuck continually fell back on public domain songs, even building entire films such as Henry King's *Alexander's Ragtime Band* (1938) around free-use musical material. The studio also aggressively pioneered the use of Technicolor in its films, while at the same time retaining a robust "B" unit that cranked out westerns, comedies, crime films, and mysteries on a regular basis.

The most prestigious director at 20th Century Fox was undoubtedly John Ford, whose films such as *The Grapes of Wrath* (1940) were both critical and commercial hits. The studio could also call on the reliable Henry Hathaway and even German émigré Fritz Lang, who adapted with surprising ease to the Hollywood system, churning out westerns and suspense films on time and on budget, after a brief and stormy stop at MGM (with 1936's *Fury*, a lynch mob drama starring Spencer Tracy, and a deeply atypical film for MGM). Ruthlessly efficient, Zanuck aimed frankly at the most commercial prospects and delivered neat, brightly colored cinematic confections to his viewers, all the while keeping an extremely tight rein on budgets and studio facilities.

At Universal, things were more chaotic. Founded by Carl Laemmle in 1915 as the Independent Moving Pictures Company, an enterprise designed to break the Edison trust that had effectively monopolized motion picture production through a series of restrictive patents until a

Supreme Court decision dissolved the Edison conglomerate), by the 1930s the company was the foremost purveyor of horror films in the industry. Universal also enjoyed great success with the arrival of slapstick comedians Abbott and Costello in the early 1940s, which eventually (if not inevitably) led to a genre/series mashup beginning with Charles T. Barton's *Abbott and Costello Meet Frankenstein* (1948). The studio also churned out a stack of program westerns, musicals and cut-rate detective films, most notably the *Sherlock Holmes* series, which the studio inherited from 20th Century Fox and transported from the Victorian era to the present day, mainly for reasons of economy.

Laemmle lost control of the studio in 1935, selling out for a paltry $5 million after his policy of hiring numerous relatives and passing control of day-to-day production to his son, Carl Jr., proved disastrous to the studio's bottom line. Reorganized as "the new Universal," with the studio logo of a crystalline globe of the earth surrounded by the words "A Universal Picture"—suggesting that the studio's appeal reached to all corners of the planet—the studio soon became the model of utterly efficient, bottom-line production that it remains today.

Warner Bros. managed to keep the wolf from its door during the Depression through its embrace of Vitaphone, an early sound-on-disc process that brought dialogue to the movies. The company was skating on perilously thin financial ice when Jack Warner and his brothers decided to bet nearly everything the studio had on the production of Alan Crosland's *The Jazz Singer* (1927), which contained only a few minutes of actual speech but brought the electrifying presence of Al Jolson to the screen; it became an enormous box-office hit. The other studios, with a sizable investment in silent films, had resisted the switch to sound, considering it just a fad, but Warner's decision to continue making talkies—driven primarily by financial considerations—forced the entire industry to adapt. Silent films were suddenly and utterly obsolete.

With this success, Warner Bros. became arguably the most hard-boiled of the Hollywood majors, creating a series of brutal gangster films, such as William Wellman's *The Public Enemy* (1931) and Mervyn LeRoy's *Little Caesar* (1931), in addition to exposés like LeRoy's *I Am a Fugitive from a Chain Gang* (1932), and racy, complex films such as LeRoy's *Three on a Match* (1932), which dealt with adultery, drug use, and kidnapping. Countering these films were the ultra-escapist musicals of Busby Berkeley, such as *Gold Diggers of 1933* (1933), which abstracted the human body into a series of kaleidoscopic compositions that surprised and delighted Depression-era audiences.

While Harry Warner ran the New York "business" and financial end of Warner Bros., Jack L. Warner was the undisputed king of the lot, pushing his contract players, such as Humphrey Bogart, Paul Muni, Bette Davis, Ann Sheridan, James Cagney, and others through one picture after another in rapid-fire succession. In addition, the Warner Bros. animation unit, initially located in a rundown building aptly nicknamed Termite Terrace for its infestation of insects and rodents, became known for fostering a newly anarchic style of cartoons, very different from the Disney "realist" model. Directors such as Isidore "Friz" Freling, Chuck Jones, Bob Clampett, and Tex Avery created the enduring characters of Bugs Bunny, Daffy Duck, Porky Pig, Elmer Fudd, and others, and the WB Cartoon unit, under the direction of producer Leon Schlesinger, was soon the only other major player in the animated short subject field, though Warners never attempted a theatrical feature cartoon, as Walt Disney did with *Snow White and the Seven Dwarfs* in 1937.

In the 1940s, Warners was home to a host of topical war films, most famously Michael Curtiz's *Casablanca* (1942), a romantic melodrama that has attained cult status over the years, and film noir crime films, with such productions as Howard Hawks's *The Big Sleep* (1946). Warners would regularly suspend actors who refused to knuckle under to their dictates, and routinely cast even top-line talent, such as Bogart and Davis, in "B" films, just to keep the production line moving. When stars objected to such cavalier treatment, they were put on unpaid suspension and forbidden to work in any medium. Eventually most capitulated to studio demands, but the true mavericks, including Davis, Bogart, Muni, and others, as well as the unlikely figure of Olivia de Havilland, who had never been seen as a studio troublemaker, eventually forced an end to the practice through the courts.

Paramount, founded by the business visionary Adolph Zukor, was in many ways the most forward-looking of all the studios. Zukor built the business up from the penny arcade level, as had Warner Bros. and other companies, but it was Zukor who first had the dream of vertical integration that became the industry model, controlling a film from first to last in the marketplace. By 1925, through a complex series of negotiations, Paramount had merged with Famous Players and Jesse L. Lasky to create Paramount Publix, a studio that by 1930 owned more than 1,200 theaters nationwide, making it the largest theater chain in America (Gomery, *Studio System* 28).

Moving smoothly to sound after Warners led the way, Paramount pushed the nascent Production Code envelope by top-lining Maurice Chevalier, the Marx Brothers (in their most effective films), and Mae West in a series of comedies and musicals that burlesqued the conventional mores of the era. The Production Code was originally created voluntarily in 1922 to avoid government censorship of films, under the guidance of the former postmaster of the Harding administration, Will H. Hays. The Hays Office had no real teeth, but when Joseph Breen took control in 1934 things rapidly changed, and the industry was brought to heel. The revised 1934 Code explicitly forbade such topics as "sex perversion," "miscegenation," "profanity," and even the use of liquor in films, resulting in a completely cleaned-up vision of the world that bore no relationship to reality. Paramount, like the other studios, bowed to Breen's dictates, because, after all, what really mattered to the moguls was the bottom line—box office receipts, ancillary products, radio programs that plugged upcoming releases, any way they could make a buck (see Dixon and Foster 130–32). If they had to soft-pedal the spicier stuff for the moment, the studios had no objections, just so long as the public kept coming to see their films.

Through the years, under the leadership of Zukor and production chief Barney Balaban, Paramount's earnings continued to accelerate, so that by 1946 the company had a net profit of $39.2 million from its films and assets of more than $170 million (Gomery, *Studio System* 34). But Balaban was shortsighted when it came to the value of Paramount's back catalogue. To raise capital in the early 1950s, he disposed of much of the studio's film library, believing that it had no future value. Thus, much of the studio's output during its formative years now belongs in other libraries, through a complex matrix of legal wrangling that is absolutely byzantine in nature.

By 1949, Paramount was forced to sell off its huge theater chain to meet the demands of the consent decree, although by then Balaban had identified television as the next distribution portal to conquer and aggressively began buying up television stations until the Supreme Court ruled against the studio (Gomery, *Studio System* 37). The studio depended on Cecil B. DeMille's historical spectacles, together with a series of comedies starring Bing Crosby and Bob Hope, to attract audiences, which they did with great success. With the loss of its theaters, however, Paramount went into steep financial decline, and by 1967 it was sold for a pittance to the Gulf & Western Corporation, continuing to make films but on modest budgets.

RKO met its downfall under the aegis of Howard Hughes, but in its earlier years, under studio head George Schaefer, RKO served as the theatrical distributer for Walt Disney's animated features and also specialized in one- or two-picture deals with star-caliber actors and directors, as opposed to building up a stable of talent like MGM. In this fashion, Schaefer reasoned, he could capitalize on stars and directors at their peak, rather than having to nurture them through their entire career. Schaefer also used "package deals" arranged by the Music Corporation of America (MCA) to fuel production needs, as well as signing Orson Welles to direct *Citizen Kane* (1941). In addition, the musicals of Fred Astaire and Ginger Rogers, beginning with Thornton Freeland's *Flying Down to Rio* (1933), proved lucrative box-office draws, but Rogers left the studio in 1941 and Schaefer was fired in June 1942.

In the wake of his departure, as might have been predicted, a much more cost-conscious regime came in, and in the postwar years RKO became known as the "House of Noir," with downbeat, pessimistic films such as Robert Wise's *Born to Kill* (1947). In addition, producer Val Lewton's horror unit, as exemplified by Jacques Tourneur's *The Cat People* (1942) and *I Walked with a Zombie* (1943), made the studio the only real threat to Universal's dominance in the horror genre, and a string of low-budget mysteries featuring the Saint, and later the Falcon, rounded out RKO's late 1940s slate, along with Lupe Velez's remarkably racist *Mexican Spitfire* series, which nevertheless made a great deal of money.

By the time Hughes had taken control of the studio in May 1948, however, RKO's fortunes were on a downward spiral. Hughes's deeply eccentric mismanagement of the studio—constant reshoots, scrapping whole films after production, wild overspending—only made matters worse. In 1955, Hughes sold his collapsing empire to General Tire and Rubber, which tried to make a go of it in film production, but only two years later it sold off the studio facilities to Desi Arnaz's fledgling television production company, Desilu. General Tire had already sold off the RKO back film library to television, effectively setting up yet another precedent that the majors had hoped to avoid—the availability of theatrical motion pictures from a major studio, now screened for free on home television. There were still some RKO films in the pipeline as late as 1957—the last film produced on the lot was Arthur Lubin's *The First Traveling Saleslady,* and the company served as the U.S. distributor for Ishirō Honda's Japanese science-fiction epic *The Mysterians,* also in 1957. But that was the end. RKO was history, and out of its wreckage had come the two things conventional moguls feared most: a working TV studio, producing *I Love Lucy* and other highly successful television series, as well as a choice library of major studio films for TV.

There were, of course, other, smaller studios: Republic, which specialized in westerns and serials; Monogram, which created low-budget horror films and westerns; and the lowest of the low, Producers Releasing Corporation (PRC), which made films for as little as $10,000–$20,000, sold them to theaters for a flat rental rather than on a percentage basis, and was referred to throughout the industry as "Poverty Row Crap." But in the midst of the low-budget activity centering on Gower Street in Los Angeles—known as Gower Gulch for its proliferation of westerns and low-budget programmers—one company was determined to make it out of the minor leagues and into the majors.

———

Columbia Pictures, founded by brothers Jack and Harry Cohn with partner Joseph Brandt, was a struggling minor studio with great aspirations. Harry Cohn, in particular, who had started as a song plugger during the sheet music era, wanted to see Columbia compete with the Big Five on an equal basis. Columbia would never own theaters, but by cutting costs to the bone and possessing an intuitive knowledge of public taste at its most plebeian level, Harry Cohn kept theaters—especially non-affiliated ones—supplied with reliable programming on a weekly basis, averaging fifty-two films a year: some good, some awful, and a few quite special indeed.

One such opportunity for a prestige picture came his way in 1933, when Cohn obtained the services of Clark Gable from MGM at a fire-sale price—Gable had been demanding more say over scripts and directors, always a bad sign for an actor, and MGM sought to punish Gable by loaning him to Cohn. Cohn pulled top-line star Claudette Colbert from Paramount to play opposite Gable in Frank Capra's *It Happened One Night* (1934), which unexpectedly swept the Academy Awards, although it was produced for a paltry $300,000 (Gomery, *Studio System* 165). Columbia's status as a major studio was now within reach. And Harry Cohn—known as "White Fang" (so dubbed by prolific screenwriter Ben Hecht for his crude demeanor)—was ready to take advantage of his moment in the spotlight.

CHAPTER 2

White Fang at Columbia

In the mid-1940s, Harry Cohn was sailing on his yacht, the *Jobella*, with the distinguished film director Rouben Mamoulian, whose many credits included *Queen Christina* (1933), *Ninotchka* (1939), and *The Mark of Zorro* (1940), as his guest. Gradually, as the two men relaxed, the talk turned from business matters to uncharacteristic introspection—uncharacteristic, at least, for Cohn, who seldom let anyone see any weakness in his character. As the two men sipped drinks, Cohn suddenly demanded of Mamoulian, "You're an intelligent man; will you answer me a question?" Startled by Cohn's directness, Mamoulian agreed. "What happens to us after we die?" queried Cohn, much to the director's amazement. Though nominally Jewish, Harry Cohn had never been much of a religious man, in either his business or personal life.

Composing himself, Mamoulian responded: "Well, there are various beliefs. Some people believe that death is the end of everything; some believe life goes on." "What do *you* think?" Cohn demanded. "My personal feeling is that there is another life," Mamoulian said quietly. Harry Cohn wasn't satisfied. "What proof can you give me?" Mamoulian shrugged. "I can only say that between the two hypotheses, I prefer to believe that there is a link between this life and the next. It makes more sense than the theory that we are in something that is just temporary. People who suffer in this life can expect a better life next time." Cohn remained unconvinced.

"Rouben, I want you to prove it to me!" he pleaded. But Mamoulian could offer no proof, and Cohn remained essentially an agnostic, believing in no one but himself (Thomas, *King* 360).

By 1957, Cohn was a dying man. He had suffered his first brush with mortality in March 1954, when he was successfully operated on for throat cancer (Dick, *Merchant* 184). Now, his health was again an issue. Plagued by a heart ailment that his physicians—the top specialists in the medical profession, naturally—told him could be cured with surgery, Cohn used his connections to obtain copious footage of open heart surgery from medical schools, hospitals, and universities, and he ran the films in his private projection room for hours on end, fascinated by the procedure, but unable to face surgery himself (Thomas, *King* 360).

In the end, although he was by this time practically living on nitroglycerine tablets, he decided against an operation that could have potentially saved his life. His will, signed on Valentine's Day, February 14, 1958, left his worldly goods to his wife and children, and specified that no funeral services should be held after his death (Thomas, *King* 359; Dick, *Merchant* 186). Roughly two weeks later, Cohn died from a heart attack on February 27, 1958, while vacationing in Phoenix, Arizona. His last words, as he was rushed to the hospital, were: "It's no use. It's too tough. It's just too tough" (Thomas, *King* 363). When the ambulance reached Saint Joseph's Hospital, Cohn's wife, the former Joan Perry, a devout Catholic, had a priest baptize Cohn's body, claiming that in his last moments "he had invoked the name of Jesus Christ" (Thomas, *King* 363).

Despite his admonition that no service of any kind should mark his passing, Joan Cohn saw to it that two Columbia soundstages were converted into a memorial chapel—just like a film set—and on March 2, Harry Cohn received as ornate a memorial service as anyone could imagine. The soundstages were overflowing with freshly cut floral tributes. Danny Kaye read a eulogy written by screenwriter Clifford Odets. Danny Thomas then took the microphone, reading an abridged version of the Catholic rite of burial, as well as the Twenty-third Psalm in its entirety.

More than two thousand mourners attended. Despite the many bitter, personal disputes Cohn had conducted over the years with his numerous employees, those who had worked with him turned out in force: William Holden, Kim Novak, John Ford, Dick Powell, Tony Curtis, Glenn Ford, Jack Lemmon, Spencer Tracy, and Frank Capra were among the luminaries present for the ceremony (Thomas, *King* xiii; Dick, *Merchant* 189). The man who wanted no funeral was going out in Hollywood style, mourned by those with whom he had spent his career working in a rough-and-tumble industry, in perhaps the most notoriously fractious studio in town.

Yet Harry Cohn was a man who hated sentimentality, and perhaps he would have found it grimly amusing when Red Skelton joked about the funeral on his television show the following week. Marveling at the huge turnout for a man almost universally considered the most abrasive and belligerent studio head in the business, Skelton quipped, "Well, it only proves what they always say—give the public something they want to see, and they'll come out for it" (Thomas, *King* xvii–xviii). The studio audience laughed uncomfortably, and the joke was roundly criticized in the various gossip columns and editorial pages of the daily press, but Harry Cohn would have recognized the essential truth of Skelton's jibe. For "Harry the Horror," "White Fang," or "King Cohn," as he was variously known, was without a doubt the most hated studio head in Hollywood history.

Not that there was a consistency of opinion about him. In an interview I conducted with the director Budd Boetticher just before his death, he stated simply that "Harry Cohn was a very dear friend of mine." When I responded with a startled "You don't hear many people say that!" Boetticher laughed and agreed, "No, you sure don't, but what can I tell you? He was a great guy, and we got along great," before detailing how Cohn first met the young Boetticher, then an assistant director on George Stevens's *The More the Merrier* (1943), and the two men engaged in a lively verbal joust, during the course of which Boetticher threatened to "knock Cohn on his ass" for bothering Stevens while he was rehearsing a scene with stars Joel McCrea and Jean Arthur.

Cohn responded by calling Boetticher "a son of a bitch," at which point Boetticher responded in kind; this stopped Cohn cold. Looking at Boetticher thoughtfully, Cohn suddenly told the young man to be in Cohn's office at 6 P.M., and quietly walked off the set. Certain that he was going to be fired (a sentiment shared by Stevens, McCrea, and Arthur), Boetticher nevertheless showed up in Cohn's office at the appointed hour and was more than a little surprised when Cohn summarily asked him to take over the last two days of direction on Lew Landers's *Submarine Raider* (1942), which effectively launched Boetticher's long career as a director. "I get the impression that if you let Harry Cohn walk all over you, he would, but if you stood up to him, you were in," I ventured. "That's it exactly!" Boetticher responded. This was the essence of Cohn's character in a nutshell. A tough customer, you could only reach him by being just as tough, if you could reach him at all (Dixon, "Boetticher" 41–42).

Similarly, Fritz Lang, no shrinking violet himself, noted parenthetically during an interview with Peter Bogdanovich on the making of the Columbia crime noir *The Big Heat* (1953), "By the way, I am one of the people who liked Harry Cohn—he was always very nice to me. Mostly he is hated, very unreasonably" (219). But then Lang knew how to take care of himself in the clinches, and despite presenting an amiable face to the general public he was well known to be a single-minded martinet on the set. Other opinions of Cohn: "He wanted to pull everyone down to his level" (Edward Dmytryk); "He had great taste—it was blind, instinctive—but it was taste" (Rosalind Russell); "An impossible man, but he had complete belief in himself" (Darryl F. Zanuck); "He was a square shooter" (Ida Lupino); "He gambled on people, never on himself" (Frank Capra); "He could be cruel, kind, giving, taking, despicable, benevolent, compassionate and malevolent, all at the same time" (Glenn Ford); "He was an okay guy" (John Huston); "He was a son of a bitch" (John Wayne) (Thomas, *King* xix). This gives you some idea of the range of emotions Cohn inspired in his colleagues; crude, complex, brutal, and yet sensitive, Harry Cohn *was* Columbia Pictures, from its inception until his death, and he ran his domain like a medieval kingdom in which no one would dare question his authority.

Cohn was born on July 23, 1891, in New York City, and left school early on—he was too busy working to let anything like a normal education get in his way. His early jobs included being a chorus boy, a shipping clerk, a fur salesman, part of a vaudeville act, a streetcar conductor, and a song plugger, or salesman, who would try to sell songs by various composers to popular singers of the day. In 1918, he landed a job as Carl Laemmle's personal secretary at the fledgling Universal Studios and learned the business firsthand, though Laemmle's management style was considerably more benevolent than Cohn's (Katz 274). "Uncle" Carl was notorious for hiring his relatives for studio jobs they were essentially unqualified for, including his son, Carl Jr., leading to the oft-quoted piece of doggerel, "Uncle Carl Laemmle / Has a very large Faemmle."

Harry's brother Jack had already been working at Universal for ten years, but, unlike Jack, Harry was a young man in a hurry. Less than two years later, in 1920, Jack, Harry, and their colleague Joe Brandt set up their own shop, the C.B.C. (Cohn/Brandt/Cohn) Film Sales Company. While Jack and Joe remained in New York to raise money and sell product, Harry arrived in Hollywood and set up offices on Gower Street, "Poverty Row," and rapidly demonstrated a knack for producing low-budget westerns, comedies, and other program pictures on fractional budgets.

Harry Cohn used every tactic he could think of to keep costs down and the company afloat; he would draw money on a bank in New York and spend it in California to make a film, then cover that check with another check, and so on and so on, until a film was sold and the money actually realized and duly deposited. But C.B.C. was getting a bad reputation in Hollywood as a strictly low-budget enterprise; its nickname was now "Corned Beef and Cabbage" (Thomas, *King* 36). That had to change, and in 1924, C.B.C. was reincorporated as Columbia Pictures. From then on, Harry Cohn was unstoppable.

By the 1930s, Joe Brandt was eased out for $500,000, and Jack Cohn, who tried to go behind Harry's back to A. P. Giannini, president of the Bank of America (then the Bank of Italy, and Columbia's chief source of finance), to topple Harry and assume direct control of the studio, was demoted to the position of vice-president and treasurer. All this left Harry in complete control of production at the studio, which is what he had always wanted, but it set up a longstanding battle of wills between the two brothers. Jack, still on the East Coast, with a huge farm in Connecticut, a wife and children, more and more the family man, took charge of all financial matters, while Harry was the hard-nosed West Coast production head. They would remain locked in combat for years, each hoping to catch the other in some business error.

Frank Capra was witness to one particularly violent argument between Harry and Jack during one of Jack's visits to the Gower Street studios, during which he was sure that Jack and Harry would soon resort to physical violence. Suddenly, Harry heard the unmistakable sound of a Good Humor ice cream truck chiming in the street below his office. Calling a halt to the argument, he nonchalantly strode to the window and ordered two ice cream bars, one for him and one for Jack, and the vendor tossed them up for Harry to catch. Harry dropped down two dimes, handed one ice cream bar to Jack, took a bite of his own chocolate crunch bar, and only then resumed the battle with his brother, screaming, "Now listen, you son of a bitch," as Capra looked on, amazed (Thomas, *King* 80).

The story illustrates what distinguished Harry Cohn's business style more than anything else: his ability to switch gears almost instantaneously. If he found that his current strategy wasn't working—at least, when he was trying to woo a prospective employee—he would try something else. Brute force not effective? Try flattery. Flattery not cutting it? Use threats. Still not getting results? Then Harry would do anything—bribe, cheat, lie, steal—anything to get what he wanted. Once Cohn had them under contract, it was a different story; Cohn's true, dictatorial personality would emerge, leaving little doubt as to who was in charge.

Over and over again, Cohn would intone a phrase that almost became his personal mantra, "I kiss the feet of talent," but that was only during the honeymoon stage. Cohn was a shrewd negotiator, a superb judge of talent, and a ruthless businessman. He knew how to run a studio, and he knew what the public wanted. In short, he knew how to make movies.

With the success of *It Happened One Night* in 1934, Harry Cohn was ready to move into the big leagues. Always on the lookout for new talent, with Frank Capra (for the moment) firmly in his hip pocket, Cohn went after director Dorothy Arzner, whose previous films included the feminist aviation drama *Christopher Strong* (1933) for RKO. When Arzner became a free agent, Cohn lured her to Columbia as a producer/director—unheard of for a woman during this era—and oversaw the production of *Craig's Wife* (1936), starring Rosalind Russell on a loan-out from MGM. Shot in four weeks for $280,000, *Craig's Wife* was a smash hit, and Arzner continued with Columbia for the rest of her career, the only woman directing in Hollywood.

Cohn already had a history of hiring people at their peak and then firing them the moment their box office value began to drop even slightly. Arzner was no exception: her last film for Columbia was the deeply feminist World War II resistance drama *First Comes Courage* (1943), by which time her star was perceptibly waning. When Arzner fell ill during shooting, she was summarily replaced with a Columbia contract director, and though the film was released to good reviews, Arzner never again directed a theatrical motion picture.

As an early admirer of Benito Mussolini—Columbia released a patched-together "documentary" feature, *Mussolini Speaks*, in 1933, when fascination with the fascist dictator was still in vogue, realizing profits of more than $1,000,000 on a $10,000 investment—Cohn realized that power had to be exercised in order for it to be retained. Others were always waiting in the wings, ready to take your place. When *Mussolini Speaks* proved a huge hit, Cohn traveled to Italy, where Il Duce received Cohn with full state honors and even awarded the producer an honorary decoration. What most impressed Cohn about Mussolini, oddly, was his office, a long hallway with a raised desk at the end where Mussolini held court. It was a long trip up the carpet to see the dictator, and as Cohn later admitted, recounting his visit to Mussolini's palatial office, "By the time I arrived at his desk, I was whipped" (Thomas, *King* 102). And so Harry Cohn designed his office at Columbia in the Mussolini manner and affected the same trappings of power over his own subjects.

Harry Cohn was tough on everyone. When Eddie Buzzell, a former Broadway star, drifted into Cohn's orbit, he pleaded with his boss to let him direct a film. Cohn allowed Buzzell to direct a series of musical/comedy shorts but refused to see them. Buzzell was convinced that if Cohn saw one of his two-reel comedies, he would be so impressed that he'd give Buzzell a feature to direct. Finally, Buzzell dragged Cohn to a preview of one of his new shorts, which Cohn seemed to enjoy. But as the crowd exited the theater, Cohn, Buzzell, and the two actresses who were their dates for the evening noticed a bedraggled man cross the street in front of them, climb up a lamppost, and then jump off headfirst onto the sidewalk below. The man was killed instantly. Buzzell and the two actresses were shocked, but Cohn simply shrugged and headed for the studio car, not missing a beat. On the way back to the studio, Buzzell, still shaken, muttered, "My God, Harry, why would a man do such a thing?" Cohn had a ready answer: "He must have seen your picture" (Thomas, *King* 242–43).

Buzzell was stunned by Cohn's callousness, but the retort was simply a measure of the man. It was Cohn's way all the time, and other people simply didn't exist unless they were useful to him. When that ended, Cohn discarded them without a backward glance. His profanity and browbeating became so ingrained that one of Columbia's top directors, Charles Vidor, actually took Cohn to court over his continual harassment, after Cohn referred to him as a "Hungarian motherfucker who would do anything for money" (Thomas, *King* 249), among numerous other gratuitous slurs, including no fewer than twenty-nine variations of "son of a bitch" (Thomas, *King* 253). The judge in the case was unmoved and amazingly found against Vidor, ruling that Cohn's habitual use of profanity was so well known that anyone who agreed to work for him would simply have to put up with it (Thomas, *King* 255).

When Vidor returned to the studio, Cohn assigned him to a string of "B" pictures, but the director retaliated by going wildly over budget on each production, forcing Cohn to remove him and replace him with another, more compliant director. Cohn continued to badger the director with inferior assignments until Jack Cohn convinced Harry that the feud was just bad business—Vidor, the director of Rita Hayworth's breakthrough film *Gilda* (1946), was simply too valuable to be used this way. Furthermore, Jack Cohn and the New York office ruled that an apology was due Vidor, and Harry was predictably livid. But because Columbia's need always came first, Cohn arranged for a trip for Vidor and himself on Cohn's private yacht and brought along a Columbia studio screenwriter, Michael Blankfort, as a witness (Thomas, *King* 257).

The three gathered on the dock before boarding the yacht. Finally, after a fashion, Cohn apologized, thus: "They say I'm supposed to apologize. If you think I'm going to say I'm sorry, you're out of your fucking mind." For some reason, Vidor realized this was the best Cohn could do and accepted, saying, "That's all right, Harry." Cohn immediately turned to Blankfort, barking, "You're the witness; you heard me apologize," before boarding the yacht—alone—and leaving Vidor and Blankfort to return to Los Angeles. Such a fragile relationship, however, was bound to shatter, and in 1948 Vidor again threatened to take Cohn to court for his unbridled behavior (Thomas, *King* 257).

This time, however, Cohn won an even greater victory. Vidor, eager to get away from his tyrannical boss no matter what the cost, finally agreed to pay Cohn $75,000 to terminate his Columbia contract. Yet ten years later, in the mid-1950s, Cohn decided that he wanted Vidor back at Columbia and began negotiations to retain his services as a director. Nothing came of it, as Cohn's career was coming to an end, but curiously, Vidor, Cohn, and their wives suddenly began seeing each other socially and were on friendly terms when Cohn died in 1958 (Thomas, *King* 257).

Cohn ran his studio like a factory—he had to. Like all the other studios, Cohn used block booking to force exhibitors to run his program pictures if they wanted Columbia's best films, but in Columbia's case, the second-tier material really was second rate—the *Crime Doctor* series, the *Blondie* films, the *Boston Blackie* detective thrillers, and an endless series of formulaic westerns. Yet mixed in with the dross were films of genuine quality, and by the late 1930s "prestige" Columbia pictures became more prevalent as the double-bill system started to collapse and feature films were sent out on their own. Harry Cohn pulled as many strings as he could, called in as many favors as he could, and arranged as many low-cost loan-outs of top-flight actors, writers, and directors as he could, and Columbia began to turn out first-rate films on a regular basis.

But life under Cohn's regime at its peak in the 1940s was difficult indeed. As Ephraim Katz notes, "Cohn was notorious for his ruthlessness and vulgarity. He ruled his studio like a despot, spying on employees through informers and a hidden microphone system, hiring and firing at will, courting the strong and humiliating the weak" (274). Or, as Bob Thomas put it, "The relationship of Cohn to his creative talent invariably followed a three-part pattern: the wooing and the honeymoon; the drive for control; the divorce" (*King* 208). Even Frank Capra, who had put the studio on the map as Columbia's first truly important director, was not immune.

Capra had been with Columbia almost from the company's inception, and such early Capra films as *The Power of the Press, So This Is Love, That Certain Thing, Submarine,* and *The Way of the Strong* (all 1928) had helped to put Columbia in the black in its formative years, to say nothing of Capra's early 1930s hits *Dirigible* (1931), *Platinum Blonde* (1931), *American Madness* (1932), and the tragic romantic drama *Forbidden* (1932). And then, as previously noted, came the overwhelming success of *It Happened One Night.* Shot in a mere four weeks at a cost of just $300,000, *It*

Happened One Night took home five Oscars, much to the surprise of everyone, especially MGM, which had lent out Gable to Columbia as punishment for his campaigning for better roles (Thomas, *King* 92–93). Gable became a star overnight, co-star Claudette Colbert, on loan from Paramount and similarly unenthusiastic about making the picture, saw her career get a similar boost, Columbia became, in one stroke, a major player within the industry, and Capra's directorial future seemed assured. There was a misstep with 1937's *Lost Horizon*, adapted from James Hilton's novel, which tested poorly with preview audiences, cost the studio a fortune, and, despite extensive recutting, struggled to find an audience. It was at this point that the first serious rupture in the Cohn/Capra relationship occurred (Thomas, *King* 121–24).

Visiting London in 1937, Capra discovered that William A. Seiter's indifferent comedy *If You Could Only Cook* (1935), starring Jean Arthur, was being sold as "A Frank Capra Production" by Columbia's British sales office, which it manifestly was not; Capra had had nothing to do with it. Cohn and Capra were already at war over the director's annual $100,000 salary; Cohn refused to pay it after the near debacle of *Lost Horizon* until Capra started work on another picture (Thomas, *King* 124). Predictably, Capra was furious. *If You Could Only Cook*, a film he had no involvement in, was being sold as his work, and it wasn't even a very good film, at that—British newspapers all noted how "disappointing" the film was compared to Capra's other work. Capra sued Columbia, setting off a long and costly court battle; Capra wanted out of Columbia, and Cohn was desperate to keep him.

When a British court seemed poised to rule in Capra's favor, and with Jack Cohn threatening to depose his brother unless Capra was reinstated, Harry Cohn went to Capra's home, unannounced, and abruptly offered a deal: if Capra would return to the studio, Cohn would purchase the rights to George S. Kaufman and Moss Hart's hit play *You Can't Take It with You* and assign Capra to direct (Arnold). Further, Cohn agreed to double Capra's annual salary to $200,000 (Thomas, *King* 148). Capra duly returned to the fold and made the film, which ended up winning the Academy Award for Best Picture; in 1939, Capra's *Mr. Smith Goes to Washington* was another massive box-office success. But now, as 1940 dawned, Capra wanted to make a Technicolor biopic on the life of composer Frederic Chopin. This time, Jack Cohn and his colleagues in New York did an about-face and strenuously vetoed the project as inherently uncommercial. Harry Cohn, never that enthused about the Chopin project, let the New York moneymen have the final say, sending Capra into a towering rage—he'd spent a year researching the Chopin project. Capra quit, but ironically, Charles Vidor made the Chopin film for Columbia in 1945 as *A Song to Remember*. It was a huge hit for the studio.

And the hits kept on coming for Columbia—including Howard Hawks's *Only Angels Have Wings* (1939), starring Cary Grant and Jean Arthur. *Only Angels Have Wings* was a turning point in the career of a very young and insecure Margarita Carmen Cansino—Rita Hayworth—who after a number of smaller roles suddenly broke through to the public at large. She would eventually become one of Columbia's biggest stars. Hayworth had broken into show business as part of her father Eduardo Cansino's dance act at the age of 12, and at 15 she was signed to a contract by Fox Films, appearing in a small role in Harry Lachman's modern version of *Dante's Inferno* in 1935. Fox soon let her go, but Rita's then-husband, Edward Judson, got her a contract at Columbia on the rebound, where Harry Cohn anglicized her name, lightened her skin, and forced her to undergo electrolysis to get rid of facial hair, all so that she would be more acceptable to contemporary audiences.

Gradually Hayworth became a star, but she was a total Hollywood construct and her tenure at the top would be brief. She appeared in Rouben Mamoulian's *Blood and Sand* (1941) at 20th Century Fox and Raoul Walsh's *The Strawberry Blonde* (1941) at Warners on loan-out in order to gain some additional experience in front of the camera, then returned to Columbia for Sidney Lanfield's lavish musical *You'll Never Get Rich* (1941), in which she co-starred with Fred Astaire. *You'll Never Get Rich* pushed her firmly into the "A" category as a bankable commodity, and she followed up the film with two more loan-outs to 20th Century Fox, on which Cohn profited handsomely: Julien Duvivier's star-studded *Tales of Manhattan* and Irving Cummings's *My Gal Sal*, both in 1942. Indeed, Fox now saw the error of their ways in letting Hayworth leave their employ in the late 1930s and offered to buy out her contract, but Cohn, no doubt gloating a bit, flatly refused to do so. Hayworth then returned to Columbia for Charles Walters's frothy *Cover Girl* (1944). Along the way, she divorced Judson in 1942 and married Orson Welles the next year.

Cohn continued giving Hayworth a careful build-up, which culminated in Charles Vidor's noir classic *Gilda* (1946), in which she played the wife of sociopathic gambler George Macready and the love interest of ne'er-do-well drifter Glenn Ford, but after *Gilda* her star faded quickly. In 1947, Welles directed her in the ambitious thriller *The Lady from Shanghai*, now considered a classic, but it was a box office flop at the time. By this time, Hayworth and Welles's marriage was in shambles. They were barely on speaking terms during the production, and divorced shortly thereafter. Meanwhile, Hayworth was becoming generally discontented at Columbia and starting to resent Cohn's continual micromanagement of her life and career. She took several suspensions rather than appear in what she considered to be inferior pictures and tried to take more control over her career. As she told reporter John Hallowell in 1968, "I used to have to punch a time clock at Columbia. Every day of my life. That's what it was like. Honey, I was under exclusive contract—like they owned me. . . . You want to know that I think of Harry Cohn? He was a monster" (5D).

In 1949, Hayworth married Prince Aly Khan, which infuriated the aging mogul; he saw the marriage as an attempt to bring another strong man into her life, one who could stand up for her against Cohn's dictates. She left the country and traveled throughout Europe with her new husband, even arranging for a rather spectacular "home movie," Jackson Leighter's *Champagne Safari* (1952), to be made of her new life. But the marriage dissolved acrimoniously in 1953, and in that same year Hayworth impulsively married singer Dick Haymes. Hayworth's personal life became increasingly chaotic, while she continued to battle with Cohn over film assignments. Nevertheless, Hayworth remained a top box-office attraction and made a string of high-profile films for the studio, including Vincent Sherman's exoticist *Affair in Trinidad* (1952), William Dieterle's biblical spectacle *Salome* (1953), and Curtis Bernhardt's *Miss Sadie Thompson* (1953), based on a short story by Somerset Maugham. Her marriage to Haymes ended in 1955, and Hayworth finished out her Columbia contract with Robert Parrish's *Fire Down Below* (1957) and George Sidney's musical *Pal Joey* (1957), in which she co-starred with Frank Sinatra. After that, Hayworth finally left Columbia, and though she appeared in films off and on after her departure from the studio, her career, in essence, was over. She made her last film, Ralph Nelson's bizarre western *The Wrath of God*, in 1972.

In all, Hayworth was married five times but never found true love. Despondent, she tried to drown her problems in drink, which only made matters worse; eventually, Hayworth was diagnosed with Alzheimer's disease and died in 1987 at the age of 68. Hayworth's glory years, then, were the 1940s, the height of the studio era; after that, she was lost without the system that had created her, even though the transformation from Margarita Carmen Cansino had cost her dearly. Cohn, for his part, soon rebounded from the loss of Hayworth's services and signed Kim Novak, grooming her into a major star by the mid-1950s.

In 1950, George Cukor was brought to the studio to direct the film adaptation of *Born Yesterday*, the smash Broadway hit that had run for more than 1,600 performances. Judy Holliday, whose screen debut was in a supporting role in Cukor's *Winged Victory* (1944), had starred in the Broadway production and wanted to reprise her role as Billie Dawn, a crooked tycoon's unsophisticated moll in need of a tutor in order to ease her entrance into Washington society while he goes about buying congressmen (Rothman). But Harry Cohn didn't think she had the requisite sex appeal for the part. Cukor, aware of both Holliday's unique comedic gifts and the unlikelihood of changing Cohn's mind by direct appeal, conspired with Katharine Hepburn to boost Holliday's star. In *Adam's Rib* (1949), an MGM film starring Hepburn and Spencer Tracy, Holliday played the supporting role of Doris Attinger, a woman accused of attempting to murder her no-good husband. Cukor and Hepburn persuaded screenwriters Garson Kanin and Ruth Gordon to add a scene for Holliday in which Doris is interviewed in jail by her lawyer (Hepburn). By filming the scene in one continuous five-minute shot, Cukor favored Holliday over Hepburn, and the rave reviews Holliday received for the film were enough to win over Cohn (Rothman). But he still maintained his doubts about her. Introduced to Holliday before the start of filming, Cohn stared at her and muttered, "Well, I've worked with fat asses before." However crude, his comment achieved its desired objective: Holliday, always sensitive about her weight, went on a crash diet and lost fifteen pounds in three weeks (Thomas, *King* 290), looking radiant in the finished film. (Holliday went on to make four more films at Columbia, with the next two, *The Marrying Kind* [1952] and *It Should Happen to You* [1954], directed by Cukor and written by Kanin and Gordon.) Perhaps a less confrontational approach would have been equally effective, but subtlety was never part of Cohn's skill set. Flattery, wheedling, and cajoling were fine when you were signing someone up for a long-term contract; after that, Cohn's signature abrasive style was the only mode of conduct he knew. Columbia was his studio, and Cohn's word was law.

The previous year, Cohn had backed the independent Robert Rossen film *All the King's Men* (1949), starring Broderick Crawford as a ruthless career politician patterned after the dictatorial Huey Long, based on the novel by Robert Penn Warren. Though initially nervous as he watched the rushes and was startled by the "rawness" of the near-documentary location footage, Cohn saw his enthusiasm for the project justified when Crawford won the Academy Award for Best Actor, Mercedes McCambridge won for Best Supporting Actress, and the film itself won Best Picture at the 1950 Academy Awards.

Vincent Sherman's *Harriet Craig* (1950), an update of *Craig's Wife*, was also a solid box-office hit, with Joan Crawford in the leading role. Both were former employees of Warner Bros., seeking greener pastures in the wake of the de Havilland decision. The same was true of Warner alumnus Humphrey Bogart, who teamed with director Nicholas Ray to create the corrosive Hollywood noir *In a Lonely Place* (1950), as the pace of outside or "pick up" pictures increased at the studio and as the older model of studio hegemony collapsed. Sam Katzman, the most penurious of producers who nevertheless created a series of solid, low-budget successes for Columbia, continued his spate of westerns, science-fiction films, rock 'n' roll musicals, and horror films for the studio, while the reliable Gene Autry churned out "Singing Cowboy" westerns at the pace of six or seven each year.

In 1952, Stanley Kramer released László Benedek's screen adaptation of Arthur Miller's *Death of a Salesman* through Columbia, which was manifestly not a success with either audiences or critics. Fred Zinnemann's *Member of the Wedding*, based on the play by Carson McCullers, was a much more successful project, along with four other independent productions. But there was an ominous trend at work. Columbia was becoming, against Cohn's will, the model of the modern studio, financing outside packages with "first look" deals and then releasing the films as studio product. The 1953–54 season saw a further increase in the importance of outside productions, with Benedek's biker drama *The Wild One* (1953) from producer Stanley Kramer, Elia Kazan's *On the Waterfront*, and Edward Dmytryk's *The Caine Mutiny* (both 1954) all winning numerous accolades and performing exceptionally well in theaters; *On The Waterfront* and *The Wild One* also served to consolidate the appeal of actor Marlon Brando as a potent box-office draw.

By 1956, independent productions dominated Columbia's output almost entirely; such films as Robert Aldrich's suspense thriller *Autumn Leaves*, Fred F. Sear's *Rock around the Clock*, and Michael Anderson's intriguing adaptation of George Orwell's novel *1984* were all initiated and partially or wholly created as "outside" films. David Lean's *The Bridge on the River Kwai* (1957) was another major success for the company, and yet again, though it was packaged and executively produced by Columbia and bore the company's signature "Lady Liberty" logo, it was a co-production between Horizon Films and Columbia Pictures. George Sidney's *Pal Joey* (1957) was produced and directed by Sidney for Columbia, but again as an independent production. Even Budd Boetticher's low-budget westerns, such as *Ride Lonesome* (1959), were packaged by Boetticher and Randolph Scott's production company, Ranown Pictures. *Ride Lonesome* cost only $100,000 to make and was shot in ten days (Dixon, "Boetticher" 55). Once, a small picture like *Ride Lonesome* could have been knocked out on the Columbia back lot as a matter of routine; now even the most modest films were being packaged by outsiders.

Still, Cohn demanded total fealty from his employees. Future producer Tony Owen tried out a job as Cohn's assistant, but after eighteen months his wife, the actress Donna Reed, threatened to leave Owen unless he quit the job. If you worked for Harry Cohn, you were on call 24/7, and Reed refused to relinquish her husband to the overpowering mogul. Ironically, Reed would go on to play the Academy Award–winning role of prostitute Alma "Lorene" Burke in Fred Zinnemann's Columbia production *From Here to Eternity* (1953), which won a total of eight Oscars out of its thirteen nominations, including Best Picture and Best Director; later, Reed and Owen would team to create the enormously successful sitcom *The Donna Reed Show* for Screen Gems, Columbia's television production unit, racking up 275 episodes between 1958 and 1966 and becoming one of the studio's top TV money spinners. But despite remaining in Columbia's orbit for much of her professional career, Reed and Owen learned that it was important to keep their distance from Harry Cohn—get too close, and you could get burned. Working for Cohn was a body and soul commitment, but only from Harry's point of view; when he was through with you, you were out. The only way to work with Cohn was to keep him at arm's length, if you could—that way, your tenure at Columbia might last longer.

Not surprisingly, Cohn favored knockabout comedy over all other forms of entertainment—personally and professionally—and so it seems natural that he would wind up as the producer of the most brutal team in comedy history—The Three Stooges. Not for him the subtlety of Laurel and Hardy, the anarchy of the Marx Brothers (Harry Cohn always had to remain in control), or the balletic, ironic grace of Charles Chaplin. Harry Cohn wanted to see heads being knocked together, eyes being gouged out, and pies in the face in rapid succession. The Three Stooges (brothers Moe and Jerry "Curly" Howard, and Larry Fine) had been knocking around in vaudeville with an exceptionally violent comedy act since the 1920s, involving slapping, hitting, and various other forms of physical brutality. At the time, they were teamed with straight man Ted Healy, who slapped them around in their stage act with real violence. But for the moment, Healy was the bigger star, so the Stooges, with Moe Howard as their leader, bided their time, looking for better opportunities. The Stooges made some shorts with Healy at MGM, many of them in two-strip Technicolor, in addition to appearing as bit players in feature films for the studio, but the chemistry was wrong. Healy's onscreen near-sadism made audiences uncomfortable. When Healy went solo, the Stooges saw their chance and put themselves on the market as The Three Stooges in 1934.

In a real-life mix-up that could easily have served as a plot line for one of their more than 190 two-reel shorts, group leader Moe Howard directed Larry and Curly to "spread out" and look for a studio deal. Moe met with Harry Cohn—without an appointment—and secured a contract for a series of two-reel shorts at $1,500 for the team per film. Meanwhile, unbeknownst to Moe, Larry was signing a similar deal with Carl Laemmle at Universal. The next morning, Moe went to Columbia, hat in hand, and explained what had happened to Cohn, expecting the worst. To his surprise, Cohn merely laughed, remarking that "this story would make a helluva movie," and placed a call to Universal's legal affairs department.

Moe had signed his deal with Columbia an hour or so before Larry had signed the team up with Universal, so Universal agreed to tear up Larry's contract and Cohn emerged victorious. "You boys belong to Columbia!" Cohn exulted, and so they remained through 1958, when the Columbia shorts unit folded and the trio was unceremoniously canned (Howard 65–67). Leaving the studio on his final day of work, where he had labored for twenty-four years, Moe forgot his lunch pail and some other personal effects in his dressing room. When he returned the next day to retrieve them, he found to his amazement that he was barred from the lot. "Sorry, Moe," said the security guard. "As of yesterday, you and your buddies are finished here" (Fleming 101).

By this time, Harry Cohn was dead, but as a metaphor for the "here today, gone tomorrow" heartlessness of the end of the studio era, the story is emblematic. After the Stooges' exit, Screen Gems, Columbia's TV arm, repackaged their two-reel shorts for children's television, where they were a resounding success and led to Columbia's hiring them back for a string of low-budget features that grossed millions at the box office. For his part, Moe Howard, despite the team's success at Columbia, remained diffident about their long tenure at the studio, remarking that "several years [after their initial contract mix-up], Universal signed Abbott and Costello. I doubt very much if they would have joined Universal if fate had us sign there first" (67). To the end of his days, Moe saw The Three Stooges as a feature act, not strictly a two-reel proposition. But Harry Cohn felt otherwise.

No matter what the situation, Cohn had to retain the upper hand. When Cohn's longtime aide Sidney Buchman once lacked change for a Coke machine during a trip, he asked Cohn to lend him a nickel. Cohn eyed him suspiciously, flipped him a coin, and when Buchman returned from the dispensary machine found Cohn still glowering at him. "For Christ's sake, I'll give you your nickel back," shouted Buchman, but Cohn wasn't placated. "Didn't you see the change machine?" Cohn demanded— which Buchman hadn't. Eventually, Buchman shrugged the incident off, but he was still amazed that Cohn, a multimillionaire and one of the most powerful men in Hollywood, was afraid that he might be cheated out of a nickel (Thomas, *King* 211).

Cohn was always afraid of being played for a sucker, in matters both small and large. For in Cohn's world, there were only two sides to any deal: the con man and the mark. Cohn was determined that he would never be a mark in anyone's con game. But unlike the other studio bosses, Cohn took this obsession with being entirely self-reliant to hitherto unimaginable extremes. When one of Columbia's publicity men, Whitney Bolton, heard a Columbia staff producer ridicule Cohn at a sneak preview at the Pantages Theater in Hollywood, Bolton reflexively defended his boss. When Cohn heard about the incident, he summoned Bolton to his office. "You're a schmuck," Cohn began. "Who the fuck told you to defend me? You put me under obligation to you for something I didn't do. I want you to quit. If you remained here, I would never be able to pass you on a studio street without knowing I was obligated to you." And so, settling $18,000 on Bolton to buy out his contract, Cohn summarily fired his erstwhile defender. Harry Cohn refused to owe anyone anything (Thomas, *King* 213).

At the same time, Cohn, using his system of hidden microphones and loudspeakers installed on every Columbia soundstage, was omnipresent on the studio lot, even if he never left his office. Cohn would often dial up one of the surveillance microphones on even the smallest "B" picture on the lot and listen to the directors and actors at work without their knowledge. When he heard something that displeased him, Cohn wasn't shy about expressing his reservations. "That was lousy. Try it again," his disembodied voice once admonished a bit player in a program picture, booming out of the darkness without warning. Startled, the actor nervously asked, "Who was that?" "God," responded the director, by now used to Cohn's tactics, as he continued working (Thomas, *King* 214).

Nor was an actor's or director's private life off limits. When William Holden first started out at Columbia with Rouben Mamoulian's *Golden Boy* in 1939, Cohn accosted the actor one day with the preemptory comment, "I hear you're going out with some dumb broad." Holden, astonished, told Cohn in no uncertain terms that whatever he was doing, it was his private life, adding, "What I do after I leave the studio is my business." Unperturbed, Cohn countered, "That dame is poison. She's a dumb broad, and she's six years older than you are," and then, without waiting for a response, walked away (Thomas, *King* 215–16). Nothing was sacred for Cohn, and he seemed to take a perverse pride in burnishing his hard-nosed reputation.

As the 1950s dawned, however, Cohn had to admit that the film business was changing, and he didn't like the new order of things one bit. One problem was that Cohn couldn't delegate authority. In contemporary terms, Cohn was the ultimate micromanager, supervising every film, from the biggest feature to the simplest short, down to the last detail. No one, he thought, could do it as well as he could. Jerry Wald, one of Warner Bros.' top producers in the 1940s, who left WB for a brief stint at RKO, soon became disenchanted with RKO and Howard Hughes's interference there and accepted an offer from Cohn to become vice-president of production at Columbia. Wald should have known better; he soon clashed with Cohn over script supervision, production approval, and other matters, and eventually resigned. Wald was certainly a capable producer, with many successful films to his credit; that wasn't the problem.

What was wrong with the setup, as Wald explained much later in a letter to director Fred Zinnemann, was "Harry Cohn's maniacal attitude toward everyone in the studio. If I had an idea for casting, a script change or a story, it always had to be told to Cohn, and no one else. Eventually Cohn would convince everyone that [he alone] was responsible for all the films made at Columbia and that no one [else] contributed any at all" (Dick, *Merchant* 184). Cohn was entering his sixties, and as he aged, his desperation grew. He felt his hold on the studio weakening, and he wasn't going to go gently into that good night.

Columbia's major contract stars, especially William Holden and Glenn Ford, were constantly complaining about scripts or working conditions, and even the younger stars Cohn was building up, such as Kim Novak, were proving temperamental. But he couldn't let go of his old vision of the studio as it had been in its heyday; he wanted to return to the past. And most of all, Harry Cohn wanted to remain unquestionably in charge, answering to no one but himself, the final arbiter of all decisions relating to Columbia. Thus, when Jack Cohn's son, Ralph, proposed that Columbia enter the new medium of television, Harry approved financing for the project, entitled Screen Gems, but for all the wrong reasons; he simply wanted to get Ralph out of the studio on the West Coast and back to New York with his father to make deals pertaining to Screen Gems' financial structure. Cohn didn't really care about television; as with many of the old-school moguls, it was a medium he couldn't understand, or, from his point of view, control. But getting rid of Ralph was too tempting to pass up; Ralph was almost as abrasive as Harry. Cohn agreed to finance Ralph's venture into television to the tune of $50,000, reasoning that "one bastard at the studio is enough." Thus, simply because Harry Cohn wanted Ralph out of the West Coast studio, Screen Gems was born (Thomas, *King* 293).

To Harry Cohn's surprise and chagrin, Screen Gems was an almost immediate success, creating *Ford Theater* in 1952—a total of 39 half-hour films at a cost of $25,000 each, with the Ford Motor Company providing 75 percent of the financing for first-run nights and possible reruns. In return, Columbia retained all rights to the negative—a real coup—and the deal, valued at $1 million for the season, laid the groundwork for network programming produced by the majors in the decades to come (Thomas, *King* 293). But at the same time, the number of Columbia's theatrical releases was steadily shrinking, from sixty-three films in 1951 to a mere thirty-five in 1954 (Thomas, *King* 293). Theatrical films were all that Harry Cohn really cared about. The television business was just a necessary evil, and Harry Cohn could just as easily have lived without it. Ralph Cohn was the real visionary here and he had only one interest, the bottom line. If Columbia was going to continue to survive, television had to be a significant part of its future, either in a series made directly for television or the leasing and/or rental of its older films for television, both shorts and features.

In the midst of all these developments, Howard Hughes, feeling over his head in day-to-day operations of RKO, approached Cohn with a singular proposition. In addition to his duties at Columbia Pictures, Hughes wanted Cohn to take over the management of RKO and run both studios simultaneously. Such an idea had never been floated before, but Hughes, ever the eccentric, decided that Cohn had both the skills and the energy to take on the task. Cohn was flattered, but after hosting a prolonged series of clandestine late-night meetings at his house, the deal fell through. Cohn realized that he had enough trouble keeping Columbia's house in order and that RKO was facing major problems with its bottom line, which wasn't helped by Hughes's erratic production methods. It would simply be too much for one man to handle, even Harry Cohn (Thomas, *King* 294).

RKO thus continued its downward spiral into collapse, becoming the first of the majors to die. It's intriguing to think of what might have happened if Cohn and Hughes had joined forces, but ultimately it appears that the idea was doomed from its inception. Both were fiercely independent men with a need for total control—Hughes also used a microphone surveillance system on the RKO lot, just as Cohn did, for one example (Thomas, *King* 294). The two men would have inevitably clashed over Hughes's extravagance and penchant for endless post-production trickery with his films, to say nothing of his policy of endless retakes, occasionally even scrapping most of a completed film and its director only to order reshoots later and resume production with a new director at the helm (the ill-fated Hughes production *Jet Pilot* immediately comes to mind; begun in 1949, it wasn't completed until 1957 and went through no fewer than seven directors during production: Josef von Sternberg, Jules Furthman, Philip Cochran, Ed Killy, Byron Haskin, Don Siegel, and Hughes himself). Harry Cohn would never have been so indecisive or profligate. For Cohn, acquisition, production, and distribution was a straight line; a good property, a solid director, some bankable stars, and a few months later you had a film. It was as simple as that.

When offers now materialized to sell Columbia Pictures outright and retire, Cohn took them more seriously than he once had, but he still wound up rejecting them all. Cohn remembered how Mussolini had met his end, strung up in the streets by his heels like a steer after being slaughtered by his former subjects. If you turned away from someone for a second, they would stab you in the back. Cohn was determined this would not happen to him; he would go out on his own terms, and he would not be pushed. As he told one of his many minions, "Sitting behind this desk, I can always press the buzzer and get somebody to talk to me. If I wasn't head of the studio, who would talk to me? Who would come to my house for dinner? No, I won't do it" (Thomas, *King* 295). And so Harry Cohn clung precariously to power, battling on through a barrage of legal difficulties, fights with actors and his brother Jack, and the encroaching infirmities of old age.

And still he fought the new order, trying unsuccessfully to get rising star Jack Lemmon to change his name to Jack Lennon ("How the hell can I put a name like Jack Lemmon on a picture—the critics will murder you," Cohn demanded, to which Lemmon retorted, "Lennon? Great, just like Lenin—they'll say I'm a Commie!" [Thomas, *King* 337]), and throwing producer Mike Todd out of his office when Cohn arguably needed him more than the other way around. Cohn had been considering financing Todd's *Around the World in 80 Days*, and in New York Jack Cohn had approved a loan of $630,000 to partially finance the film in return for distribution rights. But Harry had been unimpressed with Todd, dismissing him as a small-time producer of vulgar burlesque shows who had also once reneged on a $2,000 bet (Thomas, *King* 346). Jack had arranged for Todd to pay a courtesy call on Harry to secure the loan; it would all be very pro forma and the deal would be done. But when Todd nonchalantly entered Cohn's office and put his feet up on the desk, Cohn was infuriated. "Take your fucking shoes off my desk," Cohn barked, to which Todd responded by removing his shoes and then putting his stocking feet right back on Cohn's desk. Cohn was apoplectic at this affront, and responded by calling Todd "a welshing son of a bitch" to whom he wouldn't loan a dime. Knowing he already had David Niven and Shirley MacLaine committed to star in his film, Todd calmly got up, walked out, and went down the street to United Artists, which was more than happy to co-finance production of the film. Cohn thus missed an opportunity to participate in one of the most profitable films of all time (Thomas, *King* 346).

As 1956 dawned, Harry Cohn was hit with an unexpected blow. His brother Jack went into the hospital for a minor operation to repair a hernia but developed an embolism and suddenly died (Thomas, *King* 353). Though relations between the two men had solidified into mutual hatred many years earlier, Harry Cohn wept at the news, as he realized that his own life was nearing its end. He still rejected any offers of friendship from his employees; when Kim Novak tried to give Cohn a box of her homemade fudge for Christmas in 1955, Cohn eyed her suspiciously and said, "You don't think you're going to get anything from me, do you?" and then chastised her for referring to him as "nice" during a radio broadcast. "How do you know whether I'm a nice man or not? You've only met me a few times. How dare you say that!" (Thomas, *King* 328).

Cohn suffered another loss when the HUAC investigation robbed him of the advice, counsel, and companionship of someone who had become indispensable to the aging mogul: Sidney Buchman. Buchman, a screenwriter and producer, had been instrumental in the rise of Columbia from its Poverty Row origins, penning the scripts for such films as Gregory LaCava's *She Married Her Boss* (1935), Richard Boleslawski's *Theodora Goes Wild* (1936), George Cukor's *Holiday* (1938), Capra's *Mr. Smith Goes to Washington* (1939), George Stevens's *The Talk of the Town* (1942), and Alexander Hall's *Here Comes Mr. Jordan* (1941), for which Buchman won an Academy Award for Best Screenplay. Buchman had one of the longest tenures of anyone at Columbia, and Cohn had a sort of rapport with him;

the two men could curse at each other for hours, almost as a sort of game.

But Buchman had been a member of the Communist Party from 1938 to 1945, when he left the party of his own volition after deciding that it was "stupid, blind, and unworkable for the American people" (Thomas, *King* 301). This wasn't enough, however, given the tenor of the times. Buchman refused to name names, and for that he had to be sacrificed. In its early years Cohn had resisted HUAC, believing that no one had the authority to tell him who to hire or fire. Unlike the strictly Republican MGM, or the socially conscious Warner Bros., Harry Cohn was never really interested in politics, only in movies, and he didn't care what any employee's political or religious beliefs were so long as the person made money for the studio. But eventually, when Larry Parks, star of Columbia's hit films *The Jolson Story* (1946) and *Jolson Sings Again* (1949), admitted being a member of the Communist Party, Cohn, too, was forced to acquiesce. Parks's contract with Columbia was cancelled, and politically tainted director Robert Rossen was also dropped from the Columbia roster. In Buchman's case, Cohn sat out the hearings, not really understanding any of it, but in 1951 Buchman was forced to resign and left the studio forever. Now Cohn was all alone at the top, with one of his closest allies cut out from his personal and professional lives, which were now (and had been, in reality, since the late 1930s) inextricably intertwined. After Buchman's departure, Cohn would often lament, to no one in particular, "Damn it, I wish Sidney was here" (Thomas, *King* 302). But Buchman was gone, and there was nothing Cohn could do about it.

To make matters worse, Columbia's stockholders seemed to be turning against him. At their annual meeting in November 1957, Cohn was trying to put on a brave front, but it was obvious to all in attendance that a seismic shift was taking place. Revenue was down on the theatrical side, and for the first quarter of the year most of Columbia's profits derived from Screen Gems through the sales and leases of old Columbia films to television—in other words, Columbia's past was more valuable than its present. Ralph Cohn, riding high on the success of Screen Gems, basked in his accomplishments, while Harry admitted that in the new Hollywood, with actors, writers, producers, and directors all free agents able to name their own price, the old system of making movies just wasn't working anymore.

In response to a stockholder's question about the ever-escalating cost of making films, Cohn replied matter-of-factly that "there's nothing we can do about these star deals. If Marlon Brando will make a deal with me tomorrow for fifty percent of a picture, I'd kiss him" (Thomas, *King* 355). Only four or five years earlier, Brando had been just another working stiff at the studio, doing whatever projects the studio assigned him without protest, even if he was moody and occasionally belligerent. Now, Brando was bigger than Columbia Pictures, the studio that Harry Cohn and his brother Jack had founded with their own sweat and hard work in 1924. This was something Harry Cohn couldn't accept or understand.

Along with the death of RKO, the end of Cohn's decades-long reign was one of the first signs of the complete collapse of the old hierarchy. Nor did this cataclysmic change go unremarked in the press of the day. In an atypically long and detailed piece in *Life* magazine, critic Eric Hodgins wondered aloud what would come next after the decline of the moguls. As he wrote, "A vast revolution has changed Hollywood from top to bottom in the course of a few explosive years. The revolution did not change merely a few externals: it changed an entire society. As always with a revolution, this one took place at the point of a gun. As always with a revolution, the times were ripe and the old order flabby" (146). Brutal stuff—but absolutely true, and, even though he hated to admit it, Harry Cohn was no longer the young man who had built a studio from the ground up nearly half a century earlier. As Hodgins noted,

Cohn himself described his current problems in his company's latest annual report: "We find ourselves in a highly competitive market for these talents (stars, directors, producers, writers). Under today's tax structures, salary to those we are dealing with is less inviting than the opportunity for capital gains. We find ourselves, therefore, dealing with corporations rather than with individuals. We find ourselves, too, forced to deal in terms of a percentage of the film's profits, rather than in a guaranteed salary as in the past. This is most notable among the top stars." . . . It is hard on the Harry Cohns, not just because their power is waning but because they are losing it to the men who were once their hired hands: the stars, the directors, the producers, and even—this last being the most galling—the writers. (Hodgins 146)

After the stockholders' meeting broke up, Cohn took his wife, Joan, out to Gallagher's, an old-style New York steak and potatoes restaurant that had been around since the early 1900s. By chance, the Cohns ran into Sidney Buchman, who was having a quiet dinner alone. Buchman had been all but barred from the industry due to the fallout from his HUAC hearing debacle; now living in New York, Buchman seemed resigned to his fate. (Buchman would later return to the business, working on the scripts for Joseph L. Mankiewicz's epic *Cleopatra* [1963] and Sidney Lumet's *The Group* [1966], but at that moment, his life was hard.) The glory days seemed gone; all that remained now was waiting around for the finish. As the two old warriors embraced, Cohn looked searchingly into Buchman's eyes. "What's it going to be, pal?" he asked. "Only what it has been, Harry," responded Buchman. "It's over" (Thomas, *King* 356).

Cohn stared at Buchman in stupefaction and realized that however much he might wish that it were not so, Buchman was right. It was over for Harry Cohn, and for Columbia Pictures as a working studio; the future was going to be outside films, financed and distributed by a studio but sold to the studio before production as a pre-packaged entity or even going to the highest bidder as a finished product. For a long, long time, the studio system had worked, until it didn't. Now Columbia was just a packaging and distribution plant, and Harry Cohn was uncomfortable in a world of independent deals. He couldn't believe that his former stars were now free agents; indeed, that all the major stars, no matter what studio, now had control over their careers. Cohn had made his empire out of packaging together stars, directors, and writers that he kept on his payroll; now, without that control, Cohn was at a loss. "Two weeks after I'm gone, they'll forget about me," Cohn predicted, always the grim pragmatist (Thomas, *King* 367). He may have been right, but then again Cohn's abrasiveness is still legendary within the industry. Beyond the man himself, however, the Columbia films of his era live on, and if today they have the appearance of medieval illuminated manuscripts that we associate with all films of Hollywood's golden age, it is because, apart from the work of the directors, actors, and writers involved, they bear the imprint of one man. Harry Cohn *was* Columbia Pictures, and all that remains now is a name, a transplanted studio (in, as noted, the former house of MGM), and a logo—which, though continually modified, remains iconic to this day.

CHAPTER 3

Z for Zanuck

Darryl Zanuck always behaved as if he had been to the manner born, so to speak, but in fact his life began in a rundown hotel in Wahoo, Nebraska, in 1902. I know; I've seen the hotel. It's a nondescript building in a nondescript town, in a state whose barren landscape is as unvaried as the surface of the moon. Wahoo is also the birthplace of composer Howard Hanson, Hall of Fame baseball player Sam Crawford, and Nobel Prize laureate and geneticist George Beadle, but of all these Darryl F. Zanuck had the humblest beginnings. His father was an alcoholic hotel clerk; his mother was the daughter of the hotel's owner. Theirs was a marriage created out of loneliness, fear, and desperation, and, of course, it couldn't last. Before Zanuck was thirteen, both his parents had deserted him.

At fifteen he lied about his age and joined the army, fighting heroically in World War I. When the war ended, Zanuck drifted from one menial job to the next, working as a boxer, as a steelworker, and in a garment factory—anything that would keep body and soul together. At the same time, though he lacked almost any formal education, Zanuck doggedly pursued his chosen career as a writer, selling his first story to the pulp magazine *Physical Culture*. Later, he adapted the story into a film script and sold it to the long-forgotten silent film actor William Russell as a possible vehicle; before long, Zanuck was pitching story ideas to Irving Thalberg, Carl Laemmle, and Mack Sennett, and proved to have a genuine flair for concocting compelling scenarios—certainly what he had seen of life, even then, gave him more than enough material.

By the late 1910s, Zanuck was working regularly for Mack Sennett and other low-budget Hollywood impresarios on a regular basis, and he eventually landed a job with the fledgling Warner Bros. studio in 1924, where, along with writer/director Malcolm St. Clair, Zanuck co-created the *Rin Tin Tin* series, about a heroic police dog who invariably saved the day in the final reel of the film. For someone who lacked a literary background, Zanuck soon became ridiculously prolific at pounding out screenplays, sometimes under pseudonyms, and soon elevated himself through sheer persistence and force of will to the role of producer. When Warners made the transition to sound, Zanuck went right along with the trend and supervised production of numerous early WB talkies, such as *The Jazz Singer* and *I Am a Fugitive from a Chain Gang*.

By 1933, Zanuck was one of the top men at Warners, making $5,000 a week during one of the worst economic downturns in American history. But Zanuck was chomping at the bit at the Warner studio, realizing that Jack and Harry Warner would never let him reach top-level status as an executive, and so he quit Warner Bros. in 1933, determined to keep moving up the Hollywood ladder. As an experienced production executive, offers of employment were almost instantly forthcoming, but Zanuck soon realized that only one thing would satisfy him: total control over a studio with no interference. He was tired of taking orders from others, and, more than that, he thought he could do a better job than any of his bosses. There was only one way to do that: Zanuck had to form his own studio, which he quickly incorporated in late 1933 as 20th Century Pictures. A young man on the way to the top, Zanuck was moving rapidly and decisively to consolidate his power in the film capital.

Financing for the new studio came from a variety of sources, demonstrating how incestuous the film business was when one reached the top of the ladder. Joseph Schenck and Louis B. Mayer, along with the Bank of America and Herbert J. Yates (then owner of Consolidated Film

Laboratories, and soon to be proprietor of the mini-major studio Republic Pictures), provided Zanuck with the cash he needed to get the studio up and running. Seeing that William Fox's Fox Studio was spiraling into financial collapse as a result of the Wall Street crash of 1929 and its lingering effects—Fox had not been the wisest investor—Zanuck moved in and merged the two companies in 1935, creating 20th Century Fox and acquiring Fox's group of theaters as part of the deal. But there was an even more important aspect to the deal with Fox: Zanuck inherited, as part of the package, the contracts for Shirley Temple and Will Rogers, then America's most popular homespun entertainer. Rogers, who coined the phrase "I never met a man I didn't like," made a string of folksy, comforting comedies that kept the nation reassured in the darkest days of the Depression and generated consistent profits for Fox. Rogers, however, was killed in a plane crash in 1935, shortly after the 20th Century Fox merger, and thus Zanuck could only release Rogers's final films with suitable fanfare. He then concentrated on Temple.

Precocious by any standard, Shirley Temple had been making two-reel comedies for Educational Pictures, perhaps the most impoverished studio in Hollywood, since the age of three. The series, entitled "Baby Burlesks," was an unsettling mixture of infantilism and prepubescent sexuality; one of her shots for Educational found her appearing as "Movelegs Sweettrick," a parody of Marlene Dietrich's character in Josef von Sternberg's *The Blue Angel* (1930) (Custen 206). These primitive shorts had something uncomfortably salacious in their presentation, and Zanuck wisely decided to concentrate on Temple's wholesome appeal instead. William Fox was paying Temple $150 a week in 1933 (her mother received an additional $25 a week for household expenses), and Fox made some fast money by loaning Shirley to Paramount for Alexander Hall's 1934 version of the Damon Runyon classic *Little Miss Marker* at $1,000 a week (Custen 206–07).

The film was a hit, and Fox put her in Hall's *Baby Take a Bow* (1934), which made a fortune for the studio. Now, with the merger in place,

Shirley Temple became a 20th Century Fox property, and Zanuck wasted no time in putting her in one film after another. All of them were modestly budgeted in the $200,000–300,000 range but reliably grossed $1–1.5 million in their first runs, doing surprisingly even better in second-run "grind houses" (Custen 207). Indeed, Shirley Temple was the top box-office star in the industry between 1934 and 1940, until the disastrous performance of Walter Lang's heavy-handed *The Blue Bird*—a combination of poor script, obvious imitation of *The Wizard of Oz*, and the lack of appeal of a rapidly maturing star, an adorable little moppet no more—brought an end to her career. In the meantime, Zanuck was shrewdly building up leading man Tyrone Power (in *Lloyd's of London* [1935]) and ingénue Alice Faye as future stars, along with Don Ameche, Victor Mature, and Dana Andrews, as well as character actors Vincent Price, Laird Cregar, and others.

Shirley Temple's departure from 20th Century Fox was a turning point for Zanuck and the studio, but by this time Zanuck, who considered the three most important elements of any film to be "story, story, story" (Custen 173), was more than ready for the challenge. He also viewed Temple's departure as an opportunity to move the studio into more serious territory, away from the light, escapist fare that she had provided. In 1940, 20th Century Fox released John Ford's grimly faithful adaptation of John Steinbeck's *The Grapes of Wrath*, detailing the flight of the Joad family and other "Okies" who headed to California during the Depression, looking for work.

Although *The Grapes of Wrath* failed to win the Academy Award for Best Picture—the film was viewed by the Hollywood establishment as too controversial, downbeat, and potentially socialist—several Zanuck films were later to receive the honor: John Ford's *How Green Was My Valley* (1941), Elia Kazan's *Gentleman's Agreement* (1947), and Joseph L. Mankiewicz's *All about Eve* (1950) (Custen 227). It's also worth noting that *The Grapes of Wrath* did win the Academy Award for Best Director (Ford) and Best Supporting Actress (Jane Darwell as Ma Joad), and was nominated in five other categories, including Best Picture. The film was a serious attempt at making a difference on the screen, and Zanuck was justly proud of what he had accomplished.

During the 1940s, Zanuck alternated between socially conscious films such as William Wellman's *The Ox-Bow Incident* (1943), about a lynching in the old West, based on the best-selling novel by Walter van Tilburg Clark, and Elia Kazan's *Pinky* (1949), a racial drama improbably starring Jeanne Crain as an African American woman who "passes" in white America; surefire hits like *Laura* (1944), one of the most effective detective thrillers of the era, and an early precursor of film noir; and John Stahl's lavish Technicolor melodrama *Leave Her to Heaven* (1945), based on the popular novel by Ben Ames Williams, centering on the homicidal impulses of an insanely possessive wife.

Yet Zanuck also produced one of the biggest flops in the history of the studio; *Wilson* (1944), Zanuck's personal paean to the life and career of Woodrow Wilson, starring Alexander Knox in the title role. Zanuck poured more than $3 million into the project and arranged a star-spangled premiere in Wahoo, Nebraska, with some of the studio's biggest stars, Betty Grable, Gene Tierney, and Tyrone Power, in attendance, hyping the film as "the most important event in fifty years of motion picture entertainment" (Custen 279). After the hoopla of the premiere died down, however, it turned out that the public wasn't interested.

Though he frequently made pronouncements against "message" films, in truth Zanuck had a message, delivered in his own messianic egocentric fashion: that the world could be a better place and that although problems presented themselves on every side, they could be solved through mutual cooperation and sustained group effort. As Zanuck noted when *Wilson* went into production (using the royal "we" to refer to a supposed corporate decision that was, in reality, his own idea alone),

We are producing *Wilson* because we believe in it. It is, by far, the biggest undertaking of the 20th Century Fox studios. What is true of *Wilson* is equally true of Wendell Willkie's *One World*, which we are also preparing for the screen [but which never made it past the screenplay stage]. Those pictures simply supplement one another. [*One World*] deals with a principle—visual proof of how the world has shrunk, and how completely the nations of the world have become dependent on one another. Those pictures, I feel, have something of importance to say to the world. They cannot say it if people do not see them in great numbers. I can tell you that unless these two pictures are successful from every standpoint, I'll never make another film without Betty Grable in the cast. (Behlmer, *Memo* 78)

Thus, when *Wilson* failed catastrophically, losing $2.2 million (Behlmer, *Memo* 78), Zanuck, still the pragmatic businessman, heeded his own advice. Notwithstanding a spate of socially conscious films in the late 1940s, he gradually drifted into the realm of sheer entertainment. Years later, Zanuck tellingly confessed that "of all the pictures I have made in my career, *Wilson* is nearest to my heart. None of my studio confreres shared my fond hope of making [the film] a box-office success. When *Wilson* was released their worst fears were realized" (Behlmer, *Memo* 78). During the lavish premiere in his hometown of Wahoo, the opening night of the film was a rousing success, and both Darryl and Virginia Zanuck were convinced that the film would be a smash. The next day, however, reality set in, for when Zanuck visited the same theater that had been so completely filled with cheering patrons the night before, he found it almost deserted.

What had gone wrong? Buttonholing a passerby, Zanuck asked him why the theater was empty. The response was brutal and cut Zanuck like a knife: "The people of Wahoo wouldn't have come to see Woodrow Wilson if he'd rode down Main Street in person, so why in Hell should they pay to see [someone play] him in a movie?" (Mosley 214). Zanuck was shattered and never forgot the ignominious failure of his pet project. In fact, when he accepted the Academy Award for Best Picture in 1948 for *Gentleman's Agreement*, he stunned the audience by telling them, "I should have got this for *Wilson*" (Mosley 215). (In actuality, despite being a complete financial disaster, *Wilson* did win five Academy Awards, including Best Original Screenplay.)

As many have observed, Zanuck's true gift as a producer was as an editor—someone who knew how to recycle formulaic plots and situations over and over and still manage to make them seem fresh. At the same time, there is in most 20th Century Fox product an air of really careful calculation—borne out by Zanuck's interoffice memos—that one should never stray too far from safely mainstream taste. Zanuck knew how to cut, and more importantly where to cut, in both scripts and rough cuts of films, to keep his films moving along with maximum velocity.

As one of many concrete examples, consider his memo of August 10, 1950, to producer Julian Blaustein and screenwriter Edmund North on Robert Wise's *The Day the Earth Stood Still* (1951), originally titled *Farewell to the Master*. Zanuck's suggestions are sharp and concise, and, most important, involve the audience from the outset. After noting that "I do not like the title. We must have an exciting, provocative title that will tell an audience what to expect," Zanuck calls for cuts in the opening scene, which takes place on the spaceship of the protagonist, Klaatu (played by Michael Rennie in the role that made him a star)—suggesting that "you should open with the second sequence and treat it as realistically as you possibly can. You should suddenly hear radio programs with startling flash announcements from Washington, New York, Los Angeles, etc. The whole nation is 'listening in.' This should be dramatized like the opening of a documentary film." This is exactly how it appears in the film itself, as real-life newsmen H. V. Kaltenborn and Drew Pearson relay "special bulletins" about the landing of Klaatu's spaceship on a baseball diamond at midday in the heart of the nation's capital (Behlmer, *Memo* 191).

Despite the obviously pacifist bent of the story—Klaatu's mission to Earth is to warn the planet that it is becoming a danger to the safety of the universe as a whole, and that mindless violence must cease—Zanuck also warns against preaching to the audience: "I don't mean to avoid [the political problems presented in the film] because that is an entire issue of the story, but I believe if we try to preach or propagandize too obviously we will defeat ourselves" (Behlmer, *Memo* 192). In its final cut, *The Day the Earth Stood Still* contains an unmistakable call for peace in the new nuclear age, but at the same time it delivers the requisite suspense, special effects, and futuristic hardware and sets that audiences expected from a science fiction film. The end result is entertainment with a message— something that Zanuck pursued in many of his films, whether he liked to admit it or not.

When postwar anti-Semitism became an issue, Zanuck, the lone gentile among the studio bosses of the golden age, went into production with Elia Kazan's *Gentleman's Agreement*, in which Gregory Peck plays a magazine writer who poses as a Jew and experiences firsthand the prejudice and ostracism of racist American society. While he was perfectly at home creating more directly escapist fare such as Rouben Mamoulian's *The Mark of Zorro* (1940), even this film, with its subtext of social injustice righted by a lone vigilante, has a subliminal message for its audience.

In Irving Cummings's *The Story of Alexander Graham Bell* (1939), we are shown the results of one man's dogged pursuit of a scientific invention for the benefit of mankind, albeit in a distinctly hagiographic manner. Henry Hathaway's *Kiss of Death* (1947), while nominally a crime thriller (and Richard Widmark's breakthrough film in the role of a baby-faced psychopathic killer), is nevertheless also a film about the mechanics of police work, the necessity of maintaining the rule of law in the uncertain postwar era, and a paean to the American justice system, which is portrayed as relentless in hunting down those who would attempt to undermine its authority. At the same time, as Zanuck demonstrated with Hathaway's *Niagara* (1953), 20th Century Fox embraced sheer suspense in its more commercial projects; there is also an undeniable air of misogyny in the film, especially in the film's treatment of Marilyn Monroe's portrayal of an unfaithful, scheming wife who is strangled to death by her estranged husband (Joseph Cotten); the film seems to imply that she deserves whatever she gets.

Yet even at the height of the Blacklist, Zanuck refused to overtly propagandize in his films. As he was readying production on Kazan's anti-communist film *Man on a Tightrope* (1953), he sent the director a letter on July 29, 1952, analyzing "*why* [original emphasis] every anti-Communist picture made so far has proven to be a box-office flop," arguing that "they were so violently anti-Communistic that they . . . managed to turn themselves into 'message' pictures [which were] 'obvious.' . . . More than ever before people are going to the theater today to escape lectures, propaganda, politics and the constant talk, talk, talk which they get on television and the radio" (Behlmer, *Memo* 215).

Ultimately, 20th Century Fox didn't join the Red hysteria bandwagon embraced by RKO and Republic because, in Zanuck's view, it simply wasn't good "entertainment." This may sound odd coming from the man who supervised the production of *I Am a Fugitive from a Chain Gang* in his Warner Bros. days and then went on to create *Gentleman's Agreement*, Anatole Litvak's *The Snake Pit* (1948, a pioneering study of mental illness), Kazan's racially conscious *Pinky* (1949), Kazan's *Boomerang* (1947, about the murder of a priest), Nunnally Johnson's *The Man in the Gray Flannel Suit* (1956, warning of the dangers of corporate conformity in the advertising game), and numerous other films that contained what can only be termed overt liberal messages in their dramatic structure, but Zanuck was first and foremost a showman, and, as his memos indicate, he kept a constant eye on the bottom line, audience tastes, as well as his own political and social views when approaching a new project.

Zanuck thus emerges as a very different mogul from the typical Hollywood stereotype; he was thoughtful, circumspect in his judgments, and, while an absolute autocrat in his dealings with his staff, ultimately interested in combining escapism with a definite edge of social activism in an era when it was both unfashionable and often dangerous to do so. Finally, it is also worth pointing out that until 1952, motion pictures were not protected as free speech under the First Amendment, being seen as a form of interstate commerce by the U.S. Supreme Court rather than as artistic expression.

This would change with the *Miracle* decision in 1952, so named after the 1948 film *Il Miracolo* by Roberto Rossellini, in which the Court for the first time recognized the cinema as a medium of ideas and values, overturning the 1915 *Mutual* decision that allowed the censorship of films across the United States at the whim of local authorities. Zanuck and his peers during this era operated under a strict code of enforced values that they were obligated by law to adhere to; even after 1952, it would take more than fifteen years until the old Production Code collapsed in 1968, affording the medium the level of freedom and production it had long deserved (Dixon and Foster 171).

Yet when one looks at Zanuck's work across the years, a definite struggle between meaningful content and audience expectations emerges, as if Zanuck, despite his protestations, was often consciously attempting to push viewers to consider areas of American society that previously had been unexamined. This is particularly true of his work during his apprenticeship years at Warner Bros. In his now-forgotten production of Archie Mayo's *Doorway to Hell* (1930), with Lew Ayres improbably cast as a criminal mastermind, aided by associate James Cagney, Zanuck argued against Prohibition, demonstrating that it was unworkable, impractical, and unenforceable.

In Alfred E. Green's political comedy *The Dark Horse* (1932), Zachary Hicks (Guy Kibbee), a clueless presidential candidate, is propelled onto the national stage with a simple strategy. When asked any question at all, Hicks is instructed to look thoughtful, stroke his chin, and then invariably reply, "Well, yes, but then again, no," and thus seem wise and reluctant to "rush to judgment." Hicks eventually makes his way almost to the White House using this one trick. Mervyn Le Roy's *Three on a Match* (1933), one of the more astounding pre-Code films, deals with adultery, drug addiction, alcoholism, kidnapping, and suicide in a neat sixty-three-minute package, which is framed against a barrage of topical headlines (a Zanuck trademark) moving from 1912 to the present era. Robert Florey's *Ex-Lady* (1933), one of Bette Davis's most impressive early vehicles, focuses on a marriage in crisis, as commercial artist Bette refuses to give up her flourishing career and submit to the phantom authority of her advertising executive husband (Gene Raymond).

Having left Warners, Zanuck produced a pioneering study of anti-Semitism that predated *Gentleman's Agreement*, Alfred L. Werker's *The House of Rothschild* (1934), starring George Arliss in the title role and, in a memorable turn, Boris Karloff as a vicious racist who opposes Baron Rothschild's banking firm at every point; the film dealt frankly with the prejudice that Jews have faced throughout history, especially in the financial industry. Again, it's telling that Zanuck, the lone gentile in the industry, would even tackle such an inherently controversial project, while his brethren at the other studios urged him to sideline the film before it even went into production. Ever the showman, however, Zanuck saw to it that the film's penultimate scene, a fancy dress ball, was photographed in two-strip Technicolor, strictly for marginal value, and then promoted the film with constant references to this technological advancement—there was really no artistic or narrative reason for the switch from black and white to color in the film's final minutes, but it did give Zanuck an excellent promotional angle.

Zanuck followed with Richard Boleslawski's *Les Misérables* (1935), a naked depiction of justice carried to absurd and tragic lengths, with Charles Laughton as the obsessive police functionary Javert. John Ford's *Prisoner of Shark Island* (1936) is a sympathetic rendering of the ordeal of Dr. Samuel Mudd, who innocently treated the broken leg of John Wilkes Booth shortly after the demented actor had assassinated Abraham Lincoln. Mudd was unjustly accused of collusion with Booth and sentenced to a lengthy term of hard labor under a particularly sadistic prison warden (played with suitable relish by the great John Carradine). *Prisoner of Shark Island* is absolutely relentless in its depiction of the lynch-mob mentality that railroads innocent men and women in moments of political and social hysteria, a theme Zanuck would return to in 1943 with William Wellman's *The Ox-Bow Incident*, in which a group of innocent men are hanged by a lynch mob after being falsely accused of cattle rustling.

Yet at the same time Zanuck was making these rather bold, socially conscious films, he was also producing such feather-weight fare as Sidney Lanfield's *Sing, Baby, Sing* (1936), David Butler's *Pigskin Parade* (1936), Lanfield's *Wake Up and Live* (1937), and Lanfield's *Thin Ice* (1937), but then again, that's precisely what Zanuck strove for in his filmic output: a balance between the serious and the superficial, so that even if a more problematic film failed, it would more than be compensated for by the next Shirley Temple film or another similarly escapist confection. It is perhaps no accident that the producer among all others whom Darryl F. Zanuck idolized was the "boy genius" of MGM, Irving Thalberg, who was known for his penchant for occasionally making loss-leader films that might not score significantly at the box office but would definitely enhance the studio's artistic reputation. Yet Zanuck also produced out-and-out pop entertainment in such films as Irving Cummings's *Hollywood Cavalcade* (1939), Henry King's *Little Old New York* (1940), Walter Lang's *The Great Profile* (1940), and Gregory Ratoff's *Public Deb No. 1* (1940), as well as several Technicolor westerns directed by none other than Fritz Lang—*The Return of Frank James* (1940) and *Western Union* (1941).

One of the hallmarks of Zanuck's style was that he, perhaps more than any other studio head, worked with the director of a film in a respectful manner, provided, of course, that the project was one of value. For the programmers, Zanuck simply wanted the script shot as quickly as possible. But with his "A" directors, Zanuck offered a great deal of artistic freedom, almost invoking the auteur theory—that the director is the primary creator of a film—just around the time that this theory was first gaining popularity among French cinéastes. Thus Fritz Lang, every bit as egotistical as Zanuck, found an unlikely ally in the cost-conscious producer. Lang's days of profligacy on the set of his epic *Metropolis* (1927) in Germany were long behind him, and he had been forced to flee his native land rather than become part of the Nazi-unified UFA films, as Hitler's minister of propaganda, Dr. Joseph Goebbels, demanded.

After a sojourn in France, Lang made his way to the United States, survived the unsatisfactory experience of a heavily censored and recut lynching drama at MGM (*Fury*, 1936), and then landed at 20th Century Fox. When Zanuck put him on *Frank James*, Lang considered the film "an assignment, but I was interested: it was my first Western. . . . I remember Zanuck was very sweet to me on that picture, contrary to later on" (Bogdanovich 193). Lang viewed the western as equivalent for an American to "what the saga of the Nibelungen is for the European" (Bogdanovich 193).

Lang had tackled the Nibelungen saga (the basis for composer Richard Wagner's *Ring* cycle) during the silent era in Germany, with the two-part epic *Siegfried* and *Kriemhild's Revenge* (both 1924), for which he was given unlimited resources and an entirely open-ended budget. Now, sixteen years later, he was on a strict schedule and forced to adhere to studio dictates. Yet Zanuck's respect for Lang—even if their relationship eventually soured, as they almost always must between two strong-willed artists— moved him to take Lang on as a director, and to realize that because of his sense of spectacle and epic drama, Lang could offer a unique perspective on the opening of the West and the dictates of Manifest Destiny. Zanuck chose Lang even though *Frank James* star Henry Fonda hated working with the hands-on director, who, in stark contrast to the relatively unobtrusive (though equally dictatorial) John Ford, actually grabbed Fonda's hands during one scene to show him precisely how he wanted the actor to perform (Eisner 375).

Lang's Teutonic attention to detail, however, was really not that far from Zanuck's incessant micromanaging, as the producer continued to pore over scripts and dictate cuts and revisions to his secretary, in addition to viewing rough cuts of up to nine films a day in various stages of production so that every detail could be worked out to his satisfaction. Indeed, Zanuck's relentless supervision of every film that went through the studio, from the highest "A" budget film to the lowliest programmer, occasioned more than one practical joke on the producer.

During shooting of *The Mark of Zorro*, for example, director Rouben Mamoulian and his cast shot one gag scene in which one of Zorro's pursuers, discovering a bold "DZ" cut into the cloth backseat of a carriage, exclaims "Zanuck!" instead of "Zorro!"—to which the film's star, Tyrone Power, adds "Damn it!" Mamoulian thought this might amuse Zanuck, who inevitably screened every frame of a film's rushes, or dailies. Instead, Zanuck issued a stern directive that no such incident should ever occur again, citing the incident as a prime example of a waste of time and money during the production process.

Every director found a different way of working with Zanuck. John Ford, for example, always shot his films "to the cut," sticking his fist into the frame at the end of a take to signify the cut point to the editor. He rarely shot material he didn't use, but, unlike Alfred Hitchcock, he didn't storyboard excessively, instead working with the actors and screenwriters on the set on blocking and dialogue and then shooting one or two takes before moving on. Ford also almost never went to the rushes on his films, precisely because he trusted his technicians and actors and could himself visualize the film in his head without looking through the viewfinder to check each setup, or without viewing the raw material the next day.

Instead, Ford would leave it to his editor, usually Otho Lovering, to pull together a rough cut, and, given Ford's penchant for shooting only the material he needed, these rough cuts were usually pretty close to the finished film. But even Ford realized that Zanuck was a superb judge of pacing and editorial construction, and he noted that during his days at 20th Century Fox Zanuck "knew I hated to go into the projection room, so I had this tacit agreement that he would cut the picture. . . . He was a great cutter, a great editor" (Mosley 225).

Elia Kazan, in a somewhat similar manner, ingratiated himself during the production of his first film at 20th Century Fox, the period drama *A Tree Grows in Brooklyn* (1945), by flatly declaring that while he was an excellent stage director, "I don't know a goddamn thing about films. I know how to direct people, but I don't know what to do with the camera. Even if I *knew* what to do with the camera, I wouldn't know what to do with the film." As a result of Kazan's (perhaps calculated) admission, Zanuck assigned him Raymond Klune, Fox's most amicable house producer, ace cameraman Arthur Miller, utterly reliable assistant director Joe Bettin, and so on down the line. Kazan's tactic paid off: the film launched his career and paved the way for future projects with Zanuck (Mosley 226).

Yet Zanuck always kept his audience foremost in his mind. Frightened by the failure of *Wilson* and the equally disastrous collapse, after years of development, of his adaptation of Wendell Willkie's book *One World*— a plea for a new, united, and socially equitable international form of government (something like the "United Planets" that later surfaced in *The Day the Earth Stood Still*)—Zanuck was more suspicious than ever of mixing politics with mass entertainment. As he told a colleague in the mid-1940s, "I am [now] naturally suspicious of deep thinkers in relation to motion pictures. They sometimes think so deep they miss the point" (Mosley 227; Wiseman 279–87).

When television began encroaching on Zanuck's domain, the producer immediately understood that the only way theatrical films could compete with the new medium was through spectacle. But how could 20th Century Fox, or any studio, create an unbroken string of eye-popping, overwhelming films without resorting to repetitious story material or costly special effects? The answer was CinemaScope, adapted from a process created by French cinema pioneer Henri Chrétien in 1928. It had been used sporadically in an experimental fashion throughout the 1930s and 1940s on a few films, but it was never widely employed by any studio (Custen 321).

Zanuck decreed in 1953 that henceforth all 20th Century Fox films would be made in CinemaScope—a process that used an anamorphic lens on the camera to "squeeze" a panoramic image onto a conventional frame of 35 mm film, and then another lens on the projector to "unsqueeze" the image into a rectangular frame that engulfed the theater audience.

Fox's first CinemaScope film was Henry Koster's biblical spectacle *The Robe* (1953), and although the film itself is undistinguished, it was a massive box-office hit. As Zanuck observed at the time, "Producing companies no longer could depend on the movie-going *habit* [original emphasis]. More powerful attractions were necessary to lure a public whose leisure time and inflation-shrunken dollar were being savagely competed for by television, pocket books, magazines, sport, hobby industries and a variety of other spare time and money distractions" (Custen 322). Then as now this holds true, and Zanuck saw to it that all 20th Century Fox films—even two-reel travelogues—were produced in the 'scope format. And 'scope had several advantages economically; unlike 3D and Cinerama, both costly and clumsy processes, CinemaScope required only two lenses—easily produced, at a reasonable cost—to create their panoramic images, along with conventional cameras and projectors. Thus, even the cheapest 20th Century Fox films shot in black and white took on an aspect of phantom grandeur. The public ate it up, and of all the "new" processes developed in the 1950s to lure audiences back into theaters—3D, VistaVision, and the multiple-screen process Cinerama—only CinemaScope survives to this day, having fundamentally changed the way that motion pictures were visually composed. Before, the screen had been pretty much a small box; now, it offered a vast panorama of spectacle to the viewer. It was a triumph of both marketing and showmanship.

But as with all self-propelled powerhouses, Zanuck's internal battery was destined to eventually run down, and Zanuck's lifelong obsession with bedding as many young women as he could (despite the fact that he was married, with children) was also becoming an increasingly troubling problem. In 1951, Zanuck and his wife Virginia met a young woman named Bella Wegier while on a trip to France, and Zanuck became infatuated with her. This in itself was not unusual, but when Zanuck, Virginia, and Bella (now rechristened Bella Darvi—the surname a combination of Darryl and Virginia) returned to the United States and lived as a threesome in Zanuck's Ocean Front Drive beach house in Santa

Monica, even the jaded Hollywood community sat up and took notice
(Custen 353).

Zanuck began grooming Darvi as a star, but her good looks did not
lend her much in the way of acting talent or even onscreen charisma, and
her appearances in Samuel Fuller's *Hell and High Water* and Michael
Curtiz's *The Egyptian* (both 1954) were ridiculed by both press and public.
She simply had no place on the screen. Even the young François Truffaut,
then a firebrand critic for *Cahiers du cinéma* and several years away from
becoming a director in his own right, felt compelled to weigh in on Darvi's
performance in *Hell and High Water*: "Why is she involved in acting? Why
do they make her act? Why her? Not that she's so unpleasant to look at,
but as soon as she moves, talks, walks, what a disaster! . . . I do not think
I will hurt her by saying this, because I would bet that she hates acting and
feels as if she is being tortured in front of the camera" (qtd. in Dixon,
Truffaut 120–21).

Virginia had apparently been turning a blind eye to her husband's
affair with Bella, but finally, after a series of public embarrassments
(including a disastrous 1954 party at Ciro's restaurant in Los Angeles with
a circus theme, during which Zanuck suddenly and without warning
stripped to the waist and attempted, without success, to perform a one-
handed chin-up—an obvious attempt to demonstrate his masculinity),
Zanuck's daughter Susan told her mother what the rest of the world
already knew: Darryl and Bella were lovers (Mosley 273; Guild 9). In
retaliation, Virginia kicked them both out of the house. Eventually he
was taken back by his estranged spouse, but the tensions that had been
building in the Zanuck household had come to a boil (Custen 354).

So it was that in 1956 a tired and burned out Darryl F. Zanuck, sick of
the new Hollywood, with "everyone [i.e., actors, directors, writers, all the
people who used to simply be Zanuck's salaried employees] becoming a
corporation, with their own managers, their own agents, their own lay-
ers," left Hollywood to move to France, where he would establish himself
as an independent producer. He still owned a huge share of 20th Century

Fox stock, drew an annual salary of $150,000, and had struck a deal with the studio to distribute his films as an independent producer (Custen 357). Zanuck was only 53 years old, but he was tired, despairing, and simply couldn't accept the new order of things. As he told his compatriot Philip Dunne shortly before his departure from the studio, and the country, "In a very short time, the business will be completely dominated by the stars and their agents. Last week in this office, a goddamn agent started to tell me how a script should be rewritten. I kicked the bastard out, but next week he, or another one like him, will be back. We made the stars, but they've forgotten that. Now they think that they're entitled to run the business" (Custen 354–55).

In a 1960 interview with gossip columnist Hedda Hopper, Zanuck again complained that "actors have taken over Hollywood completely with their agents. They want approval of everything—script, stars, still pictures. The producer hasn't got a chance to exercise any authority!" (Behlmer, *Memo* 259). Dunne noted, "I also think he was tired . . . at the rate he had gone, he had to burn himself out sometime. . . . I think he was just bored with the whole thing, and not being able to drive himself as he had in the beginning. He was very young when he started" (Behlmer, *Memo* 260). Zanuck himself noted in a uncharacteristically unguarded letter to fellow studio boss Jack Warner on January 20, 1962, that "I am not bitter, but I have just reached the age and the point where I cannot spend my days with people I would not like to have dinner with at night" (Behlmer, *Memo* 261).

It was the old mogul's lament. No one was grateful for anything. The parade had passed Zanuck by, and rather than sit on the sidelines he was getting out. This left Zanuck's son, Richard, as vice-president of the newly formed DFZ Productions, to serve as liaison with 20th Century Fox's offices in Los Angeles. Meanwhile, Zanuck churned out six films of indifferent quality between 1956 and 1962 until he hit pay dirt with Ken Annakin, Andrew Marton, and Bernhard Wicki's D-Day spectacle *The Longest Day* (1962), an enormous project that starred John Wayne,

The Warner Bros. lot in Burbank at its peak, in the late 1930s.

Archie Mayo directs Bette Davis and Leslie Howard in *The Petrified Forest* (1936).

Cecil B. DeMille on the set of *The Crusades* (1935).

Stanley Kubrick (in dark jacket, on crane) directs *Spartacus* (1960).

Charles Laughton and Otto Preminger on the set of *Advise and Consent* (1962).

Clint Eastwood (right) shows nominal director John Sturges how to frame a shot on the set of *Joe Kidd* (1972).

John Ford (on platform, shading eyes) and John Wayne (foreground) on the set of *The Man Who Shot Liberty Valance* (1962).

Howard Hawks (seated foreground left, in chair with script) and the cast of *20th Century* (1934), including (center) Carole Lombard and John Barrymore.

Orson Welles, having broken his leg during a take, directs Dorothy Comingore from a wheelchair on the set of *Citizen Kane* (1941), at RKO Radio Pictures.

Alfred Hitchcock (foreground, center) discusses a scene for *Saboteur* (1942) with stars Robert Cummings and Priscilla Lane.

The Paramount Pictures studio facility in the late 1930s.

The Paramount commissary in the late 1930s.

An overhead shot of MGM Studios in the late 1930s.

The front gate of Paramount Pictures, one of the most iconic studio entrances.

Ginger Rogers and Carol Channing in Arthur Lubin's *The First Traveling Saleslady* (1956), the last film produced by RKO Radio Pictures.

A 1916 shot of the founders of Famous Players–Lasky, which eventually became Paramount Pictures; from left to right, Jesse Lasky, Adolph Zukor, Samuel Goldwyn, Cecil B. DeMille, and Zukor's brother-in-law Albert Kaufman.

"Genial" Jack Warner with Bette Davis and Joan Crawford suddenly all smiles, after the surprise success of Robert Aldrich's *Whatever Happened to Baby Jane?* (1962).

Darryl F. Zanuck, with drill rifle, on location for the epic production *The Longest Day* (1962).

Darryl F. Zanuck lost in thought on the set of *The Longest Day* (1962).

Gossip queen Hedda Hopper on the set of *The Art Linkletter Show* dishes the dirt, March 25, 1963.

A shot from Spencer Gordon Bennet's *Blazing the Overland Trail* (1956), from Columbia Pictures, the very last motion picture serial.

Jennifer Jones and David O. Selznick; just a song at twilight.

An early portrait of Columbia Pictures chief Harry Cohn.

Louis B. Mayer in his sleek roadster on the MGM lot in the late 1930s.

The enigmatic Howard Hughes, who briefly controlled RKO Radio Pictures and nearly ran it into the ground.

Gloria Swanson and Cecil B. DeMille on the set of Billy Wilder's *Sunset Blvd.* (1950).

An aerial view of the United Artists studio facilities in the 1930s.

The Mack Sennett studios in the early 1920s, when filming was still open to the public.

The front gate at MGM.

The Warner Bros. back lot in 2011: an empty space.

Rod Steiger, Henry Fonda, Robert Mitchum, Richard Burton, Sean Connery, Robert Wagner, Peter Lawford, and many other top-rank stars.

The success of *The Longest Day* emboldened Zanuck to think that perhaps his day was not entirely past and that he still might make one last stand as a studio executive. The film had cost $8 million, the most expensive (and ultimately profitable) black-and-white film (for a flavor of authenticity) until Steven Spielberg's *Schindler's List* in 1993 (Custen 361), and Zanuck and his directors shot 360,000 feet of film—more than sixty-six hours of raw material—for a film that would eventually run precisely 180 minutes in its final cut. Naturally, it was in CinemaScope (Custen 363).

But while Zanuck was finally finding some new ground for himself, back at home the company he had founded was in deep trouble. The problem: Joseph L. Mankiewicz's *Cleopatra* (released in 1963). This mammoth Technicolor disaster, whose budget amounted to roughly $40 million—the most money spent on a single film in Hollywood history at the time—went through two directors, numerous screenwriters, a shift from production in London to Rome, and a seemingly endless series of reshoots; *its* gargantuan cost ultimately threatened to sink 20th Century Fox altogether. Studio head Buddy Adler, left in charge when Zanuck departed in 1956, was dead. In his place Spyros Skouras was running the studio into the ground, with no grasp of how to rein in production costs on *Cleopatra*. And yet, the future of the studio now rested, in large part, on that film alone because of Skouras's mismanagement. It was a losing strategy and Zanuck recognized it. Zanuck decided that the only way he could protect himself, *The Longest Day*, and the studio itself was to return to Hollywood, particularly since he was doing so at the behest of many of the studio's old guard, who saw Darryl and Richard Zanuck as their only hope.

Appointing Richard as vice-president in charge of production, Darryl F. Zanuck became chairman of the board; in short, he was now back in unquestioned command, just as he had been in the studio's heyday. With *Cleopatra* pushing Fox deeper and deeper into the red, and no way to scrap the production—Zanuck realized they were in it to the bitter end, no matter what—the Zanucks essentially shut down the studio, firing some 2,000 employees, and turned their attention to existing properties that might bring in some revenue. Out of the ashes came Robert Wise's *The Sound of Music* (1965), which became one of the most profitable films in Hollywood history—$159 million in domestic gross on a negative cost of $8.2 million—as well as Robert Altman's *M*A*S*H* (1970), George Roy Hill's *Butch Cassidy and the Sundance Kid* (1967), and Franklin J. Schaffner's *Planet of the Apes* (1967) and its numerous sequels.

But the success of these films was more than offset by the outright failures of Wise's *Star!* (1968), which lost $10 million; Richard Fleischer's *Dr. Dolittle* (1967), which lost $11 million; and Gene Kelly's *Hello, Dolly* (1969), representing another $10 million down the drain. In response, Zanuck attempted to replicate the overwhelming success of *The Longest Day* with the wartime epic *Tora! Tora! Tora!* (1970), about the Japanese attack on Pearl Harbor. Richard Zanuck remained unconvinced about the commercial viability of the project from the start. Whereas *The Longest Day* was about one of the greatest Allied victories of World War II, *Tora! Tora! Tora!* focused on one of the worst disasters in U.S. military history. The film, for Richard Zanuck, was ultimately (and accurately) "the story of a defeat, and . . . the ending, no matter how we tried to twist it to get over that, was too downbeat" (Mosley 360). Initially to be co-directed by Richard Fleischer and famed Japanese auteur Akira Kurosawa at the astronomical cost of $20 million, the Zanucks soon realized that Kurosawa's footage simply wasn't working dramatically and summarily fired him (Mosley 362–63), eventually handing over the Japanese unit to action directors Toshio Masuda and Kinji Fukasaku.

Finally released after lengthy production delays, *Tora! Tora! Tora!* barely scraped by at the box office, but Darryl Zanuck had by then moved on to his new girlfriend, Genevieve Gilles (born Genevieve Gillaizeau) and the disastrous film *Hello—Goodbye* (1970), which Zanuck prevailed upon Jean Negulesco, now in desperate financial straits, to direct for a flat

$5,000 a week. Ronald Neame had started to direct the film but backed out when the "foredoom" of the project became all too apparent; Negulesco, for his part, was simply picking up a much-needed check.

Shooting progressed at a snail's pace, because Gilles seemed unable to remember her lines or follow even the most basic direction. "How long is this going on?" a visitor to the set rhetorically asked. "Forever, I hope," replied Negulesco, now reduced to being part of a ghastly joke, while Zanuck sat at the back of the set, smoking his usual enormous, phallic cigar, presiding over the entire enterprise with an air of complete detachment (Mosley 366). Clearly, Zanuck no longer really cared about anything other than pleasing his own whims, no matter what the expense.

With the failure of *Tora! Tora! Tora!* the writing was on the wall. Richard Zanuck was forced to resign in 1970, while Darryl stayed on as chairman of the board until, in a move that surprised everyone, Virginia Zanuck used her more than 100,000 shares of voting stock to force her husband's ouster, on April 19, 1971 (Custen 369). The company threw him a "Chairman Emeritus" bone with a minimal salary, but Darryl F. Zanuck's life and career were over, and he gradually retreated into life as a reclusive retiree at the Plaza Hotel in Manhattan.

Sadly, this was not to be the last chapter in Zanuck's life; after surviving an operation for cancer of the jaw (due, no doubt, to his lifelong habit of chain-smoking enormous cigars), Zanuck suddenly seemed forgetful and deteriorated rapidly. Although no one knew what to call it at the time, Zanuck was suffering from Alzheimer's disease, and in 1973 his wife welcomed him back to their home in Palm Springs. Genevieve Gilles was summarily dismissed from Zanuck's life, and Virginia took over his daily care. Continuing to fail, Zanuck finally died of complications from pneumonia on December 22, 1979, after three painful months on a respirator. He was 77 years old (Custen 370).

If this was Zanuck's life, what, then, was his legacy? In his single-minded desire to get to the top of the industry, he created his own studio from the ground up and personally produced 192 films. Many of these films were junk, and Zanuck knew it. Zanuck, however, ultimately had great respect for his audiences, as he noted in a 1950 memo on Henry Koster's 20th Century Fox production of *No Highway in the Sky*: "I give audiences today credit for a certain amount of intelligence or native imagination. They may not be brilliant but it doesn't take them long to catch on to what we are driving at. As a matter of fact, they would rather be a trifle in the dark, than have you spell it out for them" (qtd. in Behlmer, *Memo* 170)

Darryl F. Zanuck was arguably unique among the major studio potentates. His apprenticeship at Warners was something that he shared with other future power brokers, but once he broke with that studio in 1933 and rapidly consolidated his 20th Century Pictures with William Fox's failing theatrical empire, Zanuck functioned essentially as a lone wolf, answerable only to himself. He created films that entertained and enlightened, kept a tight rein on expenses, and seemed to have an almost superhuman ability to juggle numerous projects simultaneously, while affording each one a seemingly undivided measure of attention.

Perhaps, then, the ultimate tragedy of Darryl F. Zanuck was that he cared too much, that beneath his businesslike demeanor he was, in some peculiar fashion, an idealist. After all, no one forced him to produce films like Edmund Goulding's *The Razor's Edge* (1946), *The Snake Pit, Boomerang, Gentleman's Agreement*, or even *The Day the Earth Stood Still*, which despite its science-fiction genre trappings is at its heart a deeply felt plea for nuclear disarmament, disguised as a Saturday afternoon thriller. Even the character of Helen Benson in *The Day the Earth Stood Still* is more proactive than the typical 1950s female sci-fi protagonist; she gets involved, she implicitly saves the world from destruction at the vengeful, robotic hands of Gort, and she rejects the advances of a sleazy self-promoter, her nominal "love interest" in the film, for the loftier goals of mutual cooperation that Klaatu so clearly embodies.

In Wahoo, Nebraska, there is a small museum devoted to Darryl F. Zanuck, an unprepossessing structure housing various items of Zanuck memorabilia, including faded telegrams announcing the premiere of *Wilson*, numerous photographs and civic declarations, some costumes worn by the stars of the film, as well as a hagiographic history of the producer, mounted on a series of wall placards. It is staffed entirely by volunteers, who keep the lights off inside the building until someone actually stops by, which apparently isn't that often. Admission is free, but almost no one visits. As with Woodrow Wilson, no one in Wahoo cares about Darryl F. Zanuck anymore. And, as Mosley notes, "After the disastrous affair of *Wilson*, Zanuck never returned to Wahoo" (215). The dream of returning to his birthplace in a blaze of glory had been fatally tarnished, and Zanuck seemingly would not forgive the public, or the industry, that had let him down.

CHAPTER 4

Mayer's MGM

Louis B. Mayer was one of the original founders of the film industry, and, like many of his compatriots, he came from humble origins. Born in Minsk, Russia, in 1885, Mayer was brought to New York by his parents while still a young boy. Mayer's father was a laborer, a junk dealer, and anything else that (legitimately) paid the rent; the family soon moved to Canada, where Mayer Sr.'s junk business really took off, and soon Louis joined the family concern, fresh out of elementary school. After a while, Louis struck out on his own and returned to the United States, setting up a scrap metal business in Boston. After marrying in 1904, he bought a small movie theater in Haverhill, Massachusetts, in 1907 for a modest sum, renovated it, and began his film career (as did the Warners and many other moguls) as an exhibitor.

In seven years, Mayer, always a shrewd negotiator, built up an extensive group of movie theaters in New England, and in 1914 he moved into the distribution business. In 1915, he secured the New England territorial rights to D. W. Griffith's *The Birth of a Nation* (1915) and made a fortune screening the film in his numerous cinemas. But this was just the beginning for the ambitious entrepreneur, and in 1917 he started his own production company, Louis B. Mayer Pictures, after a brief apprenticeship at Alco (later known as Metro) Pictures. In 1918, Mayer moved to Los Angeles, sensing that the entire industry was moving away from East Coast production.

By 1924, his company was a major contender in the motion picture production business and attracted the attention of Marcus Loew, who now was the head of Metro Pictures. Loew gained control of Mayer's company, as well as the Goldwyn Pictures Corporation, and the three companies were consolidated as Metro-Goldwyn-Mayer. Mayer was immediately appointed as vice-president and general manager of the new concern, positions he held from 1924 to 1951, when he was pushed out in a neatly arranged coup by his erstwhile assistant, Dore Schary (more on this later).

This last episode was particularly painful for Mayer, as he had always depended upon the loyalty of his support staff, especially Irving Thalberg, the MGM production chief who served as the model for the fictional Monroe Stahr in F. Scott Fitzgerald's *The Last Tycoon* (Katz 922). Autocratic, ruthless, and seemingly tireless, Mayer was a brutal man who could nevertheless be charming and conciliatory when the situation demanded it. Mayer was instrumental in establishing MGM's studio identity as the most mainstream movie production company, with brilliant, high-key lighting, lavish sets (even on smaller productions), and a glittering roster of stars, directors, and technicians who stood ready to turn any property into a slick piece of escapist entertainment at a moment's notice.

When Mayer joined MGM, he brought with him Thalberg, lately released by Universal, and Harry Rapf, a no-nonsense production manager (Eames 7), two men who played a key role in the future of MGM. At the time of MGM's incorporation, Thalberg was only 24 years old, and before his untimely death at age 37 in 1936 he would be hailed as Hollywood's "boy genius" and put his unmistakable stamp on the studio (Katz 1347). It was Mayer, however, who really controlled MGM from top to bottom, with the later assistance of production chiefs Hunt Stromberg, and, fatefully, Dore Schary. MGM grew rapidly; by 1934, MGM employed a total of 4,000 people, including 51 certifiable stars, 17 first-class directors, and 51 top writers. The studio itself, at that time, comprised 23 soundstages, 117 acres of back lot property, and an enormous film laboratory that cranked out 150 million feet of 35mm release prints every year (Eames 58).

Early stars included Lon Chaney Sr.—"The Man of 1,000 Faces," a wizard at makeup and character parts—as well as more conventional leading men and women, such as Norma Shearer (who soon married Thalberg, thus placing herself first in the MGM pantheon of leading ladies, at least from the viewpoint of in-house status); future gossip columnist Hedda Hopper; Ramon Novarro, an early "Latin lover" archetype; Buster Keaton, the brilliant physical comedian; and directors Fred Niblo, John M. Stahl, Rex Ingram, King Vidor, and Robert Z. Leonard, as well as writers Frances Marion and Carey Wilson and art director Cedric Gibbons, one of the key architects of MGM's high-gloss visual style.

The first film that can be considered entirely an MGM production was 1924's *He Who Gets Slapped*, directed by Victor Sjöström, a circus melodrama starring Lon Chaney, Norma Shearer, and John Gilbert. Gilbert was the reigning matinee idol of the silent screen and the great love of Greta Garbo's life, though he came to a very bad end as the result of personal profligacy as well as running afoul of studio politics.

Gilbert and Mayer hated each other: Gilbert was a heavy drinker, frequented brothels, and even persuaded the normally upright Thalberg to join him on his nightly escapades, which infuriated the straitlaced Mayer (Eyman 133). All through this period, however, Gilbert courted Garbo, and, on September 8, 1926, Gilbert and Garbo were supposed to be married in a double ceremony with King Vidor and his fiancée, Eleanor Boardman. Vidor and Boardman were indeed married, but Garbo backed out at the last minute, leaving Gilbert standing alone at the altar. Mayer, seeing an opportunity to needle Gilbert, told Gilbert he should be happy just to sleep with Garbo. In response, Gilbert punched Mayer in the face, knocking him down and breaking his glasses. That was enough for Mayer, who angrily vowed to destroy the actor (Eyman 133). Some have doubted the veracity of this confrontation (Eyman 134), but Gilbert's drunken behavior, as well as his potentially damaging relationship with Garbo, one of MGM's biggest stars, was more than enough to cause Mayer to want to end Gilbert's reign on the screen.

Gilbert, however, had signed an ironclad contract with MGM for $250,000 a picture in late 1928, just before MGM moved to talkies, which even Mayer couldn't break (Eyman 147). But when sound came in, Gilbert's voice was judged too high-pitched to fit with his onscreen persona. His films began to fail at the box office, causing the actor to drink even more as his career collapsed (Eyman 148). Gilbert's films were now losing money—they didn't even cover the cost of his $250,000 salary per film—and Mayer considered firing him. He sought the counsel of Fanny Holtzmann, a street-smart show business attorney whose opinion he respected, but she bluntly advised him to "leave [Gilbert] alone and maybe he'll drink himself to death" (Eyman 186), which is precisely what Gilbert did. Once someone had lived out their usefulness and, worse still, become a public liability, his career was over. Besides, MGM had just signed an up-and-coming actor named Clark Gable, who seemed very promising as a romantic leading man. Mayer reasoned that the public would soon forget Gilbert, and they did.

But Gilbert was an anomaly. For the most part, MGM was an efficient factory, which ground out high-gloss films that burnished the company's desired image as the Tiffany of all the majors. Among the many successful silent MGM films during this period were Robert Z. Leonard's *Cheaper to Marry* (1925), Donald Crisp's *The Navigator* (1924; independently produced, starring Buster Keaton), and numerous others. But there were employees who needed to be brought in line. Directors had to function within the MGM studio system and obey Mayer's and Thalberg's dictates or they were out. Such was the case with the mutilated version of Erich von Stroheim's classic film *Greed* (1924). Although the story of the making of *Greed* is well known, it bears repeating here. Based on the Frank Norris novel, *Greed* was an epic film in every sense of the word, with an enormous budget and a lengthy shooting schedule; according to the few who saw *Greed* in its original form, it was also one of the screen's greatest achievements. But when von Stroheim completed the film, it ran forty-two reels in length, or about 420 minutes—von Stroheim envisioned it being released in two parts, with an afternoon screening of part 1, followed by a dinner break, and then part 2 in the evening.

Needless to say, both Mayer and Thalberg found this an impossible proposition; Thalberg had tangled with von Stroheim before, at Universal, and refused to give in to the director's demands. At length, Rex Ingram, von Stroheim's friend, cut the film (with assistance from June Mathis) down to twenty-eight reels, but even this did not satisfy the new regime at MGM. Thalberg ordered that the film be cut to ten reels, roughly 100 minutes of running time, no matter what the damage, and further that all the trims and outtakes be destroyed (Dixon and Foster 44). The experience practically destroyed von Stroheim, but Thalberg was unrepentant: at MGM, everyone had to toe the line and individuality was not encouraged. Conformity and uniformity were the hallmarks of MGM, and Thalberg and Mayer saw that they were enforced.

MGM was not averse to spectacle, however, provided it was properly handled. One example is Fred Niblo's *Ben Hur* (1925), a film the studio inherited from Goldwyn Pictures. That company had bought the rights to the Lew Wallace novel and began shooting in Rome three months before the merger with MGM. But the costs for the film, which starred Ramon Novarro as Ben Hur and Francis X. Bushman as Messala, were getting out of hand; when MGM took over the project, they brought it back to Los Angeles, where Thalberg and Mayer kept a tight rein on production costs.

The production costs reached $6 million—an astounding sum for a film in 1925—and due to the fact that Wallace's deal with Goldwyn Pictures called for the author to receive 50 percent of the gross profits, *Ben Hur*, despite being a certifiable box-office hit, never fully recouped its expenditures (Eames 18). Clearly, future deals would have to be more carefully orchestrated. Fortunately, King Vidor's World War I drama *The Big Parade* was released the same year and grossed more than $15 million at the box office, versus a negative cost of a mere $250,000. Again, there was a catch; Vidor had contracted to receive 20 percent of the gross profits of the lavish film in return for directing it on such a tight budget.

Now, Mayer moved in for the kill. With a combination of flattery, threats, and tearful appeals, Mayer cajoled Vidor into surrendering his 20 percent interest in the film in favor of a flat fee, thus deftly negotiating Vidor out of a much more favorable arrangement that would have grossed the director ten times as much, all for the good of the studio (Eames 18). MGM and Mayer came first; everyone else was simply an employee.

And yet, Mayer cultivated an attitude of paternalistic concern in all his business dealings that routinely convinced his constituents that he was operating in *their* best interests rather than his own, habitually reminding his stars, directors, and writers of how MGM would look after them, keep them out of trouble if they kept their noses clean, and manage their careers with an astute eye on the bottom line—MGM's bottom line. So skillful was Mayer as a negotiator that though nearly all his employees saw through this false mask of fatherly concern, they nevertheless continued to be convinced that despite all evidence to the contrary, MGM actually had their best interests at heart. Thus, the studio prospered, despite the expense of *Ben Hur* and the daily cost of running such an enormous enterprise; in 1926, only the studio's second year, MGM realized a net profit of $6,388,200 (Eames 28).

Now secure in its power base, with sound motion pictures only dimly on the horizon (and initially dismissed by the studio as a fad), MGM piled up the silent box-office hits. George W. Hill's *Tell It to the Marines* (1926) was a Lon Chaney vehicle that also made a star of William Haines, who would soon become one of the industry's first gay casualties, as his open lifestyle directly clashed with MGM's and Mayer's distinctly conservative sensibility. Gilbert and Garbo heated up the screen in Clarence Brown's steamy drama *Flesh and the Devil* (1926). Joan Crawford scored an early and defining success in Lucien Hubbard's version of Rudolf Friml and Herbert Stothart's Broadway musical *Rose-Marie* (1928)—astoundingly, a silent film version of a musical, of which Crawford later remarked, "*Rose-Marie* was surprisingly good without the music, but I felt uneasy as a French Canadian."

King Vidor scored another hit with his populist drama *The Crowd*
(1928) before MGM finally saw the writing on the wall and capitulated,
albeit reluctantly, to sound. MGM's first part-talking film was Jack
Conway's crime drama *Alias Jimmy Valentine* (1928), which was shot as a
silent and then partially reshot (for the film's final reels) with synchronized
sound dialogue at the Paramount studios, since MGM had no facilities of
its own. At length, responding to the challenge of *The Jazz Singer*, Mayer
saw to it that two soundstages were immediately constructed on the MGM
lot, and for maximum efficiency he worked them around the clock in
eight-hour shifts on as many revamped films as possible (Eames 46).

Harry Beaumont's *The Broadway Melody* (1929) was MGM's first
all-talking film, though due to the bulky sound equipment of the era,
when dialogue scenes were recorded on eighteen-inch 78 rpm records, the
camerawork is so static as to be almost unwatchable today. But matters
had certainly improved by later the same year, when Greta Garbo seam-
lessly made the transition to sound in Clarence Brown's *Anna Christie*
(1930), which was advertised with the simple slogan "Garbo talks!" The
plunge into sound was traumatic not only for the studios, but also the
stars and directors who labored there day after day. No longer could a
director shout out instructions to actors during a take; noisy sodium arc
lights that illuminated the stage had to be replaced with incandescent
bulbs; and the camera, once free to roam the set at will, made so much
noise that it drowned out the dialogue—a 35 mm camera pushing film
through at ninety feet a minute is nearly as loud as an outboard motor.
The solution was to imprison the camera in a small, asbestos-insulated
booth from which it could observe the action from a distance rather than
participate in it. By the mid-1930s, the camera motor would be "blimped,"
or silenced, by soundproofing material; but for the moment, the sound-
proof booth was the only solution to the problem.

And yet, though a latecomer to sound, MGM adapted rapidly, and for
many the 1930s remains the studio's greatest decade. Some of its most
iconic hits during this period included the smoothly sensual Clark Gable

(MGM's "King" of the star system) and Joan Crawford in Brown's *Possessed* (1931); Thalberg's all-star production of Edmund Goulding's *Grand Hotel* (1932), which began a new trend in the industry, offering a galaxy of front-rank personalities in one film for maximum box-office appeal; Gable and sex siren Jean Harlow in Victor Fleming's steamy tropical drama *Red Dust* (1932); and George Cukor's answer to *Grand Hotel*, *Dinner at Eight* (1933). The latter was produced by a young David O. Selznick because Thalberg's health was already in decline, ruined by a combination of his congenitally weak constitution, overwork, and the habitual use of amphetamines and barbiturates to alternately wake him up and put him to sleep after one exhausting day of work melted into the next (Eames 96).

Another hit was W. S. Van Dyke's *The Thin Man* (1934), designed as a simple detective thriller and shot in an astounding twelve days. The film, starring William Powell and Myrna Loy, gave the public its first glimpse of a happily married couple who were equals in love, work, and their ability to solve seemingly baffling complex crimes, and it would lead to a slew of successful sequels.

In 1934, when Paramount dropped the Marx Brothers after the relative commercial failure of Leo McCarey's brilliant comedy *Duck Soup* (1933), Thalberg salvaged the comedians' careers—after a fashion—by advising them to include "romantic subplots and musical numbers" (Eames iii) in Sam Wood's *A Night at the Opera* (1935), and in all their subsequent films for the studio, which stretched into the late 1940s. Thalberg astutely recognized that although the Marxes' anarchic comedy did well with urban, male audiences, women felt alienated from their films because they contained no one they could identify with (except, perhaps, for Margaret Dumont, and she was always used as a comic foil to the brothers' antics). Again, rough edges had to be smoothed out for wider public acceptance; MGM was the great homogenizer of public taste.

Emblematic of this status was Mickey Rooney, star of the studio's Andy Hardy films, family entertainment promoted on a grand scale. In reality, these were "B" pictures shot on standing sets, depicting an idyllic family life in the mythical Midwestern town of Carvel and radiating wholesome American values like so much synthetic sunshine. Rooney also appeared in Norman Taurog's sentimental drama *Boys Town* (1937) along with the studio's most dependable all-purpose actor, Spencer Tracy, in a tale centering on the real-life Boys Town in Omaha, Nebraska, then as now a haven for runaways, delinquents, and others who have been thrown on the mercy of chance. By 1939, MGM was in high gear with three more celebrated films: Ernst Lubitsch's *Ninotchka*; Fleming's *The Wizard of Oz*, which has achieved through the years a status all its own as a uniquely emblematic American classic; and, most famously, David O. Selznick's production of *Gone with the Wind.* To get Gable in the film, Selznick International Pictures was required to release it through MGM, and the finished product sports a glossy MGM look throughout, in large part thanks to the work of its directors: George Cukor, whom Selznick fired midway through production, and Fleming, another MGM stalwart.

As the 1940s were ushered in, the studio continued with such critical and commercial successes as Cukor's *The Philadelphia Story* (1940), William Wyler's wartime morale booster *Mrs. Miniver* (1942), Clarence Brown's *National Velvet* (1944), introducing a young Elizabeth Taylor, and Judy Garland and Robert Walker in Vincente Minnelli's *The Clock* (1945). After the war, the Arthur Freed unit, which specialized in musicals, turned out professional crowd-pleasers like Charles Walters's *Easter Parade* (1948), Stanley Donen and Gene Kelly's *On the Town* (1949), and Walters's *Summer Stock* (1950); this last film was also Garland's last for MGM after a tumultuous twelve-year rise to superstardom and years of overwork. Spencer Tracy and Katharine Hepburn were teamed in a series of "battle of the sexes" romantic comedies, such as Cukor's *Adam's Rib* (1949), while John Huston helmed the atypically dark crime drama *The Asphalt Jungle* (1950), a definite departure from MGM's world of gloss and glamour. And then came the film that spelled the end of Louis B. Mayer's tenure at MGM, a film that, at the time, seemed like just another modest program picture, with perhaps a bit more of a personal touch than most MGM assembly line product.

John Huston had just finished his adaptation of *The Red Badge of Courage* (1951), and Mayer was not happy with the result. Though it starred World War II veteran Audie Murphy in the title role as "The Youth"—a young soldier—and seemed to be highly exploitable at the box office, the previews had not gone well. The film had been approved by Dore Schary, recently promoted to head of production by Mayer, but again, Mayer was not happy about this. He didn't like the movie, he didn't particularly like Schary, whom he thought was a pretentious phony, and he didn't like the direction that the studio, and the industry as a whole, was taking.

"Art?" he complained. "*The Red Badge of Courage*? All that violence. No story? Dore Schary wanted it. Is it good entertainment? I didn't think so. Maybe I'm wrong. But I don't think I'm wrong. I know what the audience wants. Andy Hardy! Sentimentality! What's wrong with it? Love! Good old-fashioned romance!" In Mayer's office, producer Arthur Freed listened to the mogul's tirade with resignation; he had heard it all before. "Is it bad? It entertains. It brings the audience to the box office. No! These critics. They're too tony for you and I. They don't like it" (Ross 289). But audiences had deserted Andy Hardy long ago, and Mickey Rooney was no longer a promising juvenile. He was an actor trying to shift from teenage leads to adult roles and finding it difficult. Mayer wasn't helping. He was stuck in the past.

Meanwhile, with Huston gone from the lot working on another picture (*The African Queen*), producer Gottfried Reinhardt was left to shepherd *The Red Badge of Courage* through final editing and post-production. Schary took over final editing himself, aiming to make the film into a more conventional war picture. The first element to be added was a voiceover narration by James Whitmore, firmly establishing the film as based on a literary classic. Then a multitude of other cuts were made—mostly small ones—to speed up the film, although in the end it ran only sixty-nine minutes. Reinhardt agonized over the mutilation of the film, but he couldn't do anything substantial to save it. When the final cut was released no one was pleased, and the film failed at the box office. Reinhardt would go on to direct several films, none of which were conspicuously successful. For his part, Huston, ever the savvy studio survivor, simply shrugged at the loss of a year's work and moved on; he told writer Lillian Ross, "I lied to Dore. I called Dore up and said I had seen the picture. I told him I approved of everything he had done" (343).

The Red Badge of Courage represented the studio system at its worst; the film's production had turned into a political football in the fight for power between Schary and Mayer. Although it turned out to be a thoughtful, intelligent film, even in its truncated form, Mayer's tastes still ran to sentiment above all else at a time when postwar audiences were hungering for much more. The old lion clung to the past, wanting to stick to the tried-and-true formulas: "boy meets girl," "let's put on a show," "crime doesn't pay," "the family above all," and the superiority of "small town values."

What had happened? Simply put, the MGM formula had finally run its course. Mayer's Republican vision of a monolithic, all-white society, as typified by the seemingly endless string of Andy Hardy films the studio churned out like cereal boxes, no longer fit the public's perception of postwar America. Mayer, who had served as vice-chairman and chairman of the California Republican Party in the early 1930s (Katz 922), was resolutely stuck in the past, and also stuck in the racist dream world that he himself had created. For Mayer, Andy Hardy's small-town America was the real America; it wasn't a fantasy, it was authentic.

Like every other aspect of the studio, the Hardy films were a projection of Mayer's psyche. They were wish-fulfillment on a grand scale, where one man has the power to marshal the economic forces to create his own synthetic vision of existence and then to propagate that vision to the public as being somehow an accurate reflection of their lives. And for a long time, Mayer's tactics in this regard went undetected. Just as Mayer convinced his employees that he had only their best interests at heart when he was in fact ruthlessly advancing the studio's interests alone, so Mayer sold the American public on his vision of conservative, by-the-book Americanism, until the shades of gray and the darker aspects of daily existence finally overwhelmed and subsumed the brightly lit fantasyland of Mayer's regime of dreams.

Mayer's empire was constantly under attack throughout most of his tenure at MGM, and one of his chief antagonists was Nicholas Schenck, the president of Loew's Incorporated from 1927 onward, the man who ultimately held the purse strings that made Mayer's kingdom a reality, at least on film. As contract director George Sidney aptly observed, "Mayer didn't dislike Nick Schenck. He *hated* Nick Schenck. It was the old story, the Tale of Two Cities: Los Angeles and New York" (Eyman 235). It seemed like a street fight all the way to the end, day after day, and Mayer perpetually cast himself as the victim. When Thalberg at last succumbed to years of overwork, the aftereffects of a heart attack, and pneumonia in 1936, Mayer was shaken to his core, but only because Thalberg's death made Mayer more vulnerable. "Every son of a bitch in Hollywood is waiting for me to fall on my ass," Mayer lamented to one of his underlings, unsure of what to do now that Thalberg was gone (Eyman 237).

Mayer's authority was ultimately as phantasmal as the world he had created at MGM; he was simply an employee of Loew's Incorporated, no matter how well paid. This, too, is something that separated Mayer from the other studio magnates of the era, all of whom owned a controlling interest, or at least a large chunk, of the studios they operated. For all his power within the walls of MGM, outside, in the real world, as Mayer continually warned his employees, there was danger and uncertainty. In return for their loyalty, Mayer promised protection for his enormous "studio family," but in reality it was Mayer who needed protection from Schenck, and his "studio family" who needed protection from Mayer's ruthless production tactics.

Judy Garland is perhaps the most famous exemplar of Mayer's real attitude toward the men and women who worked for him, probably because her flameout was so spectacularly public. Groomed from an early age for stardom by her show business family as part of the family trio known as the Gumm Sisters (her real name was Frances Gumm), Garland received her stage name from fellow vaudevillian George Jessel, who correctly surmised that her actual surname would prove embarrassing on theater marquees. Judy's mother was, in the young actress's own words, "the real life wicked witch of the West" (Katz 512), and she relentlessly pushed Garland toward the footlights. Between 1929 and 1935, Garland made a number of short films with her sisters for smaller production companies, but these made no impact.

Signed by Mayer at thirteen, Garland made her MGM screen debut in Felix E. Feist's eleven-minute short *Every Sunday* (1936), where she was teamed with Deanna Durbin, another precocious teen whose trilling voice also captivated the public. The film was really a screen test for both young ladies. MGM kept Garland but dropped Durbin; she would soon sign with Universal and appear in a string of frothy adolescent musicals, the first of which was Henry Koster's highly profitable *Three Smart Girls* (1936) (Katz 400). Mayer, incensed that the studio had passed up such a potential gold-mine, redoubled his efforts to make Judy Garland a front-rank star, building her up with a loan-out to 20th Century Fox for *Pigskin Parade* (1936), then recalling her for home studio work in Roy Del Ruth's *Broadway Melody of 1938* (1937),where she more than held her own against a battalion of seasoned veterans, including song and dance man Buddy Ebsen.

In 1937, Garland was cast opposite Rooney in Alfred E. Green's sentimental tearjerker *Thoroughbreds Don't Cry* (1937), and the chemistry between the two teenagers was immediately apparent. Garland and Rooney would appear together in nine films all told, and soon they were among the most popular stars on the MGM lot (Katz 512). *The Wizard of Oz*, though not a major hit when first released, nevertheless proved an excellent showcase for Garland, who won a special Academy Award in 1940 as "the best juvenile performer of the year" for her work in the film; the role had originally been intended for Shirley Temple as a loan-out deal from Fox (Katz 512). But even at this early point in her ascent to stardom, Garland was already something of a problem child for the studio.

Obsessed with Garland's weight and her slight curvature of the spine, Mayer repeatedly referred to her as "my little hunchback" and saw to it that the studio physician, Dr. Edward B. Jones, prescribed Benzedrine to perk Judy up in the morning and then barbiturates to put her to sleep at night (Higham 279). By the time she was twenty-one, she was in the regular care of a psychiatrist (Katz 512). In 1943, Garland began work on *Meet Me in St. Louis* (1944), one of her most enduring hits, under the careful tutelage of her future husband, director Vincente Minnelli. Mayer, surprisingly, had no faith in the source material for the film, a series of stories by Sally Benson that originally appeared in the pages of the *New Yorker*, but he finally acquiesced, telling studio literary scout Lillie Messenger, "You want to do it? We'll give it to Arthur Freed to produce. He should be allowed at least one failure" (Higham 336).

Production of *Meet Me in St. Louis* was plagued by frequent nervous breakdowns by Garland, and other illnesses seemed to affect every other member of the cast. Mary Astor had recurring pneumonia; juvenile Margaret O'Brien came down with a severe cold and was whisked off to Arizona to recuperate; second lead Joan Carroll had to have an emergency appendectomy; character actor Harry Davenport was also ill with a variety of maladies, and so the film shut down, reopened, shut down, and again reopened production, so that it seemed it would never be completed (Higham 337). When *Meet Me in St. Louis* was finally finished and released, it was met with overwhelming critical praise and box office success, but Mayer could never forget the production problems associated with the film and directed most of his antipathy toward Garland. In his mind, Garland alone was the reason that the filming had been so difficult, when in fact her co-stars had had their share of problems as well. Or perhaps he was just annoyed that his judgment had been so wrong; the failure Mayer had predicted turned out to be a hit.

The actress continued in a series of memorable portrayals—in Minnelli's *The Clock* (1945), about a wartime romance; George Sidney's *The Harvey Girls* (1946); cameos in Lemuel Ayers and Roy Del Ruth's *Ziegfeld Follies* (1945) and Richard Whorf's *Till the Clouds Roll By* (1946); as well as Minnelli's *The Pirate*, Walters's *Easter Parade*, Taurog's *Words and Music* (all 1948), and Robert Z. Leonard's *In the Good Old Summertime* (1949), until the pace of production was literally killing her. After numerous production delays on Walters's 1950 film *Summer Stock*, MGM and Mayer had had enough. Garland was clearly out of control. Arriving on the set late, she would begin a scene, then suddenly start crying, flee to her dressing room, and lock the door. She screamed at Walters and at her co-star, Gene Kelly, and went into tirades at the slightest provocation (Higham 399).

After principal production wrapped, Garland was brought back for an additional number, "Get Happy," which ironically proved to be one of the high points of the film. Although she carried off this brief sequence with style and energy, it was too little, too late. She failed to report for work on *Royal Wedding* (1951), a Stanley Donen film that would have teamed her with Fred Astaire, and Mayer quickly replaced her with Jane Powell. Garland was devastated. On June 20, she attempted suicide in the bathroom of her home in Beverly Hills; Minnelli broke down the door and saved Garland from fatally slashing her neck with a piece of shattered glass. This was the final straw for MGM; on September 29, 1950, MGM fired her with the terse announcement that "Judy has been with us since childhood, and our devotion to her will always remain" (Higham 403).

Though Garland went on to a series of high-profile comebacks, including George Cukor's *A Star Is Born* (1954) as well as a record-breaking nineteen-week singing engagement at the Palace Theater in New York (Katz 512), the damage had been done. Garland was born with a high-strung, nervous disposition, predisposed to emotional highs and lows. The studio system had chewed her up and spat her out. Her career at MGM lasted only fourteen years in all—fourteen years of grinding, brutal, unrelenting work. For all of Mayer's talk of the harsh realities of the real world, life inside the studio walls was equally perilous, and only the strong and the clever survived. Those who counted on the false paternalism of Mayer would soon find themselves disabused of any such notions the moment they became expendable; MGM was, above all, a factory, and the assembly line had to keep rolling at all costs.

Mickey Rooney was far luckier and much more resilient in his dealings with Mayer. Director Clarence Brown described Rooney as "the closest thing to a genius I ever worked with. . . . The little bastard could do no wrong. . . . I don't know how he did it, because he never really paid any attention. Between takes, he'd be off somewhere calling his bookmaker, then come back and go into a scene as if he'd been rehearsing it for three days" (Eyman 347). Self-destructive in other ways—gambling was one aspect of his personality that caused him a lot of trouble over the years—Rooney was nevertheless the consummate professional, always on time and prepared, no matter how nonchalant his attitude might have seemed.

Another actor who could handle herself in the clinches, both personally and professionally, was Norma Shearer. When her final two films, Robert Z. Leonard's *We Were Dancing* and George Cukor's *Her Cardboard Lover* (both 1942), flopped at the box office, Shearer took her Loew's stock and retired without a backward glance (Eyman 367). Her choice of material might not always have been sound; she turned down starring roles in both *Gone with the Wind* and *Mrs. Miniver* (the latter because she felt she was too young to play a maternal figure, and, in Janet Leigh's words, "the mother of a twenty-year-old") (Eyman 367). But when it came to financial arrangements, Shearer could go toe-to-toe with Mayer and more than hold her own.

Somewhat surprisingly, Mayer surrounded himself with strong personalities at the studio, which was unusual in that he typically brooked no interference when it came to running his feudal empire. One such person was Margaret Booth, head of MGM's editorial department, who was in charge of the awesome task of supervising all of MGM's films through post-production, though others did the actual work under her direction. When a young producer on the lot one day idly asked a male film editor why Booth was the head of editorial, he received the sharp comment "because she's *better* [original emphasis]. She knows how every cut affects the entire picture" (Eyman 213). When Mayer assigned an untested director to a project, Booth would actually attend the shooting of the film, personally approving each take on set (Eyman 213). This led to a certain facelessness in the MGM house style. For all their gloss and sheen, MGM films from the Mayer era possess a certain sameness in their physical presentation, as if, no matter who directed the film, the MGM house style—in lighting, editing, costume design, sets, and camerawork—almost obliterated all individuality. Booth was unafraid to tangle with even the biggest names on the MGM lot, though canny pros like Cukor, Minnelli, Brown, and Huston knew how to work around her. But for most of the journeyman directors who worked at MGM, their main function was really that of glorified traffic cops, who kept the film on time and on budget, controlling the actors, and pretty much making sure the film was moving forward without delay.

Mayer, for all his decorousness and piety, was a man of strong desires and passions. Married to the former Margaret Shenberg in 1904, by 1933 Mayer was restless in his relationship with her, partially due to the fact that in that year Margaret was forced for health reasons to undergo a hysterectomy, which ended Mayer's interest in her sexually (Eyman 193). Thus Mayer, feeling the cold breath of mortality as he approached his fifties, began a series of attempted seductions of young starlets, including Anita Page, who flatly rejected him, and Adeline Schulberg, the estranged wife of producer B. P. Schulberg, who accepted Mayer's advances (Eyman 194). Mayer needed to prove to the world, and to himself, that he was still a force to be reckoned with. Actress and model Jean Howard was a rumored mistress (Eyman 196), but another actress, Esther Ralston, refused to be bullied by her boss, even when Mayer told her directly, "I can have any woman on this lot—Joan Crawford—you sing your psalms, young lady, and see where you get! I'll blackball you in every studio in Hollywood, and what's more, you'll get nothing here." True to his word, Mayer soon loaned Ralston out to Universal for a string of program pictures, until MGM finally let her contract lapse (Eyman 197). Needless to say, such actions were directly at odds with the public persona that Mayer liked to project. In many ways, Mayer comes off as the most hypocritical of the studio moguls, because with Harry Cohn, Darryl Zanuck, Jack Warner, and the others, what you saw was what you got. They were utterly ruthless, using whatever they had to get whatever they wanted, no matter how they had to do it, and they made no pretense about it. Mayer cloaked himself in pieties, but in reality he was every bit as rapacious as his colleagues.

And yet, as agent and later producer Charles Feldman later noted, "Working for MGM was like working for *The New York Times*—you couldn't do any better. This was one of the strong factors that Mayer developed, and that was the source of his power" (Eyman 199). For all his ruthlessness and volatility, Mayer had built up the largest, most successful motion picture studio on earth from nothing, starting as a junk dealer, then an exhibitor, and finally clawing his way to the top of the Hollywood studio system. He hated being simply an employee of Loews, Inc., but although he threatened to quit from time to time, Schenck, who was under no illusions about Mayer's feelings toward him, refused to hear of it.

Mayer was too good at what he did to dispense with, so Schenck paid him handsomely and let him run the studio. Officially, there were no such things as "B" pictures at MGM, not even in their short films department; of course, there were the *Andy Hardy* films, but even these pedestrian productions had such a high gloss, marked by the studio's signature high-key lighting and museum-like production values, that they somehow seemed to exist on the same plane with the "A" musicals turned out by the Freed unit. You could spot an MGM film instantly. They were all lit the same—bright, flat, evenly balanced throughout the frame. The sets were designed either by Cedric Gibbons or his assistants to be white, clean, and anonymous, and the directors of photography all adhered to the house "white glove" style. The sound was always the same as well—Douglas Shearer, Norma's brother who was in charge of the sound department, saw to it that MGM's voice and music tracks were smooth, quiet, and absolutely spotless. And Booth made sure that the editing in all MGM films was completely uniform, so that everything seemed to be part of one synthetic, emotionally comforting whole, the world of MGM.

Mayer believed in all of this, which is what made him so valuable. It was Mayer's vision on the screen at MGM and no one else's. So Schenck left him alone, until Mayer got older. For the moment, Mayer reigned supreme and his intuitive understanding of the strengths and weaknesses of his stars was, for the most part, entirely on point. As he once told a writer working on a vehicle for Clark Gable, "Don't put one thought in his head. Write the story from the neck down. Action only. Keep him doing something. When he talks, all they've got to do is hear his voice. He doesn't have to say anything that means anything" (Eyman 301). Films were action, movement, power. The stars were merely components in the overall mosaic of the work.

Mayer's vision, and that of the MGM factory at its zenith, resolutely belonged on the big screen, as audiences flocked, week after week, to see the latest *Andy Hardy* film or Spencer Tracy film or Clark Gable film. MGM made movies with the entire family in mind rather than aiming at a single demographic. In the 1940s, this made sense; theaters had no direct competition, and in the evenings, and especially on the weekends, local theaters would be packed with appreciative crowds enjoying an evening's entertainment as a family, which was MGM's entire strategy in a nutshell.

A bit of romance for mother and daughters; some rousing action for father and son; and some gentle comedy for everyone, all wrapped up in a shiny, attractive package with a reassuringly happy ending and a circularity of narrative that suggested MGM's vision of American life was somehow eternal and would continue to reinforce its hold on the public imagination year after year. Even the war caused no serious disruption to MGM's activities, although many of its stars (especially James Stewart and Clark Gable, the latter heartbroken over the death of his wife, Carole Lombard) enlisted for active duty, and wartime rationing put a temporary crimp in the studio's expenditures.

World War II, after the isolationist run-up, was a "popular" conflict, with nearly everyone signing on to ensure victory over the Axis powers as rapidly as possible, thus reinforcing MGM's family ethos: "We're all in this together." Parenthetically, a notable exception to this was MGM contract star Lew Ayres, who announced that, as a pacifist, he would refuse military service. As the star of the *Dr. Kildare* series, Ayres was enormously popular with audiences, but his stand made him a pariah. Ayres was immediately written out of the *Kildare* series and replaced by his mentor, Dr. Gillespie, played by the wheelchair-bound Lionel Barrymore. Ayres's career never really recovered (Eyman 304).

But now the war was over, and MGM had to cope with a new enemy, as did all the studios: television. In addition, Mayer's personal life was in turmoil. After years of separation from his wife, Mayer filed for divorce in 1947 at a reported cost of over $3 million, one of the highest settlements in American history at the time (Eyman 386). Then came the Red Scare hearings, HUAC, and the Blacklist. As a staunch Republican, Mayer himself emerged unscathed, and the studio itself also suffered relatively minor damage. Mayer testified before HUAC on October 20, 1947, stating that "I have maintained a relentless vigilance against un-American influences" (Eyman 389), which, of course, he had.

Polemicist Ayn Rand then took the stand and excoriated MGM for producing Gregory Ratoff's pro-Soviet film *Song of Russia* (1943) as a wartime propaganda film, made at Franklin Roosevelt's behest, but on the whole Mayer—while nevertheless fingering screenwriters Dalton Trumbo, Lester Cole, and Donald Ogden Stewart as possible communists—felt that he had handled the situation with as much aplomb as possible (Eyman 391). But by 1948, everyone at MGM seemed tired, at least creatively. The studio's artificial small-town vision didn't fit in with postwar reality; you couldn't go back to Carvel, Andy Hardy's mythical Midwest hometown, anymore, even if you wanted to. Clark Gable's post-war films were minor and failed to ignite at the box office. Other than the musicals produced by the Freed unit, the studio had lost its touch with the public. As late as 1958, MGM was still trying to recapture its phantom past with Howard W. Koch's *Andy Hardy Comes Home*, in which Andy, now an adult, comes back to find Carvel awash in political corruption and cleans the town up by the last reel. Audiences, however, knew that that could only happen in the movies.

The MGM formula continued in other ways as well. When Elia Kazan directed *The Sea of Grass* (1947), he was astonished to discover that all the second-unit footage for the film had already been shot, the sets designed, the costumes finalized, and the script locked in; no changes were permitted. Kazan was simply brought in to direct the actors; when that was done, Margaret Booth and her staff would take over the editing without any input from the director. Shocked by the unreality of the physical props, sets, and costumes being used in the film, Kazan asked a studio functionary, "This story is supposed to take place, is it not, in the back country?" only to be told in no uncertain terms: "Actually, this picture takes place in Metro-Goldwyn-Mayer land, where you and I are sitting this minute" (Eyman 399–400). A newer, younger generation of actors, writers, and directors no longer wanted to be part of such a formulaic assembly line. MGM was finally out of step with the America that it had helped to create.

This is when Dore Schary entered the picture. Nicholas Schenck viewed Schary, recently released by RKO, as an up-and-comer who could take MGM into the future, and in 1951 he offered him Thalberg's old title as MGM's vice-president in charge of production. Mayer, predictably, was shaken. Schenck hadn't consulted him on the hire, and the move threatened his own hold on the studio (Higham 375). Now the question was how much power Schary would amass in his new job. In their introductory meetings, Mayer was his usually affable self, as he always was with people he was inclined to despise, but Schary, knowing he had Schenck's backing, refused to fall for Mayer's empty promises. He insisted upon total autonomy as a producer, without the need for Mayer's approval on each project. It was clear to Mayer what Schenck really wanted: to ease Mayer and his regime out the door and install Schary as the new head of production.

Mayer balked and fought back. At length, reluctantly, Schary retreated from his demand for total autonomy, and Mayer retained final veto on all projects (Higham 378). However, Schary soon began to display a notable lack of tact that would continue to get him in trouble within the company: when he spoke at the University of Colorado on August 3, 1948, he asked rhetorically, "If every other medium has a right to make us think, why doesn't the motion pictures?" (Higham 379). There was truth to this notion, but it was hardly the most circumspect pronouncement a person in his position might make. The reality was that although Schary was groomed to be the next Thalberg, he could never hope to fill those shoes. Eventually, Schary would fall victim to his self-aggrandizement; he was fired in 1956 when his more ambitious films failed to pan out at the box office.

Against this uneasy backdrop, many of the old-time loyalists departed and some rather "retro" projects were pushed through, such as Mervyn LeRoy's biblical spectacle *Quo Vadis?* (1951) and Compton Bennett's remake of *King Solomon's Mines* (1950), shot on location in Africa and in color. At the same time, Mayer had fallen in love with dancer Lorena Danker, and on December 3, 1948, the couple eloped to Yuma, Arizona, where a local justice of the peace married them the next morning in a two-minute ceremony (Higham 382). But the new marriage failed to bring the aging studio boss much solace. It was the act of a desperate man, trying to begin his life again, just as his world was about to collapse. Still, not long before Mayer was fired, he received an honorary Academy Award on March 29, 1950, for "distinguished service to the motion picture industry" (Higham 405).

Meanwhile, relations between Schary and Mayer were past the break-ing point, and the two men were openly contemptuous of each other. In the spring of 1951, events came to a head. While the machinations of the final standoff are complex, in essence, Mayer threw down an ultimatum to Schenck; either Schary or Mayer had to leave MGM. It was Schenck's decision, and he favored Schary. Mayer was furious and screamed threats at Schary, but the die was cast. When Mayer tried to leave the studio after his resignation on June 23, 1951, his car was stopped at the gate; it was a studio vehicle. Mayer was forced to wait for one of his five Chryslers to be brought from his house to collect him, standing outside the front gate of the studio he had built from the ground up (Higham 408). Though MGM was thrown into a momentary panic, Schenck moved with speed to assure one and all that in the wake of Mayer's departure, Schary's accession to the throne would be conducted in an orderly and respectful fashion. And for the most part, despite the protests of Mayer loyalists, this was the case.

Yet in the aftermath of his dismissal from MGM, Mayer, now an immensely wealthy man, almost immediately began making plans for the future. Amazingly, he now sought to purchase RKO Radio from the belea-guered Howard Hughes, as well as Republic Pictures and Consolidated Film Laboratories, and combine them into a huge studio that, he hoped, would rival MGM, using his settlement with the studio to finance the entire operation in cash (Higham 410–11). But this was not to be, and Mayer then turned his attention to the new Cinerama process, which used three cameras in frame-for-frame synchronization to photograph each scene and then three projectors, also in frame-for-frame interlock, to play the images back, to create a 3D effect that was enhanced by the use of a deeply curved projection screen.

Mayer touted it as the future of the cinema, but in fact it was a short-lived gimmick that, due to its unwieldy technical demands, soon faded from the scene—the last Cinerama film was John Ford and Henry Hathaway's sprawling epic *How the West Was Won* (1962) before the process was abandoned. Mayer himself was becoming more and more tired; while his doctors told him it was anemia, what plagued Mayer was actually an accelerating case of leukemia, which was slowly but surely killing him. But no one told Mayer this. Instead, as 1957 dawned, Mayer was receiving continuous blood transfusions. In his last years and days, Mayer remained embroiled in conflicts with his former employer, bitter to the end, continuing to fulminate against the "new Hollywood."

On September 16, 1957, Mayer was removed to UCLA Medical Hospital, where, not surprisingly, he proved a difficult and moody patient (Higham 430). His longtime doctor knew the gravity of Mayer's condition but kept it from him, simply because she knew there was nothing to be done. Soon the pain became intolerable as gastrointestinal bleeding set in, and Mayer was placed on a morphine drip; then his kidneys began to fail (Higham 431). Just before he died, Mayer pulled his long-time publicist Howard Strickling close to him and whispered fiercely, "Nothing matters! Don't let them worry you. Nothing matters!" (Eyman 491). With these final, terrible words, Louis B. Mayer rendered his ultimate verdict on all that he had created, experienced, and encompassed: nothing mattered.

On October 28, 1957, Mayer slipped into a coma, and when Lorena visited him he failed to recognize her. The next day, just past midnight, Louis B. Mayer departed this world, a fighter to the last. Along with his wife, also at Mayer's bedside were Strickling and Clarence Brown, who had remained loyal to his old boss throughout Mayer's long hospitalization. Louis B. Mayer was 72 years old (Higham 431).

The tributes predictably poured in, and the flag flew at half-mast over the Thalberg Building for a week in Mayer's honor. The funeral, at Wilshire Boulevard Temple, was predictably star-studded, as Jeannette MacDonald sang "Ah, Sweet Mystery of Life" and Spencer Tracy, somewhat against his will, was drafted into service to read the eulogy (Eyman 493). It took quite some time to unravel Mayer's estate, and when it was finally probated it became apparent that for all his work the old mogul had left behind a remarkably modest financial legacy: only $7.4 million (Eyman 502).

After individual bequests, including a sizable one to the Louis B. Mayer Foundation, Lorena was left with a paltry $750,000, which she momentarily thought of contesting until she was reminded that Mayer had included a clause in his will stipulating that anyone who challenged it in court would have their bequest dropped to $1 (Eyman 502). That ended that, at least, and Lorena quickly sold their house on St. Cloud Road for a mere $350,000 to comedian Jerry Lewis (who, ironically, labored exclusively for Paramount) (Eyman 503).

In the end, Louis B. Mayer was one of the most powerful and yet precariously positioned of all the golden age studio bosses, because despite all his efforts—though sufficient to create a dream world of phantoms and shadows—he couldn't consolidate his position within the Loews, Inc. empire into anything more than highly paid indentured servitude. Locked in constant struggle with those upon whom his empire of images depended, Mayer was kicked out of the home he had created. MGM never really recovered from Mayer's departure; in many ways, the studio's identity was Mayer's own.

Since then, the MGM library of films has been sold to Turner Television, where it soon went into heavy rotation as the core of the Turner Movie Classics Channel. Now Mayer's vision of America is on view twenty-four hours a day, seven days a week, without commercials, down to and including the shorts, two-reel films, Christmas promos (including one of Judy Garland singing "Silent Night" in an ersatz studio chapel), the *Andy Hardy* and *Kildare* films—it's all there. The studio facility itself, as noted, has been taken over by Sony/Columbia. The demise of Louis B. Mayer was, then, in every way the passing of an era. As actor Turhan Bey remarked when Mayer was forced out of MGM in 1951, "When Louis B. Mayer left MGM, that was the end of contract players, of publicity departments who nursed you through the crises of studio life, of studio life itself. In every meaningful way, it was the end of Hollywood" (Eyman 445).

CHAPTER 5

Zukor and Paramount

Adolph Zukor was arguably the first, and certainly the longest living, of the golden age studio titans. And like the others, he was crazy about the movies, both as a business and an art form, although he was far less of a public manipulator, preferring to work behind the scenes. Zukor got into the game early as an exhibitor, opening a penny arcade in 1903 in Manhattan and in 1904 a small theater (Gomery, *Studio System* 26). By 1912, Zukor had moved into production, and in 1913, recognizing the rising power of the star system, Zukor signed Mary Pickford to a $20,000 a year contract, effectively jumpstarting the entire rush to sign top talent for films (Gomery, *Studio System* 27). Zukor called his company Famous Players, and later, after a merger with producer Jesse Lasky, Famous Players–Lasky, with a roster of Broadway stars, and used the facilities of Paramount, founded by William H. Hodkinson in 1914, to distribute its films. The founders of Famous Players-Lasky were Lasky, Zukor, Samuel Goldwyn (then known as Samuel Goldfish), Cecil B. DeMille, and Zukor's brother-in-law, Al Kaufman.

Hodkinson had formed Paramount from nine smaller companies, and the studio now depended on Famous Players to produce roughly half of the 100 films it distributed nationally each year. But Hodkinson was more of an auteurist than Zukor, who was simply a businessman. As Tim Wu writes, "Zukor's plan for the film industry was predicated on achieving a system of mass production not much different from that favored by other magnates of the time, such as Henry Ford. . . . Hodkinson believed in what is sometimes called craft, or authorial filmmaking, wherein one creator did nearly everything, writing, directing, producing and casting his own film" (89). The two men were bound to clash.

Quietly, Zukor bought out Hodkinson's partners and then moved swiftly to merge Famous Players and Paramount. On July 13, 1916, Zukor completed the merger and removed Hodkinson as president of the concern (Wu 91). Hodkinson saw this coming but did nothing to stop it; as he told an associate right before his ouster, "I am right, and if I'm put out of Paramount for being right, there will be another place for me in the industry" (qtd. in Wu 90). But Hodkinson's "personal style" would soon vanish from an increasingly corporate industry; Zukor's ruthless efficiency would become the hallmark of not only his reign at Paramount, but also the motion picture business as a whole; as Wu writes, Zukor "liked to operate in secret, leaving others to wonder what he was up to until he sprang his plans" (91). Goldfish, who had repeatedly clashed with his partners on various matters and clearly wanted to move out on his own, quit the organization on September 14, 1916 (Berg 63), beginning his own upward trajectory in the film business (discussed in the next chapter).

Moving forward aggressively under Zukor's visionary management, Famous Players/Paramount went on a mission to buy as many theaters as possible to enhance their hold on the nation's box office. By 1925 the company already controlled more than 400 theaters in the United States before Sam Katz and his Publix theater chain were brought into the rapidly expanding combine (Gomery, *Studio System* 28). Katz was even more ambitious in expanding Paramount-Famous, and by 1930 Paramount Publix had become the largest theater chain in both the United States and Canada (Gomery, *Studio System* 29). Paramount theaters booked their films from a centralized office; all the first-run houses had stage shows (or "prologues") as part of their entertainment, and Katz and his associates kept a very sharp eye on the bottom line (Gomery, *Studio System* 29).

When the technology for synchronized sound came, Paramount let Warner Bros. test the waters first, but once convinced it converted to sound with typical alacrity. Quickly realizing that radio would be useful for advertising their sound films, in 1929—astonishingly—Paramount acquired 50 percent of the Columbia Broadcasting System through a stock swap (Gomery, *Studio System* 31), a deal that also allowed the studio to make use of CBS's technology to help complete the shift to sound. Not content with this arrangement, Paramount actually tried to engineer a merger with Warner Bros. to create what would have been "Paramount-Vitaphone," with assets of nearly 1,500 theaters, half a dozen movie studios, CBS Radio, and the music publishing enterprises of Warners and Paramount (Gomery, *Studio System* 31).

This last coup never took place. The Hoover administration threatened to sue Paramount for creating a monopoly, and having had two previous run-ins with the Federal Trade Commission Paramount chose another tactic, buying up as many independent movie theaters as possible— 500 additional houses between September 1929 and May 1930 (Gomery, *Studio System* 31). The Depression put a cramp on Zukor's seemingly inexhaustible quest for domination, as enormous mortgage costs forced a series of draconian cutbacks, including the sale of CBS Radio for $41.2 million and a one-third cut in the budget for all feature films, both moves engineered by John Hertz of Lehman Brothers in New York (Gomery, *Studio System* 31).

Lasky and Katz left the company, theater attendance dropped drastically because people had less money to spend, and by 1933 Paramount had a deficit of $20 million, new fiscal territory for what until then had been a profitable and growing concern (Gomery, *Studio System* 31). The years 1933 to 1936 were tumultuous for the studio, which went through a revolving door of executives and production plans, but after Barney Balaban, a longtime partner of Katz and an expert at motion picture distribution, took over Paramount's presidency in 1936, the studio posted a profit of $4 million by the end of the year (Gomery, *Studio System* 33).

The lean years were finally over and some semblance of order came to the company, which now owned a twenty-six-acre studio in Hollywood, the Astoria studio on Long Island (used for shorts and occasionally features), studio facilities in Paris, film processing laboratories, forty-two film exchanges that distributed Paramount films worldwide, and roughly 1,200 theaters (although the theaters were either leased, owned [with mortgages], or merely operated by Paramount) (Gomery, *Studio System* 34).

Balaban proved a tenacious and able executive and ran the company from 1936 to 1964, even signing off personally on any expenditure of $3,000 or more and dealing every day with a vast array of box office statistics, production reports, and other matters (Gomery, *Studio System* 35–36). Nationally, Paramount dominated the theater chains, and Zukor was content to leave the reins to Balaban while he held the position of chairman of the board, with no real power over daily production (Katz 1503). Yet even though Balaban in New York and Y. Frank Freeman on the West Coast—as head of production—controlled the day-to-day workings of the studio, Zukor remained the *éminence grise* behind the scenes, and in the end he would outlive nearly all his contemporaries: when he died at the age of 103 in 1976, he was still listed in the Paramount roster as "Chairman of the Board Emeritus" (Katz 1503). Thus, though Zukor was one of the most invisible of the moguls, his fingerprints were on every deal Paramount made.

Paramount was also one of the first studios to dabble in television, investing roughly $400,000 in the fledgling DuMont Corporation in 1938, way ahead of its competitors, and starting a determined campaign to acquire as many television station licenses as it could as early as 1943; by 1948, Paramount was operating television stations in New York (WABD), Washington (WTTG), and Pittsburgh (WDTV), with stations in the works in Cincinnati and Cleveland (Gomery, *Studio System* 31–37). However, in 1934 the Federal Communications Commission was directed by the Communication Act of that year to deny television or radio licenses to any organization "convicted of monopolistic practices" (Gomery, *Studio*

System 37). Paramount was thus blocked from further acquisitions, and in 1948 came the Paramount Decision and the consent decree that stripped the studio and several of the other majors of their theater chains (see chapter 1).

In many ways, Paramount's incessant and unrelenting empire building was ultimately responsible for the consent decree, the legal machinations of which had been dragging on since 1938, because more than any of the majors Paramount wanted to own everything and control all aspects of the motion picture process. Zukor's dream of the 1910s and 1920s, vertical integration—in which the studio controlled the production, distribution, and exhibition of its films from first to last—was a goal he and his associates pursued relentlessly, despite his public pronouncements to the contrary, as in his 1918 comment that "the evils of producing and exhibiting coalitions is one of the gravest perils that has ever confronted the motion picture industry" (qtd. in Wu 94). And yet this is precisely what Zukor was after.

The other members of the so-called Big Five—20th Century Fox, Loew's-MGM, RKO Radio, and Warner Bros.—pursued a similar strategy (while Universal and Columbia never actively pursued theater ownership), but not with Zukor's single-minded zeal. Still, after divesting itself of its theaters at a considerable profit, Paramount—as well as the other Big Five studios—remained financially healthy through the 1940s by virtue of their combined lock on feature film production. With TV station ownership blocked, Paramount tried their hand at "theatrical television," presenting the 1949 World Series, football games, and boxing matches live in theaters for paying audiences, but with little success (Gomery, *Studio System* 38).

When free television took hold, Paramount, like the other majors, fought back with new "depth" processes, such as 3D and their own VistaVision system (in which the film was exposed in the camera horizontally, rather than vertically, to create what the studio hopefully dubbed "Motion Picture High Fidelity"), but as with all the other production units, Paramount took a hit. They recovered to some extent through a variety of shrewd business practices, including capitalizing on the success of rising stars of the 1950s such as Elvis Presley, just as the Bob Hope and Bing Crosby *Road* pictures proved a profitable and reliable franchise during the 1940s.

As for studio "identity," this changed rapidly with the times. In the 1930s, with Zukor still firmly at the company's helm, the sex comedies of Mae West, the anarchic madness of the Marx Brothers, and the ineffable romanticism of Ernst Lubitsch's films reigned supreme. West's *I'm No Angel* (Wesley Ruggles, 1933) and *Belle of the Nineties* (Leo McCarey, 1934), especially, were box office hits, and the Marx Brothers scored with their very first films *The Cocoanuts* (Robert Florey, 1929) and *Animal Crackers* (Victor Heerman, 1930), both shot at Paramount's Astoria studios. Ernst Lubitsch had started as a silent director in his native Germany, but he made the shift to sound and to Hollywood studio filmmaking in general so smoothly that, for a time, he was actually head of production at the studio, perhaps the only time when a front-rank *auteur* was put in charge of a studio's entire output.

In such sophisticated romantic comedies as *The Love Parade* (1929), *Monte Carlo* (1930), *The Smiling Lieutenant* (1931), and the superb *Trouble in Paradise* (1932), Lubitsch created a smooth, slick vision of the world as a perpetual clash between male and female, and also showcased the talents of Maurice Chevalier, a rising music hall star of the era. Rouben Mamoulian's sharply observed drama *Applause* (1929) and the highly kinetic *Dr. Jekyll and Mr. Hyde* (1931), which made excellent use of subjective camerawork, imaginative wipes, and eerily effective makeup in the transformation sequences, were major hits for the studio. During this period, Paramount also utilized the talents of Cecil B. DeMille, arguably the most spectacle-minded of all Hollywood directors, one whose roots in the business reached all the way back to *The Squaw Man* (1914), at six reels one of the first feature films ever made.

DeMille started with Jesse Lasky, and as Lasky was pulled into the Paramount orbit so was DeMille. Among his many films for the studio were the first versions of *The Ten Commandments* (1923) and *The King of Kings* (1927), along with *Madam Satan* (1930), *The Sign of the Cross* (1932), and *Cleopatra* (1934). Many DeMille films pushed censorship standards about as far as they could go at the time; *The Sign of the Cross*, for example, depicted copious amounts of sin and debauchery, including nudity, sex, and implied homosexuality and lesbianism, before the director's calculated insertion of salvation in the final reel to satisfy the moral-minded. DeMille stayed with Paramount for nearly his entire career; when television came along he was already an old man, but he still fought back with the genre he knew best: the big show. In his last years, DeMille contributed *Samson and Delilah* (1949), *The Greatest Show on Earth* (1952), and, as a career capper, an ultra-lavish remake of *The Ten Commandments* (1956), which is still—in 2012—shown every spring on network television, uncut, in primetime (albeit with copious commercials). DeMille's extravagant vision was entirely his own, and entirely Paramount's to exploit; for many years he was one of the studio's most dependable resources.

Yet when the Production Code acquired teeth in 1934 under Joseph Breen, one could easily argue that of all the studios, Paramount was the one that suffered the most. The Marx Brothers, hobbled by the relative "failure" of McCarey's *Duck Soup* (1933), left for MGM and much more conventional narratives; Mae West was all but sacrificed to the Code, making her last uninspired film for the studio in 1938 (A. Edward Sutherland's *Every Day's a Holiday*) and then returning to cabaret and stage work, with only four more movies to her credit before her death in 1978; and, although DeMille readily adapted to the new regime with *The Crusades* (1935), his pace of production slowed down.

By the 1940s, Paramount found its new stride with the Hope/Crosby series, comprising Victor Schertzinger's *The Road to Singapore* (1940), Schertzinger's *The Road to Zanzibar* (1941), David Butler's *The Road to Morocco* (1942), Hal Walker's *The Road to Utopia* (1946), and Norman Z. McLeod's *The Road to Rio* (1947). At the same time, Paramount spun Crosby off in a series of solo hits, including Mark Sandrich's *Holiday Inn*

(1942), Leo McCarey's *Going My Way* (1944), Stuart Heisler's *Blue Skies* (1946), and Tay Garnett's *A Connecticut Yankee in King Arthur's Court* (1949). Similarly, Bob Hope made a series of gag-ridden light comedies for Paramount during the same period, such as Butler's *Caught in the Draft* (1941), Sidney Lanfield's *My Favorite Blonde* (1942), Lanfield's *Let's Face It* (1943), Elliott Nugent's *My Favorite Brunette* (1947), Norman Z. McLeod's *Paleface* (1948), and numerous other films, all centered around his wise-cracking persona, and each film teaming him with a glamorous female co-star (Dorothy Lamour, Betty Hutton, and Jane Russell were among some of Hope's many distaff leads). Hope introduced his signature tune, "Thanks for the Memories," in Mitchell Leisen's 1938 film *The Big Broadcast of 1938*, one of a series of "Big Broadcast" films; one should remember that in all these enterprises, music publishing was never far from the studio's mind, or pocketbook.

Paramount also had a stable of cartoon characters who were very popular in their day but whose influence has waned with the passing decades. Chief among these figures was Betty Boop, created by Max and Dave Fleischer, who signed with Paramount in 1928 for their "Out of the Inkwell" heroes, initially starring Koko the Clown. Betty, however, soon outstripped Koko the Clown in popularity and was accorded her own series, which ran throughout the 1930s. Paramount's cartoon division operated under a variety of names from 1927 (even before the Fleischer deal) to 1967, but most of these shorts have been tossed by the wayside of cinema history.

The cartoon division is of particular interest because its cartoons have all but vanished in the contemporary marketplace. Max and Dave Fleischer, in addition to the Betty Boop series, also produced a series of lavish "color classics," directly competing with Walt Disney. But the Fleischers overreached themselves when they attempted to compete with Disney's feature film output, as evidenced by their unmemorable adaptation of *Gulliver's Travels* in 1939.

Gulliver's Travels went considerably over budget, failed to find an audience, and also lacked the freshness and originality of Disney's *Snow White and the Seven Dwarfs.* A follow-up feature, *Hoppity Goes to Town* (aka *Mr. Bug Goes to Town*, 1941), also directed by Dave Fleischer, also flopped. The Fleischer studio collapsed before being reincorporated as Famous Studios in 1941, with the Fleischers as employees rather than supervisors, and then churned out a series of Superman cartoons that used vividly realistic animation to bring the famous comic book superhero to life. The Superman shorts, together with Popeye cartoons—which, though rigidly formulaic, were unceasingly popular—and the Casper the Friendly Ghost series, kept Paramount's Famous Studios humming throughout the 1940s, even if these characters never achieved the pop cultural dominance of their Warner Bros. counterparts. Similarly, Paramount also had a weekly newsreel that operated from 1927 to 1957; most of this material is also scattered to the winds today, although copies of the newsreels linger in the National Archives in Washington, D.C.

One of the 1940s most respected comic directors, Preston Sturges, found a home at Paramount in 1940, beginning with *Christmas in July* and on to *The Great McGinty* (1940), *The Lady Eve* (1941), and *The Miracle of Morgan's Creek* (1944). Another major comic figure at Paramount was W. C. Fields, the wildly irascible, alcoholic comic whose brilliance in the 1930s was at its peak in films like William Beaudine's *The Old Fashioned Way* (1934), Norman Z. McLeod's *It's a Gift* (1934), and A. Edward Sutherland's *International House* (1933), but Fields's best work was in the 1930s; by the 1940s he was firmly ensconced at Universal, where he was allowed to write his own films—and pretty much direct them, too—culminating in his masterpiece *The Bank Dick,* which was nominally directed by Edward F. Cline in 1940.

Paramount also experimented with film noir during the 1940s, making an overnight star out of Alan Ladd in Frank Tuttle's *This Gun for Hire* (1942), Stuart Heisler's *The Glass Key* (1942), and George Marshall's complex thriller *The Blue Dahlia* (1946), this last film the only direct-to-the-screen scenario mystery Raymond Chandler ever attempted. But the film that epitomizes 1940s Paramount noir is indelibly Billy Wilder's acidic *Double Indemnity* (1944), in which nice-guy star Fred MacMurray switched to the other side of the tracks to romance femme fatale Barbara Stanwyck and together knock off her dyspeptic husband (Tom Powers). As a sleazy insurance salesman all too ready to forsake whatever ethics he might have in pursuit of Stanwyck, MacMurray is almost frighteningly convincing, and as the main antagonist Edward G. Robinson pulls off a bravura performance as MacMurray's straight-arrow boss. Wilder was one of the major talents at Paramount in the 1940s, with such films as *The Lost Weekend* (1945) and *Sunset Blvd.* (1950, in which Cecil B. DeMille makes a brief but effective appearance as himself), consolidating his reputation as an artist in a business where profit often trumped all other considerations.

The 1940s also saw Mark Sandrich's war drama *So Proudly We Hail!* (1943) and Sam Wood's rather static screen adaptation of *For Whom the Bell Tolls* (1943), as well as John Farrow's snappy suspense drama *The Big Clock* (1948), with Ray Milland cast as a magazine editor unjustly accused of murder (the real culprit is his boss, the corpulent Charles Laughton, doing his best imitation of publishing magnate Henry Luce), as well as the introduction of Dean Martin and Jerry Lewis to the screen in George Marshall's otherwise forgettable *My Friend Irma* (1945).

In the 1950s, Paramount, under the aegis of producer George Pal, moved decisively into science fiction with Irving Pichel's *Destination Moon* (1950), Rudolph Maté's *When Worlds Collide* (1951), and Byron Haskin's *The War of the Worlds* (1953); William Wyler adapted the stage hit *Detective Story* (1951), offering a no-holds-barred take on big-city crime and punishment. Alfred Hitchcock made some of his deepest and most personal films for Paramount in the 1950s, including *Rear Window* (1954) and *Vertigo* (1958); Alan Ladd's performance as the title character in George Stevens's western *Shane* (1953) was also memorable. *White Christmas* (1954), essentially a repackaging of Irving Berlin tunes, was the studio's initial release in VistaVision, directed oddly enough by jack-of-all-trades Michael Curtiz, far from his hardboiled persona at Warner Bros., where he is best remembered for *Casablanca* (1942) and his masterpiece, *Mildred Pierce* (1945).

But the 1950s at Paramount inescapably belonged to Dean Martin and Jerry Lewis, who moved from cabaret to television to the big screen with lightning—or frightening—speed, and were soon cranking out a series of lowbrow comedies for the studio, among them Hal Walker's *At War with the Army* (1950), Walker's *That's My Boy* (1951), Walker's *Sailor Beware* (1952), Norman Taurog's *Jumping Jacks* (1952), Taurog's *The Stooge* (1953), George Marshall's *Scared Stiff* (1953), Taurog's *Living It Up* (1954), Frank Tashlin's *Artists and Models* (1955), and Tashlin's *Hollywood or Bust* (1956), their last film as a team. Many of these films were remakes of earlier Paramount productions, with Martin and Lewis shoehorned into a series of tired plots and situations in which Lewis would clown around while Martin crooned and Paramount made lots and lots of money.

After the duo split acrimoniously on July 25, 1956, Lewis appeared in a string of solo efforts, Don McGuire's *The Delicate Delinquent* (1957), Tashlin's *Rock-A-Bye Baby* (1958), and Tashlin's *The Geisha Boy* (1958), all of which made their negative cost back but didn't perform as spectacularly at the box office as their joint efforts had. Lewis then knocked out his roles in the Gore Vidal–scripted satire *Visit to a Small Planet* (Norman Taurog, 1960) and *Cinderfella* (Frank Tashlin, 1960) and was getting ready to leave Paramount's employ when the studio reminded him that he owed them one last film as a performer. Suddenly, Lewis saw a chance to leave Paramount, make a lot of money, establish himself as a director, and have complete creative control in the process, all at one stroke.

At the time, Lewis was performing as a solo act at the Fountainbleau Hotel in Miami, and he came up with the nearly silent "sight gag" comedy *The Bellboy* (1960), which he shot at the hotel during the day while continuing his supper club gigs at night. Working with writer Bill Richmond, Lewis crafted a film that was an homage to the silent clowns—Keaton, Chaplin, Lloyd, and others—and for the first time (not counting his odd 16mm short *How to Smuggle a Hernia across the Border* [1949], which he starred in, co-wrote, and co-directed, featuring Janet Leigh as his co-star), Lewis stepped behind the camera as director. Lewis had total creative control, but when Paramount saw the rushes they withdrew their funding for the project. *The Bellboy* was so visually sophisticated as to recall the work of the French comedian Jacques Tati, and was absolutely unlike any of his previous assembly line, genre-driven vehicles.

Lewis responded by underwriting the $950,000 budget with his own money, negotiating a deal with the studio in which he received a hefty portion of the film's gross profits. *The Bellboy* was a fresh, funny film and an immediate hit, and by 2005 it had grossed in excess of $200 million; its success made Lewis not only a bankable solo star but also a reputable director. It was also on this film that Lewis invented the video assist, which videotaped each take of a scene so that Lewis could see, immediately, whether or not a gag had worked without waiting for the dailies the next day. This, of course, is now standard practice within the industry and gave Lewis an instant advantage as director; he could reshoot immediately if necessary, thus avoiding the expense of a retake later.

Lewis continued with a string of highly successful and innovative films for the studio, including *The Ladies Man* (1961), *The Errand Boy* (1961), *The Patsy* (1964), and, perhaps his best-known film of the era, *The Nutty Professor* (1963), a riff on the classic *Dr. Jekyll and Mr. Hyde*, all of which were enormous hits. By 1966, however, Lewis's films, such as *The Family Jewels* (1965), were no longer the box office draws they once had been, and he departed Paramount with a legacy of agreeably comic mayhem in his wake.

As the 1960s dawned, Paramount seemed to be growing more and more out of touch with cinema audiences. Alfred Hitchcock, for example, was under contract to Paramount for the release of his theatrical films, but he was also contracted to Universal for his television show *Alfred Hitchcock Presents*, which debuted in 1955 (the show expanded from half an hour to an hour in 1962, and ended its run in 1965). Hitchcock usually confined his input on the series to helping to select the stories for dramatization, lending his name and image to the project, and also providing a series of delightfully droll introductions and postscripts to each teleplay, which he personally delivered in his usual laconic style. The episodes were directed by such old hands as John Brahm and Robert Florey, and shot in two to three days at most, with a Universal TV crew working at maximum efficiency in serviceable black and white. Very occasionally, however, Hitchcock would direct an episode of the series, and when he did, the speed and professionalism of the Universal crews astounded him, compared to the relative lassitude of his feature crews at Paramount. Ordinarily bored by the filmmaking process—shooting seemed almost an afterthought to his exquisitely detailed storyboards—Hitchcock now found himself caught up in the excitement of actually shooting a movie.

Having known for some time that his 1950s big-budget suspense films were fast falling out of favor, Hitchcock cast around for some fresh material and found it in Robert Bloch's novel *Psycho*. Using an intermediary to keep the cost down, Hitchcock bought the rights to the novel and pitched the project to Paramount. But Paramount's executives, just as they had with *The Bellboy*, found the material too exotic, offbeat, and problematic, and refused to finance the film. After much negotiation, Hitchcock struck a deal to shoot the film at Universal in black and white using his *Alfred Hitchcock Presents* TV crew, funding the budget of $806,947 entirely with his own money, and also deferring his standard director's fee of $250,000 in return for a 60 percent ownership of the film's negative (Rebello 26–29). But due to his contract, the film would still have to be released through Paramount.

Hitchcock shot the film on a very tight schedule, starting on November 11, 1959, and wrapping on February 1, 1960 (Rebello 128). When *Psycho* opened, it exceeded the box office of all Hitchcock's previous features and—with its sinuous synthesis of sex, violence, and hitherto uncharted psychiatric territory, at least in a major Hollywood film—signaled the beginning of the end for the Breen Code. Thus, *Psycho*, like *The Bellboy*, was essentially an independent film, backed by its maker against the objections of a studio that had been making bland mass entertainment for so long that it couldn't see that the audience no longer wanted, or needed, the old formulas.

Viewers wanted something fresh, and both *The Bellboy* and *Psycho* provided precisely that—the shock of the new. It's also interesting that neither film was shot at Paramount Studios; *The Bellboy* was shot entirely on location, using the actual Fountainbleau Hotel as a gigantic ready-made set; *Psycho* was shot at Universal, where, after all these years, as noted in the prologue, the Bates Motel still stands and remains a potent attraction for tourists. Paramount released both films, but because of its shortsightedness it reaped little financial benefit from either project. The studio, in short, was beginning to fall behind the curve.

Yet there was a new star on the horizon, and for that Paramount had producer Hal Wallis to thank. Wallis had came over from Warner Bros., where he spent the 1940s cranking out one major film after another until a rift with Jack Warner over the credit for producing *Casablanca* rapidly escalated into a full-fledged feud and drove him to seek newer pastures (see Dick, *Wallis* 77–80). At Paramount Wallis successfully shepherded the Martin and Lewis films to completion, but with the team's split he was looking around for a new sensation. Idly tuning around the television dial on the night of January 28, 1956, he chanced upon Elvis Presley performing on the CBS series *Stage Show* (1954–1956) and was immediately thunderstruck by the singer's charisma (Dick, *Wallis* 159).

Moving swiftly, Wallis signed Presley to Paramount, hoping to feature the performer in the forthcoming project *The Rainmaker*. When that idea didn't pan out, Wallis loaned Presley out to 20th Century Fox for his motion picture debut, Robert D. Webb's *Love Me Tender*. Wallis had signed Elvis at $15,000 a picture but managed to loan him out to Fox for $150,000, getting him third billing from the top of the marquee (Dick, *Wallis* 161). *Love Me Tender* was such an enormous success that Wallis tore up the old contract and put Elvis on a long-term agreement at $2,500 a week, with a $100,000 bonus (Dick, *Wallis* 161). Presley's first film for

Paramount, Hal Kanter's *Loving You* (1957), was also a substantial hit, and the singer's film career was truly launched.

Elvis's manager, "Colonel" Tom Parker, was—as everyone knows—a canny negotiator, who wanted to keep Elvis tightly controlled and ensure that each of his films yielded a sound track album for maximum exposure. He actually prevented Elvis from taking on more serious roles. Parker wanted songs, fun, and girls in all of Presley's films; it was a winning formula, and he saw no reason to deviate from it. Through a deal that allowed Elvis to make four films for Wallis and Paramount plus two outside films the first year, one outside picture the second and third years, and two in the fourth year, Wallis agreed to pay Elvis a total of $175,000 per film, for eight weeks of work in each (Dick, *Wallis* 165).

Richard Thorpe's *Jailhouse Rock* (1957) was a loan-out to MGM; Curtiz's *King Creole* (1958) was made for Paramount, as was Taurog's *G. I. Blues* (1960), made to capitalize on Elvis's stint in the army. Taurog's *Blue Hawaii* (1961) was Elvis's next Paramount film, after two successive loan-outs to 20th Century Fox, and then, after two more loan-outs to United Artists, Elvis came back to Paramount to make Taurog's decidedly uninspired *Girls! Girls! Girls!* (1962), of which the title tells all. By this time, Elvis was in a complete rut and also overexposed—he made too many movies in too little time for too many studios, and through the Colonel's "wringing every last dollar out of the merchandise" style of management, he was becoming tired, overweight, and a caricature of his original sensual vitality.

In rapid succession, Elvis cranked out Richard Thorpe's *Fun in Acapulco* (1963), John Rich's *Roustabout* (1964), Michael D. Moore's *Paradise, Hawaiian Style* (1965), and Rich's *Easy Come, Easy Go* (1966) for Paramount, in between loans to the ridiculously cheapskate producer Sam Katzman at MGM. He even made an outside picture for Allied Artists, formerly Monogram Studios, but with all this activity Elvis's career was finished. The Beatles and the Rolling Stones had come to America and conquered, and Elvis continued on as if nothing had changed. Between 1957 and 1967, Presley made a total of thirty-one movies, and even he knew that he was being ruthlessly exploited, though he seemed powerless to do anything about it.

As Presley told a reporter in 1969 of his film work, "I've been extremely unhappy with that side of my career for some time. But how can you find twelve good songs for every film when you're making three films a year?" (McLafferty 214). The answer is simple: you can't. The Beatles had the sense to make only two real films, Richard Lester's *A Hard Day's Night* (1964) and *Help!* (1965), before retreating into the studio to concentrate on their music full-time. Paramount, however, saw Elvis as a commodity and kept using him until there was nothing left.

Run it into the ground—that seemed to be Paramount's motto, and don't change things too much or people will be confused. Paramount, more than any other studio, seemed to lean toward lighter-than-air enter-tainment above all other considerations—films one would forget in an instant. True, there were exceptions, but the typical Paramount film of the 1950s is an assembly-line product, designed to fit a predestined mold. There were, to be sure, outliers: Marlon Brando's out-of-control production of *One-Eyed Jacks* (1961), his only film as director, was an anomaly; Brando took over direction after firing both Stanley Kubrick and Sam Peckinpah from the project, simply by virtue of his then-unquestioned star power.

Blake Edwards had to battle through constant front-office interference to create *Breakfast at Tiffany's* (1961); John Ford's *The Man Who Shot Liberty Valance* (1962) is now considered a classic, but it was poorly received by audiences and critics when first released. More conventional fare was offered in Greg Garrison's *Hey, Let's Twist!* (1961), George Marshall's Jackie Gleason schmaltzfest *Papa's Delicate Condition* (1963), Walter Grauman's *Lady in a Cage* (1964), and Daniel Mann's *Who's Been Sleeping in My Bed?* (1963), with the occasional spectacle—Anthony Mann's *The Fall of the Roman Empire* and Henry Hathaway's *Circus World* (both 1964)—thrown in, as if to convince customers that nothing had really changed. The old order was still dominant.

In 1966, Gulf + Western obtained control of the studio; part of the deal included the formal incorporation of Paramount Television, which took place the following year, following the acquisition of Desilu Productions. As Zukor had suggested more than fifteen years earlier, since television was inevitable the studio should learn to cooperate with the new medium and produce programming for it, and now Paramount was poised to do so. In taking this step, the studio had the considerable advantage of building on the foundation of Desilu, which Desi Arnaz and Lucille Ball had established in 1950. In addition to pioneering the three-camera television sitcom with *I Love Lucy*, Desilu also was home to *Mission: Impossible* (1966–1973), *The Andy Griffith Show* (1960–1968), the original *Star Trek* (1966–1969), and the detective series *Mannix* (1967–1975), all of which would continue under the Paramount banner. As Paramount Television gained strength, it began churning out a series of squeaky-clean sitcom hits, most notably the television series adaptation of Neil Simon's *The Odd Couple* (1970–1975); the 1950s nostalgia show *Happy Days*, which ran for an astounding ten years from 1974 to 1984; and also *The Brady Bunch* (1969–1974), *Laverne and Shirley* (1976–1983), and *Taxi* (1978–1983). Since that productive period, Paramount Television has gone through a number of corporate restructurings, but it remains a viable force within the television industry and is now moving into streaming video. After all, what is streaming video other than a different form of television? Zukor always embraced the future of the moving image medium, and he surely would have approved of any plan to capture a substantial portion of the web's global audience.

Throughout the 1960s and 1970s, Paramount's corporate fortunes declined; it survived by releasing British imports—usually horror movies from Amicus Productions—independent pickups, and routine genre fare that often imitated what the other studios were doing, such as Lenny Weinrib's *Beach Ball* (1965), a direct rip-off of American International Pictures' *Beach Party* series. Rock Hudson's *Seconds* (John Frankenheimer, 1966) was a costly failure, despite being a brilliant film, and Howard

Hawks's last westerns, particularly *El Dorado* (1967), were gently elegiac throwbacks to a lost age that failed to arouse more than passing interest with the public.

The corporate structure of the company had changed, and the studio's shotgun marriage with Gulf + Western lasted until 1989. Between 1989 and 1994, the company was spun off as Paramount Communications; in 1994 Paramount became part of Viacom, which is now CBS, and this lasted until 2006; in 2006, the company was reorganized yet again as part of the "new" Viacom, a situation that persists to this day. The balance sheet, in the early twenty-first century, remains solid; in 2005, the company had revenues of $3 billion versus $62.1 million in debt, the result of an aggressive campaign to become a major provider of television programming for the big three networks and the cable networks that arose in the 1980s.

Zukor had retired long before this, content to watch the entire business spectacle pass before his eyes almost without comment, but occasionally in his last years he would offer a few nuggets of wisdom to reporters or historians eager for some insight into his meteoric rise to fame. Zukor's death at 103 was entirely in keeping with his matter-of-fact acceptance of business affairs as they were, rather than as he might have wished them to be. When television first appeared in the early 1950s, Zukor's reaction was calm and pragmatic: "Rather than lose the public because television is here, wouldn't it be smart to adopt television as an instrument?" (Krebs).

Zukor would have been right at home in the era of streaming video; his number one mantra was always adapt, adapt, adapt. Everything changes. Keep up with it. And as long as Zukor was running the company, Paramount, perhaps the least sophisticated studio in terms of its output, followed Zukor's other mantra, which became the title of his 1953 autobiography: *The Public Is Never Wrong*. Zukor never under- or overestimated his audience; he simply wished to give them what they wanted, like any good merchant. And this is exactly how Zukor saw himself, as he told journalist Albin Krebs: "I had a vision—[a] calculated vision—and the circumstances were fortunate. I wanted to be a merchant when I was a boy. And that is what I am now and have always been—a merchant." Following his own self-defined policy of "look[ing] ahead a little and gamb[ling] a lot" (Krebs), Zukor built up his empire brick by brick until he had created an edifice, which at its height was the most powerful motion picture company on earth. As Krebs commented,

> Adolph Zukor was the completely atypical movie tycoon—unflamboyant, deliberate, mild-mannered, predictable, almost self-effacing. While other pioneers in the motion picture industry, such as D. W. Griffith, Samuel Goldwyn, and Louis B. Mayer, with their well-publicized feuds, rages and personal eccentricities, became celebrities almost as well known as the stars who appeared in their films, Mr. Zukor could have been mistaken for an ordinary businessman.

This was precisely the way that Adolph Zukor wanted it: no drama, just results, as if he were playing a gigantic game of three-dimensional chess, using theaters and film exchanges instead of pawns and queens. Indeed, Zukor's patience and foresight caused his family to tag him as rabbinic material early on, which Zukor resisted (Krebs).

Instead, Zukor set his sights on reaching the masses through the cinema. Zukor could see early on that the movies were the most egalitarian form of entertainment ever invented, and that they had a ready-made audience among those who couldn't even speak English. As he told Krebs, "You have to understand what was happening in this country to see why movies were catching on. From 1900 to 1910, about nine or ten million immigrants poured in [to the United States] and because nickelodeon movies were new, cheap, silent and set up no language difficulties, they became a popular pastime."

For most of his career, unlike Jack Warner, Harry Cohn, or Darryl F. Zanuck, Zukor was content to conduct his empire from New York, and he left the day-to-day production of films to his associates. In Paramount's scheme of things, what was most important was physical domination of the industry, which included, but was far from limited to, the product that the studio produced and distributed to the theaters Paramount controlled.

In the 1920s and early 1930s, when the Paramount logo still sported the words "Adolph Zukor presents," his influence was more deeply felt on the production end, but he soon saw that the bigger game was to control everything, not just a group of actors and directors involved in creating a shadow play. An expert card player with a preference for bridge, pinochle, and poker, Zukor would play by the hour with his colleagues, especially on the coast-to-coast train trip from New York to Los Angeles that he made once a year, just to see what was going on in the studio itself. And although he maintained a hands-off policy on actual production, preferring to delegate this to Freeman, Balaban, Wallis, and others, "he never lost interest in making—and saving—money for Paramount" (Krebs).

By the early 1950s, however, Zukor knew that for him, personally, the game was over. Sitting in his office in the Paramount Building in New York, he would relive his past glories and his mostly successful attempt to control the motion picture business from top to bottom. As producer Max Youngstein, then a young turk at Paramount, later recalled, Zukor was "this little delicate man who looked sometimes like a tailor and sometimes like a guy whose head would explode with ideas. . . . What I did see was this enormous grasp for power. He figured that unless you controlled the whole ball of wax to the furthest extent the law permitted [you were weak]. . . . He was very much of the idea that softness in this business, compromising, being the nice guy, would not get you very far. . . . There was no dream with respect to power that was too big for him" (Gabler, *Empire* 427). For Zukor, nice guys finished last, if they finished at all; you had to take what you wanted, now, before someone else did.

And Zukor wanted it all. But at the same time, Zukor assiduously cultivated an appearance of benign paternalism, somewhat akin to that of Louis B. Mayer, but with an even more sinister, insidious edge. Even in retirement, he kept a close eye on the daily workings of Paramount. "What am I doing?" he rhetorically asked one reporter.

> Well, I come down [to Paramount] everyday. I attend meetings where we discuss plays, or any other policy of the company. . . . I have a great deal of pleasure in being able to study the public reaction to certain types of pictures. Then, based on that, I realize what would be a good story for the future, and I tell [the members of the board about it] and I talk about it. I don't say that they can't get along without me—*maybe they could* [emphasis added]—but in the meantime, it keeps me busy three or four hours a day, and the week goes by. (Gabler, *Empire* 428)

Zukor's wife, Lottie, died in 1956, but Zukor continued his daily routine up until the day of his death. Zukor moved to the West Coast to be closer to the studio he had built from the ground up, and, as he fervently wished, he had seen all his former competitors in the business pass on before him. Irene Mayer Selznick noted that "there was barely anyone around to remember how rough and ruthless he could be," which suited Zukor perfectly (Gabler, *Empire* 429). Now that the game was almost over, Zukor was making a smooth exit. Even as his ninety-seventh birthday approached, Zukor still came to his offices at the studio to check the weekly box office tally while living on his own in an apartment at the Beverly Hills Hotel (Gabler, *Empire* 429).

On January 7, 1973, the studio held an enormous party to celebrate Zukor's 100th birthday. By now, Charles Bluhdorn had taken over Paramount as part of Gulf + Western, but he deferentially referred to Zukor as a man who "exemplified the American dream," while President Richard Nixon awarded Zukor a Certificate of Distinguished Achievement (Gabler, *Empire* 429). Zukor, by now the wise old man and quite comfortable in the role, told the assembled throng that he was "very grateful for this wonderful party. . . . This is the best possible medicine I could have. It will last the rest of my life." A rabbi offered a brief prayer, noting that since Moses had lived to 120, Zukor might do so as well (Gabler, *Empire* 429).

Zukor moved to a Century City high-rise apartment and took on a housekeeper, yet he still had lunch almost every day at the Hillcrest Country Club and enjoyed afternoon bridge games there (Gabler, *Empire* 429). At 102, he could no longer bite into a piece of steak, one of his favorite foods, because his teeth were becoming so weak. Still, he dressed immaculately every day, and when Adolph Zukor finally departed this earth on June 10, 1976, he did so on his own terms, as he had lived his life: alert, conscious, and still full of ambition (Gabler, *Empire* 430). It wasn't that Zukor's fire had faded. It was simply that his body could no longer sustain his dreams of empire.

Paramount's story is thus one of the most curious of all the Hollywood studios, just as Zukor's mild-mannered exterior served to conceal the vast drive and imagination of the man. The studio had only a few major stars and a few key directors, but under Zukor's guidance it knew how to turn such thinly spread talent into box office dominance, through genre-based franchise filmmaking—indeed, the Hope/Crosby *Road* pictures were the most profitable franchise films made in the classical studio era, gossamer concoctions spun out of nothing more than ancient vaudeville routines, the chemistry between the two stars, and the thinnest of narratives to hold the entire package together (Gomery, *Studio System* 43).

If Paramount's identity in the 1930s under Ernst Lubitsch as production chief was both individual and entertainingly eccentric, pushing the envelope as far as possible in matters of content and thematic structure, by the late 1930s Paramount had learned to play it safe and eschewed a distinct studio signature in favor of popular but ultimately forgettable entertainment. The strategy worked financially; by 1946, the year of highest attendance for the American motion picture industry, Paramount was absolutely debt free—an unheard of circumstance for a major studio with such far-flung interests (Gomery, *Studio System* 38).

Paramount, despite tough times in the 1960s, is still very much with us. Like the other major studios, it is now a place where films are packaged, financed, and distributed, and it retains only a few mementos of its storied past. Zukor's achievement endures in the studio's centennial year, and so, in many ways, Paramount resembles the man who created it. Through sheer persistence and force of will, as well as a certain self-effacement that Zukor himself affected, Paramount survives today as a viable entity, testimony to Zukor's tenacity, vision, and adaptability. Indeed, Paramount is now one of the industry monoliths, with 2011 revenue of $20 billion and operating income of more than $11 billion. No doubt Zukor would be proud of that—even if he wouldn't come out and say so.

CHAPTER 6

The Major Minors

In addition to what were known as the Big Five during the classical Hollywood studio era—MGM, Paramount, 20th Century Fox, Warner Bros. and RKO Radio—there were the so-called "little three," although the term can't be fairly applied to these studios in retrospect, because they rapidly became as important as any of the Big Five—Universal, United Artists, and Columbia. There were also several "mini-majors" that operated in Hollywood during this period, most notably Samuel Goldwyn Studios and Selznick International on the "A" level, and Republic, Monogram, and Producers' Releasing Corporation on the "B" level. In addition, although RKO Radio was indisputably a major studio, its history is so truncated that I'll also consider it here; in many ways, the collapse of RKO was the first real death knell of the classical studio system. Finally, there's United Artists, the first "creative combine" launched by actors Douglas Fairbanks Sr., Mary Pickford, Charles Chaplin, and director D. W. Griffith in 1919, and still active today.

———

United Artists represented the first attempt by artists to control the medium as a creative combine. All four original members were then at the peak of their creative powers, with the possible exception of Griffith, who never quite recovered from the economic disaster of his sprawling epic *Intolerance* (1916). The company didn't really get off the ground until 1920, however, and in 1924 Griffith quit the group, having problems of his own making deals for new films to direct. In any case, UA's early years were fraught with difficulties. In addition to Griffith's troubles, Fairbanks and Pickford soon realized that their individual careers were beginning to decline.

Pickford, once America's sweetheart, found that the public wouldn't let her grow up. She was forced to use oversize props in her later films to retain her "little girl" image, until she quit the business almost entirely after the critical and commercial failure of Frank Borzage's melodramatic *Secrets* (1933). Soon after, she divorced Fairbanks and married Buddy Rogers, which shocked her public, and further destabilized UA. Griffith, meanwhile, rejoined UA in 1927 and directed the static biopic *Abraham Lincoln* (1930), the director's first sound film, which was a commercial failure, notwithstanding some belated critical plaudits.

UA refused to bankroll further Griffith projects, and the director was forced to seek independent financing for *The Struggle* (1931), a film about alcoholism that mirrored Griffith's own battle with the bottle. Shot on location in the Bronx and at a cut-price film studio in Astoria, Queens, the film is almost neorealist in its threadbare intensity and has recently been restored on DVD to considerable acclaim. At the time, however, the reviews were brutal, with one critic writing that "it's a struggle to have to report that D. W. Griffith, who directed some of the greatest pictures, now presents one of the worst" (qtd. in Griffith and Mayer 209). UA, which had picked up the film for distribution, suddenly dropped it like a hot potato after a pathetic attempt to sell it as a comedy failed. Griffith would never make another film.

In the early years of UA, Joseph Schenck served as its nominal president. Though his control of the studio was less evident than that of its founders, his role there was significant, and when he quit in 1933 to work with Darryl Zanuck to establish 20th Century Pictures (two years before its merger with Fox Studio), UA was in trouble. As a result, the company was never really able to compete with the majors during what we call the golden era of the studio system. It wasn't until 1951 that Arthur Krim and Robert Benjamin contacted Pickford and Chaplin, the two surviving founders of the studio, and proposed a unique strategy. In short, Benjamin and Krim proposed to manage UA for a five-year period, with an option to buy the company afterward if they turned it around. Pickford, seeing that UA was just a shell of its former self, readily assented; Chaplin initially held out, but when his U.S. passport was revoked in 1952 at the height of the Red Scare as he was in London promoting his new film, *Limelight*, he capitulated and eventually sold out his shares. Krim and Benjamin, in the meantime, had moved swiftly to lock up John Huston's *African Queen* (1951), and the resulting success of the film put UA back on the map.

UA then became a "studio without a studio" (although it used the old Fairbanks-Pickford studio as a nominal base of production from 1928 to 1955, when Samuel Goldwyn acquired all rights to the property), relying on negative pickup deals—buying completed films from outside producers for a flat sum, and then distributing the film as part of studio product— and co-productions with such maverick filmmakers as Otto Preminger and Stanley Kramer. In 1955, UA's production of Delbert Mann's *Marty* surprised the industry by winning the Academy Award for Best Picture, Best Director, Best Actor (Ernest Borgnine in the leading role of Marty, a lonely Bronx butcher looking for love), and Best Adapted Screenplay (Paddy Chayefsky, from his television play of the same name). This low-budget, downbeat film was the direct antithesis of what Hollywood had been cranking out for decades—no glamour, no big-name stars, no color, no spectacle—and yet it was a resounding commercial and critical triumph.

In response, Pickford sold out her final shares of UA for $1.5 million. UA, then, prospered during a period when the majors and minors were shuttering their facilities; simply put, UA had no facilities to shutter. Relying as they did entirely on carefully picked outside product, UA became in many ways the model for film production as it is today; "packages" of stars, script, director, and producers putting together projects that the "studio" would then finance and distribute for a healthy chunk of the proceeds. *West Side Story* (1961), directed by Robert Wise and Jerome Robbins from the highly successful Leonard Bernstein/Stephen Sondheim Broadway musical, was another conspicuous hit for UA, and in 1962 UA financed the initial entry in the James Bond franchise, Terence Young's *Dr. No*.

In 1964, independent producer Walter Shenson brought *A Hard Day's Night* to the studio, followed by *Help!* in 1965, both starring The Beatles and both directed by Richard Lester. UA also backed the *Pink Panther* series, directed by Blake Edwards, as well as Sergio Leone's Italian westerns, which were initially made for exceedingly modest sums but made an overnight star out of former TV contract player Clint Eastwood and performed stunningly at the box office. So, in a very real sense, UA was essentially moribund from the beginning of the sound era in 1927 through 1948, springing to life with such films as Fred Zinnemann's *High Noon* (1952), Delbert Mann's *Marty* (1955) and the James Bond series, only as its more established competition floundered. UA would enter a period of great difficulty in the 1970s, however, culminating in the production of Michael Cimino's epic film *Heaven's Gate* (1980). Originally released at 219 minutes in length, the film sent the company into a financial tailspin from which UA has yet—despite a seemingly endless series of buyouts, negotiations, and restarts—to recover. At present, its future is uncertain.

———

Samuel Goldwyn was born Schmuel Gelbfisz in Warsaw, Poland, probably in July 1879—in later years, Goldwyn would do everything he could to assert that his actual birthdate was August 27, 1882, but this, like many of the other "facts" of his early life, was simply an invention (Berg 5). From an early age, Goldwyn had a burning desire to shed his impoverished upbringing and emigrate to the United States, which he viewed as the promised land, and in 1895 he began a long pilgrimage to America, moving first to Germany, then to London, then across the ocean to Canada, and finally to the United States (Berg 9–13).

Working at first in the garment business, Goldwyn hustled his way to New York, and in 1913 he was one of the four founding members of the Jesse L. Lasky Feature Play Company, along with Cecil B. DeMille, Arthur Friend, and Lasky himself. Paramount signed a deal with the Lasky Company to distribute Lasky's "photoplays," starting with DeMille's *The Squaw Man* (1914). But from the start, Adolph Zukor was angling for control of the entire Paramount/Lasky setup, and Goldwyn (who at this point was still using the *nomme de cinéma* of Samuel Goldfish) quit the Famous Players/Lasky combine on September 14, 1916 (Berg 63), and shortly thereafter partnered with Archibald and Edgar Selwyn to create the Goldwyn Pictures Corporation (merging the names of its founders); Goldwyn immediately took the company name as his own legal name.

However, though the Goldwyn Pictures Corporation was modestly successful, a series of internal power struggles forced him out of the new company on March 10, 1922 (Berg 103), and Goldwyn was on his own again, with two strikes now against him. But the ever-industrious Goldwyn realized that his future lay in production, in a company that he alone would control, rather than in a partnership. He shrewdly spent the next several months with ghostwriter Corinne Lowe "writing" his auto-biography, *Behind the Screen*, in which Goldwyn took advantage of the opportunity to rewrite his personal and business history as he wished it to be seen, "expunging the mistakes of the past" (Berg 109). The book was a substantial hit, serialized in the widely read journal *Pictorial Review* for an audience of two million readers, and Goldwyn made sure to flatter every celebrity whose path he had crossed and to place himself at the center of the infant medium.

With financial backing—albeit reluctantly—from A. P. Giannini's Commercial National Bank, okayed by DeMille, and a distribution deal with First National, Goldwyn established his own company, Samuel Goldwyn, Inc., though not before his former partners at Goldwyn Pictures Corporation tried to stop him from using the Goldwyn name. The case wound up in federal court, where Justice Learned Hand proclaimed that "a self-made man may prefer a self-made name" and ruled against Goldwyn Pictures in favor of Samuel Goldwyn, with the following stipulation: when he used the phrase "Samuel Goldwyn Presents" in his advertising and promotional materials, he would also have to attach the disclaimer that he was "not now connected with Goldwyn Pictures," setting up a confusion among historians and viewers that exists to this day (Berg 115).

In retrospect, it's rather amazing that Goldwyn won the favorable ruling, given that his new name was created with the formation of Goldwyn Pictures, and that, as Goldwyn Pictures pointed out to the court, the company existed "before Samuel Goldfish became Samuel Goldwyn" (Berg 115). But with the ruling and the court-mandated disclaimer, Goldwyn had won a double victory; he now "owned" his name outright and was *required* by the verdict to use the phrase "Samuel Goldwyn Presents" in the credits, advertising, and promotional materials for each of his films, along with the disclaimer, which made it seem as if he was deliberately distancing himself from his former associates. In 1923, Samuel Goldwyn, Inc., opened its first office on Madison Avenue in New York City.

Meanwhile, the original Goldwyn Pictures Corporation had fallen on hard times and was absorbed into Metro-Goldwyn-Mayer. Louis B. Mayer was given the role of vice-president and general manager, and Goldwyn's stock, which he had received as his settlement during his departure, was bought out for a cool $1 million in the spring of 1924 (Berg 117). Goldwyn wasn't happy with the deal, but he took it. He was now an independent producer, working on projects that he carefully selected, usually shooting only one film at a time. But at MGM, Mayer was watching Goldwyn's rise with mixed emotions, though he essentially regarded Goldwyn as an upstart. After all, the company's full name was Metro-*Goldwyn*-Mayer, offering another source of confusion, even if Goldwyn's personal success could benefit MGM by association.

Soon enough, Goldwyn and Mayer hated each other with a passion; a final blowup between the two men over the rights to some literary property in which Goldwyn told Mayer in no uncertain terms that he was a "son of a bitch" (Berg 199) exacerbated an already tense situation. MGM could do nothing about the name confusion, and Goldwyn himself didn't really want to—it offered additional advertising for his own product. But Goldwyn always referred to MGM as "the Metro-Goldwyn company," leaving out Mayer's name for the rest of his life (Berg 119). As for his own films as producer, Goldwyn was sure of his ground, and he liked the independence that sole proprietorship of his organization offered him. As he said near the end of his life, "My pictures were my own. I financed them myself and answered solely to myself. My mistakes and my successes were my own" (qtd. in Berg 119).

Goldwyn moved to Hollywood, setting up offices at 7200 Santa Monica Boulevard, the site of the old Pickford-Fairbanks studios, founded in 1920. He immediately set about building up a talent roster, declaring that "God makes stars. It's up to producers to find them" (qtd. in Berg 120). Through the years, he worked with such stars as Danny Kaye, Gary Cooper, Ronald Colman, Walter Huston, Barbara Stanwyck, and numerous others. Among his many standout films were William Wyler's *These Three* (1935), an early adaptation of Lillian Hellman's play *The Children's Hour*, considerably sanitized for the screen; Wyler's *Dodsworth* (1936), based on Sinclair Lewis's popular novel; Wyler's *Dead End* (1937), based on Sidney Kingsley's hit Broadway play, staring Humphrey Bogart and introducing the Dead End Kids to the screen; and King Vidor's *Stella Dallas* (1937), one of Barbara Stanwyck's most effective maternal melodramas.

These films were followed by Wyler's *Wuthering Heights* (1939), starring a young Laurence Olivier, Merle Oberon, and David Niven; Wyler's *The Little Foxes* (1941), with Bette Davis at her most poisonous; Howard Hawks's *Ball of Fire* (1941), a raucous comedy with Barbara Stanwyck; Sam Woods's *The Pride of the Yankees* (1942), with Gary Cooper as baseball great Lou Gehrig; Elliot Nugent's *Up in Arms* (1944), with Danny Kaye at his most manic; and his crowning masterpiece, Wyler's *The Best Years of Our Lives* (1946), in which real-life World War II veteran

Harold Russell, whose hands had been blown off in a training accident, played one of three returning veterans (the others played by Dana Andrews and Fredric March), who are forced to readjust after the adrenalin rush of combat to the even more brutal realities of peacetime existence.

Goldwyn continued into the late 1940s and early 1950s with Henry Koster's fantasy/comedy *The Bishop's Wife* (1947), starring Cary Grant, David Niven, and Loretta Young; the Danny Kaye vehicle *Hans Christian Andersen* (Charles Vidor, 1952); and the lavish Technicolor musical *Guys and Dolls* (Joseph L. Mankiewicz, 1955), which top-lined Marlon Brando, Frank Sinatra, Jean Simmons, and the rotund comedian Stubby Kaye. Goldwyn's last film as a producer was Otto Preminger's 1959 version of *Porgy and Bess*, starring Sammy Davis Jr., Sidney Poitier, Dorothy Dandridge, and Pearl Bailey. The NAACP, rightly feeling that the film encouraged racial stereotyping of African Americans, fiercely opposed production of the film, and the result was both a critical and commercial failure.

Rouben Mamoulian had been the initial director for *Porgy and Bess*, but constant fights with Goldwyn took their toll on both men and Mamoulian was summarily fired, with nearly all his footage scrapped. To top it off, the film's main set burned down during production, and when *Porgy and Bess* finally limped into theaters (Preminger proving no less fractious in his dealings with Goldwyn than Mamoulian had been), at an over-budget cost of $7 million, everyone knew the film would be a tough sell. It was, taking in only half its negative cost—$3.5 million—not including prints and advertising. It was an ignominious end to an illustrious career, driven by talent and perfectionism. *Porgy and Bess* was Goldwyn's eightieth and final film. Said Goldwyn after the smoke had cleared, "No one is waiting breathlessly for my next picture" (qtd. in Berg 488).

There followed a protracted retirement, as Goldwyn sold the television rights to fifty of his films to CBS's key television stations in New York, Chicago, Los Angeles, Philadelphia, and St. Louis (Berg 496), and then fought with William Wyler over the net profits of *The Best Years of Our*

Lives (Wyler owned 20 percent of the film), and with Lillian Hellman over the rights to *The Children's Hour* and *The Little Foxes* (Berg 499). On March 27, 1971, President Richard M. Nixon bestowed the Medal of Freedom upon Goldwyn, but by this time the aging mogul was no longer fully cognizant of the events that transpired around him. Nixon made the unusual gesture of going directly to Goldwyn's house to present the medal, remembering that when he lost his presidential bid in 1960 Goldwyn was one of the few who telephoned him and urged him to "stay with it. You'll win" (qtd. in Berg 506).

Goldwyn died at the age of 94 on January 31, 1974, more than two decades after producing his last film (Berg 507). Goldwyn is also legendary for his numerous malapropisms, or "Goldwynisms" as they came to be called, many of which are apocryphal. Confronted with a sundial and told that it was used to tell time, Goldwyn purportedly exclaimed, "My God, what'll they think of next?"; he was also credited with such gems as "a verbal agreement isn't worth the paper it's printed on," the infamous rejoinder to "include me out," and winning an argument by asserting that "we are dealing in facts, not realities!" (qtd. in Berg 396–98). Some of these remarks are genuine, but most are simply part of the Goldwyn legend. Nevertheless, for a self-made man Goldwyn cut a wide swath in Hollywood, and he created some of the most meticulously crafted films of the studio era. Though his company survives today, with Goldwyn's last film in 1959 its true identity was sealed forever; after *Porgy and Bess*, there would never again be a new film with the court-mandated logo "Samuel Goldwyn Presents."

———

David O. Selznick—the "O" was simply an invention of Selznick's and stood for nothing; Selznick had no middle name—had a similarly indomitable personality. (The "no middle name" story has been so widely circulated and embellished as to enter the realm of myth, but Selznick himself stated that "I have no middle name. I briefly used my mother's maiden name, Sachs. I had an uncle, whom I greatly disliked, who was also named David Selznick, so in order to avoid the growing confusion between the two of us, I decided to take a middle initial and went through the alphabet to find one that seemed to give me the best punctuation, and decided on 'O'" [qtd. in Behlmer, *Memo* 3].)

Selznick's career in Hollywood was brief but incandescent. Born in Pittsburgh, Pennsylvania, in 1902 to movie distributer Lewis J. Selznick, young David attended Columbia University in New York while also working for his father, but Lewis Selznick's bankruptcy in 1923 abruptly ended this arrangement, and by 1926 David was in Hollywood laboring as an assistant story editor for MGM through 1927 (Gomery, *Studio System* 69). Always restless and possessed of enormous energy and self-confidence, Selznick moved to Paramount in 1928 in search of better opportunities for advancement. He further honed his skills as a very hands-on producer; he was on the set all the time, constantly keeping an eye on the production, marching the cast and crew toward the finish line.

On April 29, 1930, Selznick married Irene Mayer, an advantageous match since Irene was the daughter of Louis B. Mayer. During their marriage, David and Irene had two sons, Jeffrey and Daniel. But Selznick was always playing around on the side, and he gambled recklessly, in addition to his habit of consuming large quantities of pep pills to keep him going through long days at the studio. When Selznick began pursuing actress Jennifer Jones with a single-minded passion—more on this later—Irene had enough and left Selznick; their divorce was finalized in January 1949. Irene went on to a long career as a theater producer, starting with the 1947 production of *A Streetcar Named Desire*, directed by Elia Kazan.

In 1931 Selznick moved again, this time to RKO, as head of production. During his tenure there he presided over numerous films, most notably Katharine Hepburn's screen debut in George Cukor's *A Bill of Divorcement* (1932), Ernest B. Schoedsack and Irving Pichel's classic adventure film *The Most Dangerous Game* (1932), and Schoedsack and Merian C. Cooper's epic *King Kong* (1933), which took motion picture special effects to a new level for the era. But in 1933, Irving Thalberg, MGM's boy wonder, was in ill health, and Selznick returned to MGM to assist in production chores there, supervising such films as Cukor's all-star melodrama *Dinner at Eight* (1933), Cukor's *David Copperfield* (1935), and other prestige productions.

Selznick, much like Goldwyn, wanted his own organization that he could run entirely without interference, and so in 1935 he founded Selznick International Pictures, using the old Pathé Pictures lot in Culver City, which was then part of the RKO Radio facility. It took quite a bit of financing to make it work. Selznick's brother Myron contributed $200,000, and Irving Thalberg and his wife, the actress Norma Shearer, kicked in another $200,000 (Thalberg was probably delighted to see Selznick leave MGM, viewing him as a potential rival; see Behlmer, *Memo* 103). Financier Jock Whitney put in an additional $2.4 million, and with a final $300,000 garnered from other investors Selznick was on his own (Schatz 177).

Correctly judging that "there are only two kinds of merchandise that can be made profitably in this business; either the very cheap pictures or the very expensive pictures," Selznick chose "to compete with the very best" (qtd. in Schatz 178), an ambitious agenda for any independent producer. And, as noted, Selznick intended to continue as a very hands-on producer, stating at the outset of the company that "in the making of good pictures [it is] so essential for a producer to collaborate on every inch of script, to be available for every conference, and to go over all the details of production," adding that it would be "impossible for [such a producer] to give his best efforts to more than a limited number of pictures" (qtd. in Schatz 179).

Thus, as with Goldwyn, Selznick concentrated on making one film at a time, pouring all his resources and energy into each. Despite an early, unrealistic slate of ten pictures per year, all to be released through United Artists, Selznick soon realized that it was far better to make one or two major films per year—otherwise he would be spreading himself too thin

(Schatz 179). And so David O. Selznick embarked on what he termed "a tradition of quality," though in fact his glory years were brief indeed.

Selznick's films during the early years of the company included Richard Boleslawski's *The Garden of Allah* (1936), photographed in luscious Technicolor; William Wellman's Hollywood melodrama *A Star Is Born* (1937); Wellman's *Nothing Sacred* (1937), a screwball comedy starring Carole Lombard and Fredric March; John Cromwell's *The Prisoner of Zenda* (1937), a classic adventure/romance film that has proven a reliable staple for remakes ever since; and Norman Taurog's suitably censor-scrubbed *Tom Sawyer* (1938), all of which scored substantially at the box office. But Selznick had his eye on what would be the biggest prize of all: a screen version of Margaret Mitchell's novel *Gone with the Wind*, which was released after years of production and preparation in 1939.

Selznick first became aware of the property when Kay Brown, SIP's New York story editor, sent him a copy of the manuscript in May 1936, a month before the novel's publication, along with a detailed synopsis and a note enthusiastically recommending the property for a film adaptation. Selznick, busy completing *The Garden of Allah*, gave the manuscript to Val Lewton—later to become a producer in his own right with a series of original and distinctive low-budget horror films at RKO—who was then working as SIP's Hollywood story editor. Lewton hated the novel, labeling it "ponderous trash," but Selznick by now had had a chance to read the novel and was favorably disposed toward the project (Schatz 180).

At MGM, Thalberg famously passed on the project, telling Louis B. Mayer, "Forget it, Louis; no Civil War picture ever made a nickel," but Selznick, undeterred, closed the sale with Mitchell for $50,000. In addition, through Merian C. Cooper's Pioneer Pictures, Selznick made a series of unrelated but propitious deals with Technicolor, whose proprietary 3-strip color process—which Technicolor controlled from start to finish, furnishing their own cameras and directors of cinematography, and then processing the resultant footage in their own laboratory—was far and away the best color process available. Selznick acquired a six-picture commitment from Technicolor, which would first be used on *Gone with the Wind* (Schatz 180), and the producer was justifiably proud of his coup (Schatz, *Genius* 180).

Gone with the Wind's long and extensive production, including the numerous directors who worked on it—from action director B. Reeves Eason for the burning of Atlanta sequence, to George Cukor, who was famously fired and replaced with Victor Fleming, to Sam Wood for retakes—has been well documented elsewhere. The film was the pinnacle of Selznick's career, winning eight Academy Awards, including Best Picture, and he was never able to equal it, though his production of Alfred Hitchcock's *Rebecca* (1940) did win Best Picture the following year.

An extravagant man who pushed himself far beyond the endurance of an average man, Selznick was driven during the production of *Gone with the Wind*, and in its aftermath he was burned out, tired, and unsure of what to do next. To pull the film together, he had to offer to release it through MGM and allow the studio to take a hefty slice of the film's profits in return for the loan-out of Clark Gable for the leading role of Rhett Butler; the final opening title of the film reflects in microcosm the complexity of the entire project: "Selznick International in association with Metro-Goldwyn-Mayer has the honor to present its Technicolor production of Margaret Mitchell's story of the Old South *Gone With the Wind*." The film has multiple fingerprints all over it, from production designer William Cameron Menzies to an uncredited F. Scott Fitzgerald, who worked for a few days on the screenplay of the film, along with a host of other writers, including Selznick himself. *Gone with the Wind* has become a touchstone of Hollywood history, from the year that many consider to represent the industry's zenith, 1939, which also produced *The Wizard of Oz*—another film principally directed by Victor Fleming.

After *Rebecca*, Selznick for the most part confined himself to loaning out the services of the directors and stars he had under contract, especially Alfred Hitchcock, who chafed at the arrangement to such a degree that when he was finally free of Selznick's contractual obligation, he cast

Raymond Burr as a Selznick look-alike in *Rear Window* (1954) in the role of a man who murders his long-suffering wife. Selznick's later productions include Hitchcock's psychological thriller *Spellbound* (1945) and William Dieterle's treacly romance *Portrait of Jennie* (1948), starring SIP contract star Joseph Cotten and Selznick's new wife, Jennifer Jones (born Phyllis Isley), whom he had been grooming as a star since 1941. She won the Academy Award for Best Actress in Henry King's *Song of Bernadette* (1943) for 20th Century Fox on loan-out, and subsequently appeared in Selznick's production of John Cromwell's *Since You Went Away* (1944), a wartime tear-jerker that is painfully memorable for the circumstances surrounding its production.

Jennifer Jones was married at the time to actor Robert Walker, but when Selznick came into the young actress's life he almost immediately began having an affair with her that soon became public knowledge. Walker was unable to offer her what Selznick could: fame, fortune, and stardom. Cast as young lovers in *Since You Went Away*, Jones and Walker were required to film take after take of scenes of passionate romance, as Selznick took sadistic pleasure watching from the sidelines. In April 1945, Jones filed for divorce from Walker, which precipitated his torturous journey into years of alcohol use, mental instability, a failed marriage to director John Ford's daughter, Barbara, and a sense that his career was disintegrating before his eyes. Finally on August 28, 1951, Walker died of a combination of alcohol and amobarbital, a barbiturate administered by a psychiatrist to assuage Walker's alcohol-fueled rage. He was 32 years old.

In 1946, in an attempt to recapture the grandeur of his past productions, Selznick mounted the expensive and overwrought western *Duel in the Sun*, directed by King Vidor. By this point, Selznick was promoting Jones and Joseph Cotten as a screen "love team," although the chemistry between them was never more than lukewarm. The film failed to capture the dynamism of Selznick's earlier pictures, but with its lavish budget, extravagant production values, sensationalistic plot line, and all-star cast—including Lionel Barrymore, Gregory Peck, Herbert Marshall,

Walter Huston, and even Butterfly McQueen, late of *Gone with the Wind*—it became a box office hit. Vidor's overall direction of the project was supplemented by uncredited assists from William Dieterle, William Cameron Menzies, Josef von Sternberg, and even Selznick himself.

Selznick also wrote the film's screenplay—in which "half-breed" Jones is torn between brothers Peck and Cotten—from Niven Busch's novel, while Ben Hecht punched up the script for final shooting. *Duel in the Sun* was, in a peculiar fashion, the quintessential Selznick film—excessive, melodramatic, sprawling, and extravagant, with the producer in complete, though erratic, control throughout. But after *Duel in the Sun*, Selznick's energies almost vanished. As he wrote many years later, "I stopped making films in 1948 because I was tired. I had been producing, at the time, for twenty years. . . . Additionally it was crystal clear that the motion-picture business was in for a terrible beating from television and other new forms of entertainment, and I thought it a good time to take stock and to study objectively the obviously changing public tastes" (qtd. in Behlmer, *Memo* 423).

These "obviously changing public tastes"—the rise of teen films and films aimed at an even younger audience; the demise of the family film that the entire family would attend together, to be replaced by "niche" films that targeted one audience segment at a time; the rise of horror and science fiction films, genres that Selznick knew little about; plus audiences' lessening interest in Selznick's manufactured love team of Jones and Cotten—were passing Selznick by. There were a few other films that followed; Selznick co-produced Carol Reed's *The Third Man* in 1949 in exchange for the services of Cotten in the film; there was the disastrous *Indiscretion of an American Wife* (1953), a U.S./Italian co-production directed by Vittorio De Sica, which was cut to a mere sixty-three minutes when previews proved unfavorable; and finally Charles Vidor's adaptation of Ernest Hemingway's *A Farewell to Arms* (1957), with Jones and Rock Hudson in the leading roles. Despite a decent budget and solid production values, the film remained static and unconvincing, particularly when compared to Frank Borzage's 1932 version starring Gary Cooper and Helen Hayes.

Selznick continued to live lavishly but, despite lucrative theatrical rereleases of *Gone with the Wind* over the years, seemed perpetually out of funds. Throughout his career, Selznick was in the habit of writing lengthy memos and letters, which became legendary within the film community; in his final years, these missives, always insistent, took on a pleading, hectoring tone, as if Selznick were trying to order a life that had spun out of control. In 1962 and 1963, Selznick tried in vain to get a new project off the ground. In April 1964, he suffered the first of five heart attacks that would occur over a fifteen-month period. Finally, on June 22, 1965, Selznick died from a heart attack at the age of 63. All told, Selznick had spent his entire adult life in the motion picture industry, but his period of independence and complete control lasted little more than a decade, from Selznick International Pictures' inception in 1935 to *Portrait of Jennie* in 1948. After that, there were only memories, debts, and countless memos and letters to be catalogued and indexed. Selznick's legacy, as he knew it would, rests on *Gone with the Wind* above all his other work; he spent the rest of his life trying to recapture one moment in time.

———

Republic Pictures, in contrast, was considerably more down-market than Selznick International, but their energetic and unpretentious serials, westerns, and second features reached an enthusiastic audience throughout the United States, particularly in rural areas. Known particularly for its pulse-pounding action serials, such as William Witney and John English's *The Adventures of Captain Marvel* (1941), Witney and English's *Jungle Girl* (1941), Witney's *Spy Smasher* (1942), and Witney and Fred C. Brannon's *The Crimson Ghost* (1946), Republic made a name for itself providing low-cost, high octane thrills for the masses.

Serials were chapter-plays, running twelve to fifteen episodes per production, and usually played in movie theaters as part of the Saturday morning matinee. Republic was also home to singing cowboys Roy Rogers and Gene Autry, and the company's ability to churn out fast-moving, slick product made it the biggest and most visible of the minor studios. Republic budgets were tight—very tight. Director Joseph Kane recalled that the early Gene Autry westerns were made on budgets as low as $12,500 and shot in a six-day week (McCarthy and Flynn 320). The budgets for serials came in between $87,000 and $223,000, not counting prints and advertising; *Captain America*, directed by John English and Elmer Clifton in 1944, remained Republic's most expensive serial up until the serial format's demise in 1956 (Hurst 77). The studio's cadre of stunt men, contract players, and special effects experts (the redoubtable team of brothers Howard and Theodore Lydecker) excelled at squeezing every last dime out of every production dollar, yet they still managed to bring a sheen and polish to Republic's films that the two other minor studios of the era, Producers Releasing Corporation and Monogram, could not hope to match.

Republic was born in 1935, created out of the detritus of six smaller studios, all of which used Consolidated Film Laboratories to process and print their films. Consolidated, in turn, was owned and operated by Herbert J. Yates, a tough customer in the Harry Cohn mold who began his career as a "tobacco marketing executive with American Tobacco and Liggett and Meyers" (McCarthy and Flynn 21). Yates then moved into the film processing business, building up Consolidated as the lab of choice for independents. When the Depression hit, many of the smaller companies, which were very thinly capitalized, often making a profit of only a few thousand dollars per feature, found themselves unable to pay their lab bills. Thus it was that Liberty, Majestic, Mascot, Invincible, Chesterfield, and, surprisingly, Monogram Pictures became part of the Republic combine in 1935, though Monogram executives Trem Carr and W. Ray Johnston soon tired of working with the overbearing Yates and split off in 1937 to rejuvenate Monogram Pictures Corporation as an individual entity (McCarthy and Flynn 20).

Nat Levine's Mascot Pictures was one of the prime parts of the newly formed company. Levine, who was known (and not very well liked) for his

penurious production practices, was adept at producing serials and westerns for pennies on the dollar, such as Ford Beebe and B. Reeves Eason's
The Shadow of the Eagle, a 1932 twelve-chapter serial starring a young
John Wayne. Between 1929, when Mascot was first organized, and 1935,
when Yates took control, Mascot released no fewer than twenty-four
serials, or four complete chapter plays each year. Mascot produced the
genuinely bizarre science fiction/western/musical serial *The Phantom
Empire*, directed by Otto Brower and Eason in 1935, a truly mind-bending
genre mash-up that managed to blend country and western songs, cattle
stampedes, fisticuffs, a lost underground civilization complete with a
despotic femme fatale ruler, and Gene Autry's dubious talents as an actor
to create a jaw-dropping film that is oddly enjoyable.

Yates built on Levine's skills as a producer—it was Levine who devised
the strategy of using two directors on each serial, one for action sequences,
the other for dialogue scenes—but spent more money, time, and care with
Republic productions and then produced a technically superior product
in every department. Yates soon forced out or alienated his new "partners";
Johnston and Carr, as mentioned, left in 1937 to restart Monogram; and
Levine was unceremoniously dropped after Yates stripped him of his
entire production facility and his roster of cut-price talent. Though Yates
bought him out for $1 million, Levine was an inveterate gambler and soon
squandered his money at the racetrack. Louis B. Mayer came to Levine's
rescue momentarily, employing him at MGM as a second unit director,
but Levine soon tired of being a hired hand and he and Mayer had a falling
out besides. Penniless, Levine took a job managing a movie theater in
Redondo Beach, California, but by the 1960s his health forced him to enter
the Motion Picture Country Home (the film industry's long-established
retirement facility, which is now, sadly, in jeopardy due to financial
problems), where he died in 1989.

With his "associates" gone Yates was the top man at Republic, a position he was to retain until the company's demise on July 31, 1959 (McCarthy
and Flynn 324). The assets of Republic are now owned by Viacom, often

channeled through Spelling Entertainment and National Telefilm Associates after Republic ceased production. But in its heyday, from the late 1930s through the early 1950s, Republic's name was synonymous with slick, undemanding program filmmaking, and the sheer volume of Republic's output alone demands respect.

Republic pioneered numerous innovations in action filmmaking; it was director William Witney, for example, who came up with modern fight choreography as he watched Busby Berkeley direct musicals at Warner Bros. in the late 1930s. Witney saw that Berkeley staged the action in short bursts, cutting the segments together to create the illusion of continuous, flowing motion. Adapting this to fight sequences, Witney perfected the intercutting of stunt men and women with the stars of the films he directed, creating a seamless flow of propulsive motion that has earned him the respect of director Quentin Tarantino, among others, who routinely cites Witney as one of the major influences on his work. Then, too, the Lydecker brothers specialized in one-fifth scale miniatures, filmed in slow motion, to effectively stage spectacular crashes, explosions, and other action sequences, with a fleet of miniature planes, trucks, rocket ships, and submarines, not to mention standard automobiles, all built to scale and photographed against natural backgrounds to create a convincing illusion of real destruction.

If serials and westerns were Republic's mainstays, the studio also produced some "A" films, such as John Ford's *The Quiet Man* (1952), which won Ford an Academy Award for Best Director, shot on location in Ireland in Technicolor; Nicholas Ray's bizarre western *Johnny Guitar* (1954), starring Joan Crawford as Vienna, the hardboiled owner of an Old West casino; and Orson Welles's minimalist version of *Macbeth* (1948), which was a financial disaster upon first release but now is regarded as a minor masterpiece.

Yates established four budget categories for his productions: Jubilee, Anniversary, Deluxe, and Premiere. Jubilee films were mostly low-budget westerns; they were shot in six or seven days on budgets of $50,000 or so.

A good example of this is Phil Ford's *The Dakota Kid*, shot in seven days starting on January 3, 1951, for a total negative cost of a mere $52,471, exposing only 23,000 feet of film. Moving up to the Anniversary level, William Beaudine's *Havana Rose* (1951) cost a hefty $183,744, took fourteen days to film, and used 45,000 feet of raw stock. Joseph Kane's Deluxe film *Fighting Coast Guard* (1951) cost $532,111, took twenty-two days to shoot, and used 55,000 feet of film. John Ford's Premiere budget for *Rio Grande* (1950) came to $1,214,899, thirty-two shooting days, and 80,000 feet of film (McCarthy and Flynn 26–29).

But there was a fatal flaw in Republic's system; it failed to take into account the fact that many of Republic's films played in theaters for a flat rental rather than a percentage of the box office, so when Republic had a hit it couldn't really capitalize on its successes. But there were other problems as well. Yates refused to pay residuals to the Screen Actors Guild for the sale of his films to television, and so SAG declared Republic "not in compliance," boycotting the company. And as the icing on the cake, Yates fell in love with ice skater Vera Hruba Ralston; convinced that she was star material, he put her in twenty-six films from 1945 through 1958, only two of which made a profit, and both of those featured John Wayne as co-star.

Simply put, Vera Hruba Ralston had almost no screen personality; watching her on screen, it's clear that she was in over her head, a complete nonprofessional thrown in at the deep end, left to fend for herself as best she could. John Wayne wanted to make a film about the Alamo at Republic (he later did, directing it himself, with assists from Ray Kellogg and John Ford, as an independent production in 1960), but he refused to co-star with Ralston in the project, which Wayne considered a losing proposition from all points of view. As he told an interviewer, "Yates made me use Vera Hruba. . . . I don't want to malign her. She didn't have the experience. . . . Yates was one of the smartest businessmen I ever met. I respected him in many ways, and he liked me. But when it came to the woman he loved—his business brains just went flyin' out the window" (Hurst 19).

Republic's stockholders agreed, and in 1956 sued Yates for continuing to star Ralston in big-budget feature films when it was obvious the public didn't accept her, despite Republic's assertion as early as 1945 that Ralston was one of the "names which go above the title . . . real marquee names now" (Hurst 16). By 1957, the writing was on the wall; Republic lost $1,362,420 in that fiscal year alone (Hurst 23). In 1958, at the annual Republic stockholders' meeting, Yates peremptorily announced that the company was ceasing production, stating flatly that "we have one problem—getting out of the motion picture business." One stockholder asked timorously, "What happened to your vision, Mr. Yates?" but Yates had no reply (Hurst 23). Republic was out of the running, another casualty of the collapse of the studio system. Yates sold his library of films and the Republic physical plant for a bit less than $6,000,000 and retired from the business; he died in 1966 at the age of 88. Today, the former Republic plant is CBS Studio Center.

———

Monogram Pictures was similar in many ways to Republic, but its overall production plan was more modest. Monogram films lacked the polish and punch of Republic's work; their films were hurried, cheaply produced, and show obvious economies in nearly every respect. Formed in 1931 from W. Ray Johnston's Rayart (aka Raytone) Productions and Trem Carr's Sono Art-World Wide Pictures, Monogram operated as an independent entity until 1935, then briefly became part of the Republic combine only to break away again in 1937 and restart production on its own.

Trem Carr, however, went over to Universal, leaving Johnston in charge of the operation, assisted by Steve Broidy as general sales manager from 1937 onward. Broidy had no illusions about Monogram's output, telling an interviewer that "not everybody likes to eat cake. Some people like bread, and even a certain number of people like stale bread rather than fresh bread" (McCarthy and Flynn 269). Monogram was content to be the "stale bread" of the film industry, knew its place, and never tried to reach too high. Yet Monogram was one of the most prolific studios in Hollywood. Between 1940 and 1949, Monogram released an astonishing 402 pictures, or roughly 40 per year, all of which were produced in-house. However, because, as with Republic, many of their films went out for a flat rental rate, Monogram's average profit for this nine-year period was an astonishingly low $1,932.12 per film (McCarthy and Flynn 24). At Monogram, perhaps more than anyplace else save Producers Releasing Corporation, this razor-thin level of profitability required that every penny be counted and every possible production shortcut utilized.

Monogram never made serials; that would be too costly. Instead, they relied on "series" pictures, which today we would call franchise films. The Bowery Boys films (aka The East Side Kids), featuring a group of comic toughs who originated in Samuel Goldwyn's production *Dead End*, led by the volcanic Leo Gorcey with Huntz Hall as his perennially clueless sidekick, was a dependable series for the studio, eventually racking up a total of forty-eight films. Monogram would also revive properties that other studios felt were used up just to get a little more mileage out of them. When 20th Century Fox dropped the Charlie Chan series, Monogram was there to pick up the pieces and put a very tired detective through his final paces.

Boris Karloff appeared as Mr. Wong, a Charlie Chan knockoff; the Cisco Kid was on hand, as well as Bomba, the Jungle Boy. Bela Lugosi, down on his luck and addicted to morphine, starred in a seemingly endless series of rock-bottom horror films for the studio. Monogram films were cheap—cheap to make, cheap to rent, cheap to see. But they were never pictures that audiences lined up for; they were just "there," on the bottom half of the double bill, and people sat through them simply to kill time. As Broidy told an interviewer, "I [knew] nobody was coming in to buy our pictures—we had to go out to sell them" (McCarthy and Flynn 276–77).

Broidy recounted one particularly dispiriting visit to the offices of the Fox West Coast theater group in the early 1940s, when the film buyers for the chain bluntly asked him, "What would we want to buy this crap for?"

Broidy kept pitching regardless. The head of the theater chain, Charles Skouras, overheard Broidy relentlessly pushing Monogram's threadbare wares, called Broidy into his office, and asked him to deliver his pitch all over again. Broidy complied and Skouras turned on 20th Century Fox's own salesmen, the very ones who had been deriding Monogram's product, and delivered his verdict. "Look. He sells a bunch of junk. Just look at his pictures. But you see how hard this man fights to sell his product? And I give you the best pictures that the market has and you complain that this is wrong, that's wrong, something's always wrong. With him, with the worst pictures on the market—nothing's wrong! Give him some business" (276–77).

In 1946, in an effort to pull out of the low-budget market, Broidy and future producer Walter Mirisch created the Allied Artists brand name for higher-price Monogram product; by 1953, Monogram had transformed itself into Allied Artists in totality. As Allied Artists, the company continued on much as before, knocking out an additional 443 films under the AA banner between 1947 and 1978. Mirisch tried to convince Broidy to move into more prestigious films, such as William Wyler's *Friendly Persuasion* (1956) with Gary Cooper, and Billy Wilder's *Love in the Afternoon* (1957), starring Cooper and Audrey Hepburn, but both films failed at the box office and Mirisch moved over to United Artists.

Perhaps AA's highest-profile films were Bob Fosse's *Cabaret* (1972), which opened to great critical and commercial success—earning over $20 million in domestic gross on a $6 million budget, and Franklin J. Schaffer's *Papillon* (1973), which grossed over $53 million domestically on a budget of $12 million.

But even this was not enough to save the company. With the high production, distribution, and marketing costs, AA failed to recoup significantly on either film and, in 1979, filed for bankruptcy. Most of the Monogram library is now part of the Warner Bros. back catalogue, but the company's influence lingered on long after its demise. This influence was perhaps most notable when French New Wave director Jean-Luc Godard dedicated his debut film, *Breathless* (1960), to Monogram Pictures because, in his mind, Monogram, more than any other studio, epitomized the "B" picture aesthetic, which was what Godard was trying to emulate in that film. If Monogram's films were always shabby and rundown, they were, in an odd sense, comforting. A Monogram film made no demands or waves, reliably fulfilled the requirements of its genre, whether western, horror, or comedy, and wrapped everything up in a neat little package with a running time of roughly seventy minutes. Monogram films promised little and delivered it, but they accurately gauged the tastes of American moviegoers for more than forty years, with some gaps in between. In the rough-and-tumble world of the film business, that's no small accomplishment.

———

But if Monogram was cheap, it wasn't the bottom rung of the studio system in the 1940s. That dubious honor belongs to Producers Releasing Corporation, or PRC, better known in the industry at the time as Poverty Row Crap. PRC's average shooting schedule was six to seven days; budgets were as low as $20,000 for a feature film, using only eighty minutes of raw stock for a sixty-five-minute feature film; in short, the first take would be the only take. Founded in 1939 by Sigmund Neufeld out of the ruins of Producers Distributing Corporation, a short-lived concern operated by Ben Judell, PRC used recycled scripts, sets, costumes, scenery, and anything else to get a film in the can, working on an assembly line basis. Their most prolific director, and also the most prolific director in sound motion picture history, was Sam Newfield, Sigmund Neufeld's brother, who was so fast (he could shoot a western in two to three days, using stock footage and a nearly nonexistent script) that Sigmund forced Sam to adopt two aliases to cover his tracks: Sherman Scott and Peter Stewart. Today, this "triple identity" is well known, but at the time it was a closely guarded secret, allowing PRC to keep its most dependable director working at top speed.

It has been alleged that Newfield used these aliases on a "genre" basis—using Newfield for westerns, Scott for crime films, and Stewart for more serious dramas—but there seems to be little foundation for this (Dixon "Fast Worker"). Scott, for example, was the director of record for *Billy the Kid's Fighting Pals* (1941), while Stewart was credited with *Billy the Kid in Texas* (1940) and Newfield for *The Lone Rider Fights Back* (1941). Further, Newfield abandoned this "triple threat" strategy early in 1943 with only one exception (1946's *The Flying Serpent*, which he directed as Sherman Scott) until PRC itself collapsed. Newfield then began the final phase of his career, freelancing for William Pine and William Thomas (known as "The Dollar Bills" for their unflagging production economy) at Paramount and producer Maurice Conn at 20th Century Fox, among Newfield's few brushes with a major studio.

Obviously, Newfield wasn't the only director on the PRC lot. Edgar G. Ulmer, whose films have since been recognized as some of the most interesting and influential genre films of the 1940s, was PRC's "prestige" director. Such films as *Detour* (1946), *Bluebeard* (1944), *Strange Illusion* (1945), and *Her Sister's Secret* (1946) have long since developed a cult status among aficionados of 1940s Hollywood cinema. Even so, Ulmer had minimal resources to work with: a strict schedule of five or six days per feature, a 2:1 shooting ratio (shooting only twice as many feet of film as there are in the finished film, an extraordinarily tight amount of raw footage, and something unheard of in the major studios), and an average of sixty or more camera setups a day.

Ulmer adopted a style of shooting the close-ups in his PRC films against a neutral gray background to disguise the fact that all close-ups were shot with one setup in the final hour of shooting every day. Ulmer would direct the actors to look "camera right" or "camera left" as they read off dialogue from all the day's sequences, and even put his hand over the lens to separate the takes. This draconian economy did not come naturally to Ulmer, who had been used to the relative production luxury of such films as Universal's *The Black Cat* (1934) earlier in his career. For Sam Newfield, however, such tactics were an everyday occurrence. Newfield's many westerns are straightforward and violent, with a minimum of character development; his big-city dramas, such as *Queen of Broadway* (1943), and his horror films, in particular *Dead Men Walk* (1943) and *The Flying Serpent* (1946), are grimly procedural, moving with inexorable assurance toward their generically predestined ends (Dixon "Fast Worker").

The Black Raven (1943), a crime drama set in a rundown inn, is unrelentingly bleak and fatalistic; *I Accuse My Parents* (1944), an early juvenile delinquency film foreshadowing Nicholas Ray's later *Rebel without a Cause* (1955), offers a similarly grim view of wartime absentee parenthood and its social consequences. *Swing Hostess* (1944) is a typically cheerless PRC musical, simultaneously tacky and tawdry, while *Murder Is My Business* (1946) is a grimy crime thriller that embraces its shoddy world with world-weary certainty.

The pace of production at PRC was unrelenting. In 1943 alone, Newfield directed no fewer than eighteen feature films, in 1945, twelve films, and in 1946 fifteen full-length features. Sometimes PRC would cut corners a bit too tightly. One of Newfield's most controversial projects was his riff on Billy Wilder's *Double Indemnity* (1944), which he directed as *Apology for Murder* (1945); the original title of the project, amazingly enough, was *Single Indemnity*. Paramount, Wilder's home studio, wasn't fooled and slapped an injunction on the finished film, which remains in force to this day.

At PRC, it was a constant fight to find story material, hire actors at cut rates, recycle sets from existing flats, and then push through forty to fifty setups a day to get the finished film in the can. PRC was involved in a continual struggle for mere survival on an everyday basis, much like the rest of the country during World War II. Life in the 1940s was hard; life at PRC was hard. Unlike the major studios, where luxury and privilege were a way of life for many of the most valuable players, at PRC everyone from the top down worked for their living. However, in 1947, PRC was completely absorbed by the newly formed Eagle-Lion Films, which Sigmund and Sam both viewed as a serious mistake—PRC was very successful as a "bread and butter" studio, making simple genre films for an undemanding public. Upgrading PRC's product, given the extremely tight budgets the company had to work with, created much more risk. Eagle-Lion, which was eventually folded into United Artists in February 1951, started out with an ambitious slate of productions, such as Ulmer's *Ruthless* (1949) and a series of atmospheric noirs directed by a young Anthony Mann, but soon became overextended (Dixon "Fast Worker").

When PRC went out of business, the negatives for its entire catalogue were sold to a television syndicator for a flat $1,750 each, and in the early days of the medium, when the majors shunned television as a threat to their hegemony, PRC's films were ubiquitous. In time, the copyrights on all the PRC films lapsed when no one bothered to renew them, and the films entered the public domain for anyone to screen, copy, or sell to the public. And so, ironically, PRC has become one of the most visible of all the minor Hollywood studios of the 1940s, simply because their films are easily available. It's an odd fate for PRC; its entire catalogue has now been digitally archived, the only studio that can make that claim (Dixon "Fast Worker").

———

We have only one last "major minor" studio to consider: RKO Radio. While it's unfair to characterize RKO as a minor player in the 1940s studio system, the studio's spectacular demise in the late 1950s and the concomitant collapse of the RKO theater chain place RKO in an unusual position for historians. Once a vibrant, bustling film factory, RKO was gradually stripped of both its vitality and its assets under the eccentric ownership of industrialist Howard Hughes, and RKO's extensive library of films is now all that remains of the once-influential studio in the present day. As Richard B. Jewell and Vernon Harbin note, "Throughout its history, RKO generally took a back seat to such competitors as MGM, Paramount, and Warner Bros. in the area of contract performers. Consequently, it was often forced to borrow leading actors from these and other companies" (7).

This, and other factors, led RKO to be the least stable—in terms of talent—of all the majors. RKO Radio was born in 1928 out of a consortium of several different companies: Joseph P. Kennedy's Film Booking Offices of America, or FBO; the Keith-Albee-Orpheum (KAO) circuit of theaters, originally designed for vaudeville, but now looking for a way to transition to sound motion picture exhibition; and David Sarnoff's Radio Corporation of America (RCA), which wanted to break into the talkies with their sound-on-film process, Photophone, but faced stiff opposition from Western Electric, whose own sound process had been adopted by Fox and Warner Bros., with Paramount, MGM, Universal, and First National also clamoring to get on board.

Sarnoff realized that Photophone, with its optical sound track system, was inherently superior to the sound-on-disc process used by Western Electric, but he also knew that the realities of the marketplace would dictate who ultimately emerged as the victor in the battle between Western Electric and RCA. Unless RCA could find a major studio to adopt its system, Photophone would make no inroads in the industry at all. Thus, Sarnoff set his sights on FBO and KAO, and on October 23, 1928, RCA acquired Kennedy's interests in FBO and KAO, creating Radio-Keith-Orpheum, with Sarnoff as chairman of the board.

Kennedy stepped back from this new conglomerate, keeping his own studio, Pathé; but by 1931, Kennedy sold Pathé to the new RKO combine, which thus acquired Pathé's studio space in Culver City as well as a newsreel company and a group of contract performers. In the meantime, former FBO vice-president Joseph Schnitzer was installed as head of production and distribution for the new organization, named Radio Pictures. With Kennedy out of the picture, Sarnoff had achieved his ambition: to create a new studio and distribution system that would blanket the country with Photophone "talking" pictures (Jewell and Harbin 9–10).

Early trade ads for the new company were typically immodest. One declared, in all capital venues, that "A TITAN IS BORN . . . ECLIPSING IN ITS STAGGERING MAGNITUDE AND FAR REACHING INTERESTS ANY ENTERPRISE IN THE HISTORY OF SHOW BUSINESS . . . ONE MAMMOTH UNIT OF SHOWMANSHIP . . . FULFILLMENT OF DARING DREAMS . . . [A] COLOSSUS

OF MODERN ART AND SCIENCE" (qtd. in Jewell and Harbin 10). Clearly, RKO had a lot to live up to, but Sarnoff kept expanding, buying out the Proctor Theater chain in New York and New Jersey, as well as six theaters controlled by the Pantages Corporation (Jewell and Harbin 10).

Establishing studios at 780 Gower Street in Los Angeles, Sarnoff spent lavishly on the studio, buying the rights to the Florenz Ziegfeld musical *Rio Rita* for $85,000 and paying more than $100,000 for the rights to another Broadway musical, *Hit the Deck*. Sarnoff sank $500,000 into upgrading the Gower Street studio for talkies and bought 500 acres of land in the San Fernando Valley as a huge back lot for westerns and period sets. As 1929 dawned, the future looked bright indeed for the new company (Jewell and Harbin 10). Sarnoff envisioned his new combine as "a giant entertainment conglomerate that would someday combine films, vaudeville shows, radio broadcasts, and [even] television (then in the experimental stage) in a symbiotic package" (Jewell and Harbin 10).

But despite all Sarnoff's grandiose plans and the literally millions of dollars poured into the new enterprise, his dreams of empire were never really realized. As Jewell and Harbin note, "Throughout the 27 years of activity that followed, RKO existed in a perpetual state of transition: from one regime to another, from one group of filmmakers to an altogether different group. Being a less stable studio than its famous competitors, the company never 'settled down,' never discovered its real identity. . . . This uncomfortable state of affairs, marked by continual financial fragility as well as creative turmoil," would eventually bring about the collapse of the studio in 1957, signaling more clearly than any other major industry event the clearly defined end of the classical Hollywood studio system (Jewell and Harbin 10–11).

William Le Baron headed the first RKO regime, but his films proved too indebted to silent filmmaking, so Sarnoff replaced him with David O. Selznick. But Selznick butted heads with RKO's corporate chief, Merlin Aylesworth, and left in 1933—later, of course, to start his own company. Merian C. Cooper, creator of *King Kong*, replaced Selznick, but when illness sidelined him, Pandro S. Berman took over, presiding over the first Fred Astaire/Ginger Rogers musical, Thornton Freeland's *Flying Down to Rio* (1933), which established the team overnight as perhaps RKO's most bankable stars.

In 1934, Berman stepped back from running the studio, handing the reins to Ben Kahane through 1935. But corporate machinations soon led to Kahane being replaced with Samuel Briskin, a veteran of Columbia Pictures. Briskin lasted until 1937, and Pandro Berman again found himself in the top slot, but he left RKO for MGM in 1939, leaving George Schaefer in charge of the studio. It was under Schaefer's watch that Orson Welles moved onto the RKO lot to make *Citizen Kane* (1941), having scored a tremendous success in radio with, among other things, his infamous broadcast of H.G. Wells's *War of the Worlds* on October 30, 1938, resulting in an unprecedented degree of freedom—including the right of final cut—for the fledgling director. *Citizen Kane* is, of course, a masterpiece, but Welles's thinly disguised biography of yellow journalist William Randolph Hearst caused the studio considerable difficulty. Indeed, *Citizen Kane* almost didn't see the light of day. At Hearst's behest, Louis B. Mayer tried unsuccessfully to buy the picture outright through Nicholas Schenck and destroy the negative (Crowther 258), and thus what is usually at or near the top of any list of "best films ever made" was preserved. But whatever the eventual success of *Citizen Kane*, Schaefer's insistence on making "quality" films above all other considerations soon put RKO on the brink of bankruptcy; he quit the studio in 1942 (Jewell and Harbin 11–12).

Next up was production chief Charles Koerner, who, in direct opposition to Schaefer's policy, established a regime committed to fast, commercial films designed to please mass audiences, such as the *Falcon* series of detective thrillers, or the Mexican Spitfire comedies with Lupe Velez. It was under Koerner's watch that Val Lewton was hired away from Selznick International to create his landmark series of low-budget, intelligent horror films, using the talents of Jacques Tourneur, Robert Wise, and others to create legendary fantasy films on minuscule budgets; this is perhaps Koerner's most lasting legacy.

When Koerner died of leukemia in 1946, studio executive N. Peter Rathvon took control, but he soon hired future MGM production chief Dore Schary to head production duties for RKO. Schary was instrumental in making more realistic films for the studio, especially the postwar noirs for which RKO is famous, but he left in 1948 for MGM when Howard Hughes bought the studio and essentially ran it into the ground with ruinous overspending and sheer despotic incompetence. A fervent supporter of the House Un-American Activities Committee, Hughes didn't seem to care as executives, directors, and stars fled to more stable studios, and finally, bored with RKO—which to him had been nothing more than a toy—Hughes sold out to General Teleradio in 1955.

General Teleradio's main interest in RKO was its back catalogue of films, which were eminently exploitable in the new medium of television (ironically fulfilling Sarnoff's dream of multimedia dominance, though Sarnoff himself was now long gone from RKO). RKO's final chief of production, William Dozier, was at the time too inexperienced and thus ill suited to his position (Dozier would later go on to much greater success with the camp television series *Batman* [1966–1968]), and in 1957 RKO shut down production for good (Jewell and Harbin 13–14). This was really the end of RKO Radio Pictures as a functioning Hollywood major/minor, the only prominent studio to utterly collapse in the wake of the consent decree, television, and other postwar challenges to the established studio system.

Despite all the changes in artistic direction and ownership, RKO Radio managed to rack up more than 1,000 feature films between 1929 and 1957 in an atmosphere that was always uncertain, and often left a widely disparate group of authentic talents alone to create work of lasting beauty and significance. Unlike the other major studios, RKO never had a guiding vision or house philosophy. RKO's films are all over the map, and the studio's commercial and artistic direction literally varied from year to year. This built-in instability was what made the studio ripe for a Hughes takeover, because it lacked one strong personality at the top—Harry Cohn at Columbia, Zanuck at 20th Century Fox, Jack Warner at Warner Bros.—to set a compass for the studio's future.

Instead, RKO kept reinventing itself from moment to moment, until its constant state of flux caused the studio to implode. Still, any studio that could produce as disparate and significant a series of films as George Stevens's *Swing Time* (1936), Wesley Ruggles's *Cimarron* (1931), Howard Hawks's *Bringing Up Baby* (1938), Sam Wood's *Kitty Foyle* (1940), Alfred Hitchcock's *Notorious* (1946), George Cukor's *Little Women* (1933), Dorothy Arzner's *Christopher Strong* (1933), John Cromwell's *Of Human Bondage* (1934), Rouben Mamoulian's *Becky Sharp* (1935; the first complete feature in three-strip Technicolor), John Ford's *The Informer* (1935), Jacques Tourneur's *Out of the Past* (1947), or Orson Welles's *The Magnificent Ambersons* (1942), to name just a few of RKO's many prestigious films, is a major part of Hollywood's history.

Although RKO closed down in 1957, its film library remains the company's most valuable asset, and as of 2011 RKO was in production, in a modest fashion, with Yaron Zilberman's film *A Late Quartet*, a drama starring Philip Seymour Hoffman, Christopher Walken, and Catherine Keener, as well as licensing their past properties, such as Mark Sandrich's Astaire/Rogers musical *Top Hat* (1935), for stage presentations. RKO is thus one of the most singular of the classic Hollywood studios, one that started with perhaps the best funding of any of the majors or minors, but a studio that, through uncertain management and lack of direction, crashed and burned in a truly spectacular fashion, a harbinger of the end of the classical studio regime.

CHAPTER 7

Universal Goes Corporate

Universal was one of the earliest and most influential of the major Hollywood studios and remains so to this day. Founder Carl Laemmle came from the exhibition side of the business, and by 1909 he and a partner owned a profitable chain of film theaters as well as a distribution exchange, the Laemmle Film Service, the largest in the United States at the time. But Thomas Edison's Motion Picture Patents Company—the "Trust"—was set on controlling every aspect of the fledgling film industry and wiping out the competition.

Edison wanted every film producer to pay him a fee for using cameras, which, Edison argued—and the courts initially agreed—all derived from patents devised entirely by the Thomas A. Edison Company. In addition, all distributors, or film exchanges, had to pay Edison a fee for simply distributing their films (again, because they were supposedly possible only because of Edison's patents), and exhibitors were required to pay a weekly fee to use Edison's projectors. If producers failed to pay Edison, he sued. If distributors failed to pay Edison, he sued. If exhibitors failed to pay Edison, he sued. In short, Edison wanted to control every aspect of the business (Hirschhorn 9).

Laemmle fought back and broke off all dealings with the Trust on April 12, 1909. He then rented a studio in New York at 11 East 14th Street, hired actor/director William Ranous and actress Gladys Hulette, and, using a second-hand camera, shot a one-reel adaptation of *Hiawatha* on location in Coytesville, New Jersey. Though production of *Hiawatha* took four months before a final print was struck, Laemmle soon got the feel for film production and was quickly cranking out a new one-reeler every week (Hirschhorn 9).

Laemmle called his new production company the Independent Moving Pictures Company—and Edison reacted predictably, filing no fewer than 289 lawsuits against Laemmle. But Laemmle countersued, seeking relief from a "multiplicity of suits" while running elaborate display ads that beseeched theater owners to "come out of it, Mr. Exhibitor," with a cartoon depicting a group of starving theater owners lining up to pay a hugely overweight figure labeled "Film Trust" two dollars a week for the "right to run my own theater and use my own goods" (Griffith and Mayer 22). The Trust, which created the General Film Company to threaten exhibitors, distributors, and production companies, even physically, stepped up their intimidation tactics, sometimes wrecking film labs or studios to bring malcontents into line.

But Laemmle soldiered on, and in 1910 director Thomas Ince joined IMP, followed by the actress Florence Lawrence. Until then she had been known simply as "The Biograph Girl," after the Biograph studio, where she had broken into the film business and became a star, all without being named in the credits of her films. Laemmle paid Lawrence $200 a week and promised her more publicity for her work, in an era in which the Trust refused to identify the players in their films for fear that once they became box office draws they would demand higher salaries. This made primitive economic sense, but neither the actors nor the public were pleased with the arrangement, and so Laemmle shrewdly played up Lawrence's defection from Biograph by planting a false rumor in the newspapers that Miss Lawrence had been killed in a streetcar accident in St. Louis, Missouri. Of course, nothing of the sort had happened—the entire affair was an invention of Laemmle's, and yet he then took out full-page ads in the trades declaring "We Nail a Lie," denouncing the false reports as "the blackest and yet at the same time the silliest lie yet circulated by enemies of the 'Imp'"—when all the time Laemmle had designed the entire stunt to build up Lawrence's public, identify her by name, and further challenge the Trust (Griffith and Mayer 46–47).

By April 15, 1912, Laemmle's efforts were paying off, as the federal government filed a petition against the Motion Picture Patents Company and the General Film Company, demanding that they both be dissolved immediately as "corrupt and unlawful associations" (Hirschhorn 10). At the same time, IMP continued to grow and Laemmle hired star King Baggott, as well as future superstar Mary Pickford, who had been working for Biograph, to make the one-reel short *Their First Misunderstanding* (1912). Pickford soon left IMP for greener pastures, even though Laemmle doubled her Biograph salary and gave her star billing, but the star system was already too firmly entrenched with the public and it was Laemmle, ironically, who had largely created it (Hirschhorn 10).

Then, on June 8, 1912, Laemmle joined up with four other small production companies to create what was then the world's largest film production company—Universal. Moving to Los Angeles, Laemmle next set about building the world's largest film studio, Universal City, which from the start was really and truly a city unto itself, including a hospital, barber shop, restaurant, film lab, two production stages, a zoo, and numerous other facilities. Ironically, it was Thomas Edison, who had so bitterly opposed Laemmle's trust-busting activities, who threw the switch that electrified the new facility—Laemmle figured it was good publicity to let bygones be bygones (Hirschhorn 8). The inaugural festivities lasted two full days, and then Laemmle got down to the business of making as many films as possible, as rapidly as possible, to meet the demand of the literally tens of thousands of exhibitors in the United States and around the world who were clamoring for product in the wake of the Trust's demise.

Universal's first full-length feature was George Loane Tucker's white slavery drama *Traffic in Souls* (1913), and the first feature produced at Universal City proper was Otis Turner's drama *Damon and Pythias* (1914), shot when the studio was still under construction. But Laemmle was onto something else—from the start, he designed Universal City not only as a movie studio, but also as a tourist attraction, placing ads that asked, "Are you going to come out to Universal City on March 15th or not? Are you going to give your wife and kids a treat by bringing them to the wonder city of the world—or not? [Universal City] is a fairyland where the craziest things in the world happen. . . . See how we blow up bridges, burn down houses, wreck automobiles and smash up things in general in order to give the people of the world the kind of pictures they demand" (qtd. in Hirschhorn 12–13).

Laemmle charged 25 cents per person for a studio visit, which included a box lunch, and, since filmmaking was still silent, visitors were allowed to sit in bleachers and watch several movies being shot on adjacent stages simultaneously, in addition to touring the studio grounds. When sound came in, the tours had to be discontinued, as the spectators inevitably interrupted the filming with sneezes, coughs, or idle chatter. Formal tours were reinstated in 1964 on a much more organized basis, and today the tours are a vital part of the studio's profits, as they were at its inception (Hirschhorn 13).

In contrast to the other major studios, where the public was viewed as a nuisance, at Universal City the public was part of the action. Once the facility was launched, events at Universal City unfolded at a rapid pace. John Ford made his directorial debut in 1917 with a two-reel film entitled *The Tornado*; Rudolph Valentino made an early appearance with Carmel Myers in Paul Powell's *A Society Sensation* (1918). Also in 1918, the 19-year-old Irving Thalberg began working at Universal's New York office; in 1919, Thalberg was shuffled to Universal City, and by 1920 he was promoted to head of production at Universal—"Uncle" Carl certainly did have an eye for talent (Hirschhorn 13).

Universal's studio identity soon became apparent. Although Erich von Stroheim captured much of the public's attention with his extravagant productions of *Blind Husbands* (1919) and *Foolish Wives* (1920), it was

Universal's association with Lon Chaney Sr. that firmly set the studio on its signature genre path: the horror film. Wallace Worsley's *The Hunchback of Notre Dame* (1923) and Rupert Julian's *The Phantom of the Opera* (1925) both made a fortune for the studio, and *Phantom* even contained a brief segment in two-strip Technicolor, adding to the film's box office appeal. But there was another factor to consider. Unlike Paramount or MGM, Universal owned no theaters, and so Laemmle was forced to rely upon rural movie houses and down-market metropolitan venues to screen its product (Hirschhorn 15).

Laemmle, however, quickly figured out that although the choicest American theaters were closed to him, American films were welcome everywhere in Europe. As such, Universal rapidly adopted a "package" system of offering a full program—"a feature, a newsreel, a serial, and a one-or-two-reel short" (Hirschhorn 15)—to both his American and European customers, with great success. Then, too, when most of the world ceased film production during World War I, the United States continued production apace, locking up foreign markets with Hollywood product, so that the gloss of American commercial cinema became the worldwide template for genre entertainment. Universal thrived because no matter what obstacles were placed in Laemmle's path, he instinctively found a way around them and often turned adversity to advantage by thinking outside the box. This, then, was the origin of Universal Pictures, a resolutely commercial enterprise from the outset, making movies for the common person.

Early commercial and critical successes in the sound era included Lewis Milestone's antiwar film *All Quiet on the Western Front* (1930), but with Tod Browning's *Dracula* (1931) and James Whale's *Frankenstein* (1932) the studio struck gold. Boris Karloff and Bela Lugosi became the two signature horror stars of the early sound era, though Lugosi would soon be left behind because of his lack of business acumen and later a crippling morphine habit (the drug was prescribed to him for ulcers, and before he knew it Lugosi was hooked). These two iconic films led to a wave of sequels;

for Dracula, there was Lambert Hillyer's *Dracula's Daughter* (1936), Robert Siodmak's *Son of Dracula* (1943), and Erle C. Kenton's *House of Dracula* (1945); for Frankenstein, Whale's *Bride of Frankenstein* (1935), Rowland V. Lee's *Son of Frankenstein* (1939), and Kenton's *The Ghost of Frankenstein* (1942). George Waggner's *The Wolfman* (1940) added another monster to the Universal stable, building on Stuart Walker's earlier *Werewolf of London* (1935), and soon there was Roy William Neill's *Frankenstein Meets the Wolfman* (1943) and Kenton's *House of Frankenstein* (1944).

Karl Freund's *The Mummy* (1932) gave birth to Christy Cabanne's *The Mummy's Hand* (1940), Harold Young's *The Mummy's Tomb* (1942), Reginald Le Borg's *The Mummy's Ghost* (1944), and Leslie Goodwin's *The Mummy's Curse* (1944), each less inspired than the previous effort. Universal also cranked out a series of "Inner Sanctum" horror films, all starring Lon Chaney Jr., who, after an auspicious Universal horror debut in *The Wolfman*, rapidly became Universal's utility man for all things supernatural, eventually playing Dracula (or his "son," Count Alucard— "Dracula" spelled backward), the Frankenstein monster, and anything else the studio threw at him.

In similar fashion, James Whale's *The Invisible Man* (1933) led to Joe May's *The Invisible Man Returns* (1940), A. Edward Sutherland's *The Invisible Woman* (1941), Edwin L. Marin's wartime thriller *Invisible Agent* (1942), and Ford Beebe's *The Invisible Man's Revenge* (1944). There were also numerous non-series horror films, such as Edgar G. Ulmer's *The Raven* (1935), Arthur Lubin's *Black Friday* (1940), George Waggner's *Man Made Monster* (1941), and many others to keep less discriminating audiences entertained.

But behind the scenes, changes were taking place. When Irving Thalberg left Universal in 1923, Carl Laemmle appointed his son, Carl Jr., as interim and eventually permanent chief of production. While Carl Jr. had initially waited to produce prestige films to bring Universal up to the level of Paramount or MGM, as the boom times of the Roaring Twenties became the raw reality of worldwide economic collapse "Junior" began slashing budgets and developing more cost-conscious films. Historians have viewed Carl Laemmle Jr. as an inept studio executive, deeply unsuited to his administrative role that he received through nepotism alone. But as Thomas Schatz notes, Carl Jr. "held Universal's losses to $1.7 million in 1932 and $1 million in 1933, during a period that saw Warners lose $20 million" (228). Indeed, Universal "actually finished 1934 in the black—just barely showing a profit of $200,000" (Schatz 228), so although he was no visionary Carl Jr. was hardly the incompetent that conventional lore would have him be. For example, *The Bride of Frankenstein* was shot in forty-six days for a final negative cost of $397,000, very cheap for an "A" feature, while other, less important Universal films of the period came in for less than $200,000, before prints and advertising (Schatz 229). Carl Jr. also supervised John Stahl's melodrama *Imitation of Life* (1934), which was significantly more expensive, requiring twelve weeks of shooting, at a negative cost of $665,000. Nevertheless, the film was a huge hit, and it seemed Universal was finally closing in on the majors (Schatz 231–32).

But then Carl Jr. made a fatal mistake, allowing Stahl to produce a pet project, *Magnificent Obsession* (1935), while James Whale, sick of making horror films, got the go-ahead to remake *Show Boat* (1936), which had been a great success for Universal in 1929 in a limited sound version under the direction of Harry Pollard. Both films went significantly over budget; *Magnificent Obsession* wrapped with a total negative cost of $947,697 after ninety-two days of shooting; *Show Boat* was completed after six months of production at a cost of $1,275,000.

Strapped for cash by the tremendous overhead of both films, in 1936 Carl Jr. convinced his father to take out a loan for $750,000 from Standard Capital Corporation, headed by Wall Street financier J. Cheever Cowdin, under the onerous condition that the money had to be repaid in ninety days or Cowdin could exercise an option to buy the studio outright for $5.5 million in stock purchases (Schatz 234). The Laemmles hoped that incoming revenues would cover the load, but they didn't; ninety days later, on April 2, 1936, Cowdin acquired control of the company by purchasing 80 percent of Universal's stock. Carl Sr. got a $1.5 million "golden handshake" and became a figurehead chairman of the board; Carl Jr. was simply fired. Both men were crushed. Carl Sr. died in 1939, his empire now owned by an impersonal conglomerate; Carl Jr., only in his late twenties when he was ousted from the company his father had founded, never worked in the industry again; he died in 1979 (Schatz 234–35).

Standard Capital installed Robert Cochrane as the new Universal president and Charles Rogers, late of RKO, as head of production. The immediate effects were obvious; costs were cut to the bone. Ironically, *Show Boat* was a substantial hit, more than earning back its production costs, but new projects faced tight-fisted fiscal scrutiny. Carl Jr.'s last project was *My Man Godfrey* (1936), a screwball comedy starring William Powell and Carole Lombard and efficiently directed by Gregory LaCava; the new regime told LaCava that the film's projected budget of $586,000 was sacrosanct. LaCava went over slightly, finishing at $656,000 for thirty-five days of shooting, but the film was a huge hit, eventually garnering no fewer than seven Oscar nominations (Schatz 235–36). If only Carl Jr. had had a little more time, he might have prevailed: in the end, despite cost overruns, *Magnificent Obsession, Show Boat,* and *My Man Godfrey* were all hits, vindicating Carl Jr.'s "quality" instincts. But Universal's new management saw too much risk and decided "the New Universal" (which was how the company now advertised itself) would specialize in serials, westerns, science fiction, and horror films, all made for the lowest cost possible.

Universal now depended almost exclusively on genre films, such as the Deanna Durbin vehicle *Three Smart Girls,* directed by Henry Koster in 1936, which was a huge and unexpected hit for the studio. But history began to repeat itself when the budgets for the Durbin musicals escalated in production costs, and at the end of 1937, despite the success of *Three Smart Girls* as well as Koster's follow-up feature *One Hundred Men and a Girl* (1937), Universal finished 1937 more than $1 million in debt. Now Cowdin moved again, firing Cochrane and Rogers and installing an even more parsimonious team to run the studio: Nathan Blumberg as president, William Scully as sales manager, and Cliff Work as vice-president in charge of production (Schatz 242). Then, in 1940, another shift came; J. Cheever Cowdin quit the company, which left Nate Blumberg running the show.

It was in this period that the studio introduced Bud Abbott and Lou Costello to the public in A. Edward Sutherland's otherwise unremarkable *One Night in the Tropics* (1940). With the pair's second film, Arthur Lubin's *Buck Privates* (1941)—made for a pittance but a box office bonanza—Universal quickly realized it had tapped into a goldmine. The comedians then embarked on a long and profitable string of vehicles for Universal, such as Lubin's *Hold That Ghost* (1941) and *Ride 'Em Cowboy* (1942) and Charles Barton's *Abbott and Costello Meet Frankenstein* (1948), in which the studio paired up their two most profitable franchises—their rogues' gallery of monsters and the low comedy of Abbott and Costello— leading to Charles Lamont's *Abbott and Costello Meet Dr. Jekyll and Mr. Hyde* (1953) and Lamont's *Abbott and Costello Meet the Mummy* (1955).

Another profitable franchise was the Sherlock Holmes series, which Universal picked up from 20th Century Fox, updating Sir Arthur Conan Doyle's classic sleuth to the present for economic reasons. In the first film of the series, John Rawlins's *Sherlock Holmes and the Voice of Terror* (1942), Holmes outwitted the Nazis, leading to a string of sequels of uneven quality. Overall, Universal was a busy factory throughout the 1940s, adding musicals, program westerns, and even a few classic comedies with W. C. Fields to the mix, Edward Cline's 1940 *The Bank Dick* being perhaps the comedian's finest film.

Now Universal was really dedicated to low-cost filmmaking, and never again—at least for the 1940s—stepped out of line. Cliff Work, a studio pro, made sure that shooting schedules were brutally quick and budgets remained low. Arthur Lubin, for example, directed the Karloff/Lugosi vehicle *Black Friday* starting on December 28, 1939, and finishing on January 18, 1940, for the astonishingly low negative cost of a mere $125,750; *Buck Privates*, Abbott and Costello's breakthrough film, was shot in a few weeks in December 1940–January 1941 for an approximate cost of only $180,000 and grossed over $4 million in the United States alone. Between 1940 and 1945, Universal released almost 350 features, and, astoundingly, none of them lost money. As World War II ended, Universal had shed the last vestiges of the Laemmle era and was firmly in the black as a productive, conservative, low-cost studio, clearly in the entertainment business with few, if any, pretensions about its product (Hirschhorn 99).

However, Universal was about to undergo the biggest shift of its long history: a path back to more ambitious films. J. Arthur Rank, the British producer who had built up the Rank Organization in the United Kingdom as one of the country's largest studios, acquired a stake in Universal in 1945 (Macnab 176), and, after a bit of shuffling at the top, Universal became Universal-International on July 30, 1946, with Leo Spitz (a former president of RKO, and a skilled business lawyer) and William Goetz (Louis B. Mayer's son-in-law, and a former production executive at 20th Century Fox) in charge (Hirschhorn 156). Spitz and Goetz laid down some new ground rules. No film could be less than seventy minutes long. More films would be made in color (the studio splurged on a series of Technicolor exoticisms starring the self-proclaimed "Queen of Technicolor," Maria Montez, who can be seen to best advantage in the outrageously campy *Cobra Woman* [1944], directed with typical flair by Robert Siodmak). Serials, twelve- to fifteen-minute chapter plays for Saturday mornings, were out (Universal's last serial, Ray Taylor and Ford Beebe's *Lost City of the Jungle* [1946], went conspicuously over budget, and was further compromised by the death of its star, Lionel Atwill, halfway through production). "B" westerns also got the ax (Hirschhorn 156).

Rank used the Universal-International arrangement to imprint his productions of Carol Reed's *Odd Man Out* (1947) and David Lean's *Great Expectations* (1947), among other films, including Sir Laurence Olivier's 1948 version of *Hamlet*. The contract players who had served Universal so well in the 1940s were unceremoniously dropped. Still, Universal seemed to do best with low-end fare, such as the Francis the Talking Mule series, which started with the simply named *Francis* in 1949, directed by Arthur Lubin in assembly-line fashion and featuring veteran character actor Chill Wills as the voice of Francis and Donald O'Connor as Francis's sidekick.

In similar fashion, the lowbrow comedy of the Ma and Pa Kettle films, starring Marjorie Main and Percy Kilbride as stereotypical hillbillies who, with their family of fifteen children, rumble through a series of supposedly amusing adventures, also became a profitable franchise. What turned into a nine-film series started with Chester Erskine's *The Egg and I* (1947), which shocked Universal by racking up more than $5.75 million on a relatively minuscule investment (Hirschhorn 157). Claudette Colbert and Fred MacMurray were the nominal stars of the film, but audience research revealed that Main and Kilbride were the real draw. In response Universal put together *Ma and Pa Kettle* in 1949, directed by Charles Lamont, for a very modest $200,000, and the seventy-five minute film went on to earn more than $2.25 million at the box office (Hirschhorn 157). It seemed that no matter how hard Universal tried to shake its low-rent image, it just kept coming back.

The Paramount Decision of 1948 was, oddly enough, a boon to the studio, which still owned no theaters. While Paramount, MGM, 20th Century Fox, and Warner Bros. had to sell their theaters, Universal was unaffected, and it realized that a whole new market was opening up for the company; now they could get into the first-class theaters to which they had for so long been unable to gain access (Hirschhorn 157). In a series of complicated deals, Rank sold out his interest in Universal-International to Milton Rackmil, the owner of Decca Records. Decca eventually acquired a 28 percent share of Universal for $3.8 million, which included Leo Spitz and William Goetz's 150,000 shares of stock. In July 1952, Rackmil took over as Universal-International's president, Spitz and Goetz quit, and Edward L. Muhl was appointed as head of production (Hirschhorn 157).

Muhl, a savvy businessman, found an effective way to bring quality projects to the studio by working with independent producers such as

Albert Zugsmith, Robert Arthur, Ross Hunter, and Aaron Rosenberg. Zugsmith produced Jack Arnold's science-fiction classic *The Incredible Shrinking Man* (1957) and Orson Welles's last Hollywood film, *Touch of Evil* (1958); Rosenberg guided Anthony Mann's *The Glenn Miller Story* (1954) and Jesse Hibbs's *To Hell and Back* (1955), the story of World War II hero Audie Murphy, through the production process; Robert Arthur produced Blake Edwards's naval comedy *Operation Petticoat* (1959), which netted $9.5 million in theaters. Ross Hunter excelled at delivering sudsy melodrama to the screen under the gifted direction of Douglas Sirk, with sumptuous Technicolor remakes of *Magnificent Obsession* (1954) and *Imitation of Life* (1959), properties to which Universal still held the rights and so could make for a reasonable cost in a competitive market.

Hunter also was instrumental in teaming Doris Day and Rock Hudson in a series of innocent sex comedies, starting with Michael Gordon's *Pillow Talk* in 1959, which surprised everyone by grossing $7.5 million in domestic rentals (Hirschhorn 157). Muhl had successfully broken the low-rent Universal-International image at last, and under his administration glossy, big-budget romances flourished, while Abbott and Costello and Ma and Pa Kettle finally faded into the distance. Universal-International still made program pictures, to be sure; Audie Murphy westerns and exoticist throwbacks to the Maria Montez era, like George Sherman's *Veils of Bagdad* (1953) with fading stars Victor Mature and Mari Blanchard; but more often than not, the films were in color and at least seemed to belong to a more modern era of filmmaking.

But once again, the rules of the game were changing, and Universal was about to move into an entirely new arena: television. At the same time, with actors becoming free agents, the entire contract system of stars, directors, composers, and other creative artists being under long-term contracts to the studios was beginning to collapse. Lew Wasserman, an agent at Music Corporation of America, was instrumental in pushing the old system into the past in favor of profit participation deals for his clients. MCA, started by Jules Stein in the 1920s to arrange bookings for orchestras and singers, had rapidly expanded into the movie business, largely through Wasserman's efforts; by the late 1940s, MCA represented the bulk of Hollywood's now freelance stars.

It was Wasserman who pioneered the idea of packaging a star or two, a director, and a script, all from MCA clients, and then selling the complete project to a studio as a "ready to shoot" product. But Wasserman's most famous deal in his early days in the film business was the 1950 contract he arranged for star James Stewart with Universal. Stewart's going rate in 1950 was $200,000 per film, but Wasserman felt that since Stewart's films routinely grossed $4–5 million per picture, the actor was being well underpaid. Wasserman's deal called for Stewart to be paid his regular salary for making Henry Koster's version of the Broadway play *Harvey*, which Stewart had played onstage as a replacement for the production's original star, Frank Fay. When Stewart took over the lead in 1947, the play, which had been running since 1944, took on new life. Stewart was a perfect fit for the role. Studios began frantically bidding for the rights to the play, as well as for Stewart's services as the lovable alcoholic Elwood P. Dowd, whose imaginary companion is the eponymous Harvey, a six-foot rabbit. Wasserman was in the enviable position of being able to supply both: $150,000 for the screen rights to Mary Chase's play and $200,000 for Stewart. But there was a catch: Universal also had to make a routine western, Anthony Mann's *Winchester '73* (1950), and on this film Stewart would take no salary—but he would get above-the-title billing and 50 percent of the net profits (McDougal 154).

Such an arrangement was unprecedented, but Wasserman knew what he was doing. *Winchester '73* was a substantial hit, and Universal and Stewart both benefited from the deal. Stewart became a wealthy man overnight, Universal was able to make films with significantly less cost "above the line" (i.e., for star salaries), and the Universal/Stewart/Wasserman deal rapidly became the template for the new Hollywood. It's also important to note that Stewart's deal with Universal was non-exclusive; he could, and did, work for other studios at the same time, and it was during this period that Stewart appeared in such Alfred Hitchcock classics as *Rear Window* (1954), *The Man Who Knew Too Much* (1956), and *Vertigo* (1958), all for Paramount, under a separate deal also arranged by Wasserman, who also counted Hitchcock as one of his many clients (Schatz 472).

Theatrical audiences were waning. People were staying home and watching television for free, following *The Adventures of Ozzie and Harriet*, the zany antics of *I Love Lucy*, or the manic ad-libbing of Milton Berle. Additionally, a large library of "B" films and foreign product, especially from England, flooded television screens in major metropolitan areas, and many people were content to stay home and bask in the glow of the new electronic hearth. Although Hollywood fought back with CinemaScope (20th Century Fox), Natural Vision 3-D (first at Warner Bros. with André de Toth's *House of Wax* in 1953, then at all the majors), VistaVision (Paramount), and the three-camera, three-projector Cinerama process—all developed to give moviegoers an experience they couldn't get at home—audiences continued to dwindle. In 1958, Universal lost $2 million on its annual slate of pictures. Wasserman had changed the rules of the game, and it seemed impossible to run a studio in the classical manner, with rosters of talent in all departments on call. Everyone was now freelancing.

Seeing the writing on the wall, Milton Rackmil sold the Universal-International lot to MCA for $11.25 million in February 1959. MCA was aggressively moving into the television business with its Revue Productions and needed studio facilities; Universal, in turn, reserved the right to lease back any part of the facilities it might need for feature production (Hirschhorn 159). It's important to note, however, that MCA at this point did not own Universal-International itself, as a company; it owned the physical plant, but not UI as a corporate entity. What MCA did was essentially take over the lot by providing ready-made packages for Universal to produce; it was during this period, for example, that Hitchcock began his television series at Universal/Revue and used its facilities to shoot *Psycho* (1960), signaling the end of the director's association with Paramount and an older, more traditional style of filmmaking.

By 1962, MCA had acquired controlling interest in Universal-International by purchasing Decca Records; in 1963, MCA dropped the "International" part of its corporate name, and the company again became simply Universal Pictures. MCA was forced to abandon its position as an agency, but it got around that problem by signing nearly all its clients to non-exclusive contracts with Universal. The first completed film under the new Universal regime was Hitchcock's *The Birds* (1963), which, while not performing as well as *Psycho* at the box office, still garnered a respectable $4.6 in domestic box-office receipts (Hirschhorn 256). With varying degrees of profitability, Hitchcock would remain at Universal for the remainder of his career.

The Universal studio tours, which had been dropped some years earlier, were resumed on a commercial scale in 1964; as of 2011, this lucrative enterprise has accommodated an average of more than 30,000 patrons a day. In addition, MCA shifted Universal to television production, away from a rapidly diminishing feature marketplace, becoming one of the most prolific producers of programming in the industry. The studio pioneered low-cost, made-for-television movies, starting with the ninety-minute TV series *The Virginian*, which was actually seventy-five minutes long plus fifteen minutes of commercials. Essentially a series of "B" westerns in color, *The Virginian* ran from 1962 to 1971 for an astounding 249 episodes—paving the way for a string of low-cost instant movies, one of which was Steven Spielberg's *Duel* (1971).

NBC was a prime customer for Universal's series output, and soon Universal dominated small-screen entertainment. Edward Muhl stayed on as head of production; Jules Stein, MCA's founder, became chairman of the board; and Lew Wasserman, not surprisingly, was installed as president (Hirschhorn 256). Universal, however, was still deeply immersed in theatrical motion pictures, as evidenced by Stanley Donen's *Charade* (1964)—often mistaken for a Hitchcock film—starring Cary Grant and Audrey Hepburn and tallying up more than $6 million at the box office, while Andrew V. McLaglen's late western *Shenandoah* (1965), starring

James Stewart, racked up another $7.8 million in rentals for the studio. Ross Hunter continued to produce a string of hits, most notably George Roy Hill's period musical *Thoroughly Modern Millie* (1967) starring Julie Andrews, Mary Tyler Moore, and John Gavin, which grossed $16 million, and George Seaton's sudsy aviation drama *Airport* (1970), which brought in an astonishing $45.3 million, proving once again that Hunter was an extremely shrewd judge of public taste (Hirschhorn 257).

Moving firmly into the 1970s, Universal seemed to be firing on all cylinders, cranking out George Roy Hill's *The Sting* (1973), which made $79 million on a relatively modest budget; George Lucas's *American Graffiti* (1973), taking in $56.7 million on an even smaller initial outlay; and Spielberg's *Jaws* (1975), which astounded everyone by becoming an enormous summer box-office sensation, raking in $133.4 million in theaters (Hirschhorn 258). All these films benefited from a distribution strategy dubbed "saturation booking," in which a film opens in hundreds of theaters simultaneously to forestall negative word of mouth. This idea was first introduced by American International Pictures in the 1950s and 1960s for their horror, science-fiction, and "Beach Party" pictures. AIP wanted to get every dollar out of their cheaply budgeted films, and by saturating the market with a film they ensured that no one could miss it, and that they would get their money back within the first week or two of release. Universal took AIP's strategy and expanded it, reaching hundreds and later thousands of theaters simultaneously worldwide; indeed, saturation booking has now become the norm for major theatrical releases. *Jaws* also benefited from another strategy that Universal borrowed from AIP: somewhat astoundingly, AIP had been the first company to realize that summer offered a lucrative window for first-run release, since their films were mostly aimed at teenagers, who had the summer off and were looking for cheap entertainment. By the time *Jaws* was dominating the box office, however, Rackmil had left Universal, Jules Stein had essentially retired, and Lew Wasserman had become MCA's new chairman of the board.

Wasserman also worked conscientiously at expanding the Universal physical plant to 430 acres in 1982, almost double its size in the 1910s. The improved facility included thirty-six soundstages, the industry's largest back lot, a fourteen-story administration building, a 200,000 square-foot office complex, a Technicolor lab, a 6,000-seat covered amphitheater, a bank, and a twenty-story hotel (the Sheraton Universal) with 500 rooms. Carl Laemmle's Universal City was now home to over 10,000 employees (Hirschhorn 259).

When Tom Pollock became president of Universal in 1986, he instituted a new policy in which major stars, accustomed to receiving a hefty upfront paycheck along with a percentage of the "back end" (gross or net points) of a film, would now accept reduced salaries in return for a larger chunk of the gross earnings. In 1988, Universal opened Universal Studios Florida in Orlando, a combination theme park and production facility. Then, in a move that surprised everyone, Wasserman sold MCA for $6.13 billion in 1990 to Matsushita Electric (better known by their brand name Panasonic [McDougal 484]) in a deal brokered by Hollywood agent Michael Ovitz, who at the time was spearheading the Creative Artists Agency. Ovitz had built CAA from the ground up into the most influential talent agency of the 1980s, with a client list that included Kevin Costner, Dustin Hoffman, Tom Cruise, Robert De Niro, Steven Spielberg, and many, many others. Ovitz was, in short, a very powerful man—as powerful in the New Hollywood as Wasserman had been in the 1940s through the 1980s.

The deal almost collapsed, however, when word of it leaked out prematurely in the *Wall Street Journal* (McDougal 481), underscoring how complex and delicate the entire transaction was. When it finally went through, Wasserman emerged as an extremely rich man (he was already wealthy by any standard, but with the Matsushita deal his personal fortune improved considerably), and MCA would still be his personal domain (McDougal 491). Soon Wasserman and Sidney Sheinberg, who continued to control day-to-day activities for the company, came into conflict with Matsushita, which simply couldn't understand the inherent

ter the Matsushita
ndly suggested that
was to "make more
if such a thing were
ws anything, trends
th the best talent in
n a project from its
ht seem on paper.
r comprehend this.
iness, once a major
amatically; in 1994,
Wrote (1984–1996)
us when Wasserman
y for sale—CBS was
isney had purchased
er Bros. had created
with Fox emerging
d (McDougal 496).
of CBS. Wasserman
t their parent com-
with the *New York*
and Sheinberg were
ith Edgar Bronfman
to sell off Universal
ita was so anxious to
stment (McDougal
he deal was the fact
had been the master
this was happening

ed, but he gradually
en give Wasserman

a courtesy call on the deal, ev

Wall Street Journal, Wasserman

about the sale after meeting wi

popular hotspot for Hollywoo

stemmed from the fact that he w

a fight. In an interview with

safely noted that "there's nothi

it is to reflect on the past, I've

future. The only reason I wis

the beginning of this industry. I

be around to see all these chang

Wasserman was certainly righ

the permanency of change wou

sal. Tom Pollock left the com

retired the MCA name: from no

known simply as Universal. K

Katzenberg, who had done mu

nence, split off to form their ow

DreamWorks, which rapidly be

Wasserman was still chairman e

istration building was formally

Wasserman finally resigned

died on June 3, 2002, at the a

ultimate power broker was ove

assets, both physical and intan

chased PolyGram Entertainme

television arm and the USA cabl

to the surprise of many, purch

Vivendi, becoming Vivendi U

Universal to sell off 80 percent

facilities and their attendant am

then owned NBC.

unpredictability of the movie business. Shortly after the Matsushita takeover, one executive of the electronics company blandly suggested that to be consistently profitable, all Universal had to do was to "make more hit movies and stop making flops" (McDougal 494), as if such a thing were possible. It's an axiom of the profession: no one knows anything, trends come and go like a flash of lightning, and, even with the best talent in the room, factors that no one can foresee may doom a project from its inception, no matter how promising the idea might seem on paper. In short, every film is a gamble. Matsushita could never comprehend this.

Meanwhile, Universal's share of the television business, once a major source of the company's revenue, had decreased dramatically; in 1994, Universal had only two network shows, *Murder, She Wrote* (1984–1996) and the sitcom *Coach* (1989–1997) (McDougal 496). Thus when Wasserman and Sheinberg heard that a TV network was potentially for sale—CBS was supposedly in play—they jumped at the opportunity. Disney had purchased ABC some time back, and Fox, Paramount, and Warner Bros. had created their own networks, with varying degrees of success, with Fox emerging as the clear winner as the twenty-first century dawned (McDougal 496). Matsushita, however, rejected the proposed takeover of CBS. Wasserman and Sheinberg were livid, publicly lashing out against their parent company; Sheinberg blasted Matsushita in an interview with the *New York Times* in late 1994 (McDougal 500). But if Wasserman and Sheinberg were furious, so was Matsushita, which began secret talks with Edgar Bronfman Jr. of Seagram, makers of Seagram's Scotch whiskey, to sell off Universal and get out of the movie business altogether. Matsushita was so anxious to consummate the deal it even took a loss on its investment (McDougal 506–7). But perhaps the most amazing thing about the deal was the fact that Lew Wasserman, the man who for so many years had been the master of everything he touched, had no idea that any of this was happening (McDougal 501; Fabrikant).

When apprised of the deal, Wasserman was shocked, but he gradually accepted the situation. Though Matsushita didn't even give Wasserman a courtesy call on the deal, even after it was publicly announced in the *Wall Street Journal*, Wasserman seemed uncharacteristically philosophical about the sale after meeting with Bronfman over dinner at Morton's, a popular hotspot for Hollywood executives. Perhaps his muted reaction stemmed from the fact that he was now 82 years old and no longer relished a fight. In an interview with *Variety* shortly after the sale, Wasserman safely noted that "there's nothing so permanent as change. As tempting as it is to reflect on the past, I've always had a tendency to look toward the future. The only reason I wish I were younger is because this is just the beginning of this industry. The possibilities are limitless. I wish I could be around to see all these changes" (qtd. in McDougal 509).

Wasserman was certainly right about one aspect of this entire situation; the permanency of change would continue to influence events at Universal. Tom Pollock left the company in 1996, and Seagram permanently retired the MCA name: from now on, the entire conglomerate would be known simply as Universal. Key executives David Geffen and Jeffrey Katzenberg, who had done much to bring the studio back into prominence, split off to form their own company with director Steven Spielberg, DreamWorks, which rapidly became a major player in the industry. Yet Wasserman was still chairman emeritus of a sort, and the studio's administration building was formally renamed after him (McDougal 521).

Wasserman finally resigned from Universal on February 4, 1998, and died on June 3, 2002, at the age of 89. His long reign as Hollywood's ultimate power broker was over. But the mad scramble for Universal's assets, both physical and intangible, continued unabated. Seagram purchased PolyGram Entertainment in 1999, but then sold off Universal's television arm and the USA cable network to raise cash. Seagram was then, to the surprise of many, purchased by the French media conglomerate Vivendi, becoming Vivendi Universal. By 2004, debt forced Vivendi Universal to sell off 80 percent of its holdings, which included the studio facilities and their attendant amusement parks, to General Electric, which then owned NBC.

By 2007, the company was known as NBC Universal, of which GE owned 80 percent while Vivendi held on to 20 percent, which it finally sold out to GE in 2010. To finance the deal, GE sold 51 percent of NBC Universal to cable television operator Comcast, which in turn reorganized its holdings into the latest version of NBC Universal on January 29, 2011. So, as Lew Wasserman said, there's nothing so permanent as change, and as Universal grows larger and larger, and the dollar amounts attached to the company and its assets escalate with the passing years, we can be certain that the current NBC Universal deal will also be superseded by other, even more complex negotiations.

Universal has survived by getting bigger and bigger; in the entertainment industry, as in all big business operations, one must either get bigger or die or be swallowed up by a larger entity. The Universal of the 1930s and 1940s is barely recognizable within the vast corporate structure that now surrounds the studio, and yet, at Universal City, it is the legacy of the Frankenstein monster, Dracula, the Wolfman, and the other classic monsters that still dominates. Indeed, when most people think of Universal, they instinctively think of the classic Universal horror films as emblematic of the studio, although Universal itself doesn't seem to know what to do with its iconic creations.

To illustrate Universal's troubled relationship with its own legacy that continues until this day, it is instructive to go back to the late 1950s. It was at that time when England's Hammer Films decided to try its hand at horror movies with Terence Fisher's *The Curse of Frankenstein* (1957), the first Frankenstein film to be made in color, and the picture that launched the careers of horror icons Christopher Lee (as the monster) and Peter Cushing (as Baron Frankenstein). Universal did everything in its power to stop the project, claiming that it alone had a lock on the Frankenstein monster, Dracula, and the other members of its monster gallery. But Hammer simply pointed out that since their film was based on Mary Shelley's 1816 novel (which was published anonymously in London in 1818; Shelley's name was first publicly attached to *Frankenstein* when the novel was printed in France in 1823), and that since the novel was firmly in the public domain, there was nothing Universal could do about it.

Undaunted, Universal continued to threaten Hammer all through the production of the film, insisting that they alone had the rights to "their" monsters. Hammer, however, assiduously avoided any thematic or visual resemblance to any of the films in the Universal series and thus avoided any legal problems. When *Curse of Frankenstein* (released through Warner Bros.) was a massive hit, Universal finally saw the light and made a deal with Hammer to remake the entire stable of Universal monsters, without any legal threats. Thus *Curse of Frankenstein* became the first in a long line of Hammer horror productions that, unlike most British films, successfully competed in the American marketplace, Their next film was Fisher's version of *Dracula* (1958), known in the United States as *Horror of Dracula*, again top-lining Christopher Lee (this time as the bloodthirsty Count) and Peter Cushing (as Dracula's nemesis, Dr. Van Helsing). Photographed in lurid Technicolor and released through Universal, *Horror of Dracula* was an even bigger hit than *The Curse of Frankenstein*, and soon Hammer followed up with Fisher's *The Mummy* (1959), *The Curse of the Werewolf* (1961), *The Phantom of the Opera* (1962), and numerous other titles, all of which made a pot full of money for both Hammer and Universal. In agreeing to this, Universal implicitly acknowledged that they had run out of fresh approaches to their own creations, and if Hammer could come up with a new interpretation, it was better to get a slice of the action rather than none.

After all, the studio had effectively killed off the monsters once and for all in *Abbott and Costello Meet Frankenstein*, which was just like the earlier "monster rally" films *House of Frankenstein* and *House of Dracula*, in which the Frankenstein monster, Dracula, and the Wolfman were all brought together in a hectic genre mash-up; but with the Abbott and Costello film, what once had been played straight was now played for comedy, the last stop on any genre's development cycle (first the original concept; then the classical stage; then the baroque or rococo stage of calculated excess; and finally parody). In the climax of *Abbott and Costello Meet Frankenstein*, Dracula attempts to escape the clutches of the Wolfman by turning into a bat and escaping from a castle balcony, only to be caught by the Wolfman's paws in midair before both creatures fall to their deaths on the rocky cliffs below. It was as if Universal wanted to free itself of the burden of its horrific creations, but in reality it was simply that it had run out of ideas for the iconic characters that had made the studio famous, established its most enduring identity, and were dependably profitable from 1931 to 1945, all the way through the Depression to the end of the Second World War.

By 1964, the classic monsters were again viewed as comic foils rather than fearsome opponents, as Universal unveiled the TV series *The Munsters* (1964–1966), a horror/comedy sitcom featuring Fred Gwynne as Herman Munster, an obvious knockoff of Karloff's original Frankenstein monster, and Al Lewis as Grandpa, a Bela Lugosi-esque Dracula clone. (In 1974, Mel Brooks took this parodic intent one step further with his affectionate comic tribute to the original Universal films, *Young Frankenstein*, featuring Peter Boyle as the monster and Gene Wilder as Dr. Frankenstein. Though the film was produced for 20th Century Fox, the "mad lab" sequences used some of the original electrical equipment Kenneth Strickfaden had designed for the Universal series in the 1930s and 1940s.)

When Universal tried to restart the monsters in the late 1990s, the results were decidedly mixed. Most successful was Stephen Sommers's version of *The Mummy* in 1999, but his attempt to re-create one of the "monster rally" films with *Van Helsing* in 2004 was much less interesting. Similarly, Joe Johnston's 2010 version of *The Wolfman*, with Benecio Del Toro and Anthony Hopkins, was a critical disappointment, though the film did score an Academy Award for Best Makeup. The project started out in 2006 with the enthusiastic participation of Del Toro, a fan of the classic 1940s series of films, under the direction of Mark Romanek, who reportedly wanted to do most of the special effects prosthetically rather than using computer-generated imagery (CGI). But Universal disagreed with this approach and Johnston was brought in to replace Romanek, the script was rewritten, and makeup artist Rick Baker's work was amped up with extensive computer enhancement. Additionally, in the rewrites, not only Laurence Talbot (Del Toro) but also his father, Sir John Talbot (Hopkins), become werewolves, and the climax of the film is a father-and-son smackdown that is both risible and unconvincing.

No one was pleased with the result, but the film eventually grossed more than $140 million worldwide. Yet since cost overruns pushed the budget of the film to $150 million, *The Wolfman* failed to make back its initial investment, to say nothing of prints, advertising, and promotional expenses, earning only $139 million worldwide. *The Wolfman* was designed to be a reboot in the tradition of Christopher Nolan's 2005 *Batman Begins*, which had successfully relaunched the DC Comics Batman franchise for Warner Bros. But Universal's failure at reviving one of its signature creations epitomizes in a sense what happens when a company loses sight of its genuine identity; indeed, Universal's next move with the *Wolfman* franchise was to aim for the straight-to-DVD market with a cheap new version shot in Bucharest, Romania, starring Stephen Rea as the unfortunate lycanthrope. Once again, the studio devalued one of its most valuable franchises—the monsters—due to a lack of imagination and originality.

Thus, one might argue that Universal died with the ouster of the Laemmles, but that isn't entirely true; Carl Laemmle had created Universal, but when he and his son were pushed aside the company persevered under numerous regimes through the 1960s as a prolific provider of low-cost, predictable entertainment. With the rise of MCA and the Wasserman regime, the entire Universal operation became more interested in the bottom line than in any part of the creative process. As budgets soared, the initial spark that drove the studio in the thirties, forties, fifties, and sixties was replaced by a series of corporate strategies that emphasized expansion over creation, domination rather than inspiration. Wasserman, who controlled the destiny of the studio from the late 1950s through the early 1980s, was the consummate dealmaker, but he was not essentially a creative person.

It can certainly be said that Universal has always been, as all Hollywood studios are and must be, a commercial enterprise. But Universal is now trading mostly on its past, and it seems uncertain as to how to handle its cinematic legacy. So while Universal City is a bustling tourist attraction, and production of television shows and even some theatrical projects continue apace, one could say that the studio died when its most famous creations died, and that although it continues to exist as a corporate entity, the original Universal aesthetic has long since expired. Universal survived by going corporate, but the contract player system, which Wasserman helped to dismantle, is long gone, and the studio is now simply a production facility, its only real identity inextricably rooted in the days when it was a vital, creative idea factory, making compelling films for a price. By the mid-1960s, those days were over, and all that was left was an endless succession of deal making, of interest only to those who view film solely as a business and nothing more.

CHAPTER 8

That's All, Folks

JACK WARNER'S LOST KINGDOM

There were four Warner brothers: Harry, the eldest, and also the most serious; Albert, who took life as it came and never worried too much about anything; Sam, an extrovert who sadly died much too soon; and Jack, the most charismatic, ruthless, ambitious, and driven of the four and the one who became their ringleader, but, as his own son, Jack Warner Jr., noted, "a man driven by fear, ambition, and the quest for absolute power and control" (xi)—a quest that would eventually destroy the Warner family in a fraternal betrayal so sensational that even hardened observers of Hollywood were shocked. As Jack Warner Jr. added, "If ever two people were born on a collision course, Harry and Jack L. Warner were those men. Some time at the midpoint of their lives their basic moral outlooks took violently opposite turns. . . . The most terrible kind of warfare, the battle of brother against brother, . . . transformed the great company they had created and nurtured into the betrayal of a dream" (xi). Harry was the president, in charge of all the fiscal decisions, while Jack ran the production end. One brother, Jack, would emerge victorious; the other, Harry, would be essentially destroyed. The story of the brothers Warner and the studio they built is rife with conflict, ambition, and dreams of empire, but the only member of the family ruthless enough to pull it off was Jack, without whom the Warner Bros. studio probably wouldn't have even existed in the first place.

The sons of Polish émigrés—their actual last name was Wonskolaser—the four brothers started out as exhibitors, as many of the moguls did, rather than producers. From their first theater, the Cascade, in New Castle, Pennsylvania, in 1903, the brothers soon established the Duquesne Amusement and Supply Company, located in Pittsburgh, as a distribution service. Soon they were serving as an exchange for movies across four states, but conditions at the Cascade remained primitive for more than a decade. As Richard Schickel and Gerald Perry note, the chairs for the Cascade were "rented from an undertaker. Jack [sang] songs between the short pictures (and when the film broke) [while] Sam [cranked] the projector" (22). They had an early success as distributors with Francesco Bertolini and Adolofo Padovan's 1911 Italian color-tinted version of *Dante's Inferno* for which Jack provided sound effects behind the screen, and in 1918 they broke into actual production with *My Four Years in Germany*, directed by William Nigh, who would go on to a long, if not particularly illustrious, career working mostly for Monogram Pictures.

My Four Years in Germany was a considerable success, but the brothers didn't really capitalize on their coup. Harry and Albert were in New York, Sam was in Los Angeles, and Jack was in San Francisco (Schickel and Perry 22), so even after they set up Warner Bros. Pictures in April 1923 in Culver City, California, the brothers still hadn't coalesced into an effective unit. Finances were so tight that one studio supervisor "was obliged to take . . . camera[s] home with him to avoid [them] being repossessed; other employees [collected] paychecks on Friday but [were] told by Jack not to cash them until the following Monday," while Jack himself went around the studio at night turning off all the lights to save money—at one point, the electric company actually shut down the studio's power for nonpayment of the bill (Schickel and Perry 22).

Jack and his brothers persevered and began cranking out films at a furious pace. The studio's first big star was Rin Tin Tin, a German Shepherd dog trained by Lee Duncan. Rin Tin Tin appeared in a series of outdoor action films, of which Chester Franklin's *Where the North Begins* (1923) is a typical example. In 1924, the brothers hired a young Darryl F. Zanuck to write for the Rin Tin Tin films; Zanuck was only 22 at the time but was ready to make his mark in the business. By 1929, Zanuck had moved into management within the company; in 1931, he was named head of production, working under Jack Warner. Of course, none of this was enough for Zanuck, who would soon depart the studio to start his own company (Silke 25). In 1923, the brothers scored a real triumph when they convinced the sophisticated German comedy director Ernst Lubitsch to sign with the studio for five films in 1924, starting with *The Marriage Circle* (1924), followed by *Three Women* and *Forbidden Paradise* (both also 1924), which helped the brothers to advance the studio's fledgling reputation (Silke 27).

Meanwhile, after years of playing the field with the ladies, Jack Warner decided it was time to marry and start a family. On October 14, 1914, he married Irma Solomons over the objection of her parents, who didn't think that Jack, or motion pictures, had much of a future. On March 27, 1916, Irma gave birth to Jack Warner Jr., the couple's only child (Thomas, *Clown Prince* 29–30), but their marriage did not, in the end, turn out happily. Like other moguls, Jack continued to carry on affairs on the side, including one with actress Marilyn Miller, and by the late 1920s it was clear to Irma Warner that her marriage was doomed (Thomas, *Clown Prince* 94–95). Irma was a very traditional wife who stayed home, looked after Jack Jr., and waited for her husband to come home, which he seldom did.

By the early 1930s, Jack had fallen in love with Ann Page, a vivacious minor actress who was married as well, but this proved to be no obstacle for the headstrong studio boss. At Jack Warner's urging, Ann divorced her husband, Don Page, in Chihuahua, Mexico, in order to obtain an immediate decree and keep the entire divorce secret. On September 15, 1933, he left Irma and Jack Jr. to pursue his new love, and Ann and Jack began openly living together (Thomas, *Clown Prince* 95). Finally, in January 1935, Irma finally filed for divorce. The charge, quite reasonably, was desertion, and she was given a property settlement while retaining sole custody of Jack Jr., who was now 18 (Thomas, *Clown Prince* 102).

In 1936, Ann and Jack Warner were married, but brothers Harry and Albert and their respective families refused to attend the ceremony. "Thank God our mother didn't live to see this," said Harry, summing up the general disapproval of the rest of the Warner clan (Thomas, *Clown Prince* 102). Ann was more Jack's new style: someone to show off at parties, not a homebody like Irma. But since Jack Jr. remained with Irma, Jack Sr. grew to dislike his son, which, as we will see, ultimately led to a complete breach between them. But the breach was only personal; as a business, Warner Bros. went on as if nothing had happened at all.

In the early 1920s, Jack and his brothers had acquired the services of Broadway star John Barrymore, then at the height of his fame, for such films as Harry Beaumont's *Beau Brummel* (1924), and the studio's identity of mixing quality pictures in with obvious programmers was beginning to take shape. In a shrewd move, Warners began to make phonograph records of the orchestral music played in major cities, where Warner Bros.' films were presented in first-run situations, and then offered the recordings to second-run theaters as a way of increasing the presentation value of their films (Silke 29).

This was, of course, a prelude to Warners' embrace of sound, which put the company way out in front of the competition—and a good thing, too, for the studio was perennially strapped for cash. Warners made a deal to use Western Electric's sound-on-disc system, Vitaphone, and presented a program of synchronized sound shorts on August 6, 1929, along with a music and sound effects version of *Don Juan*, directed by Alan Crosland, starring John Barrymore in the lead.

This was merely a curtain raiser for Crosland's 1927 *The Jazz Singer*, starring musical comedy idol Al Jolson, which, although it contained only brief snippets of dialogue, took the public by storm and is considered by most historians to be the first widely distributed talking picture. Inventor Lee de Forest had already been experimenting with his far superior optical track, or "sound on film," method with great success as early as 1923, and both Thomas Edison and French cinematic pioneer Alice Guy had previously sought to give the screen a voice with "sound on wax cylinder" technology, but de Forest lacked the money and business skills to successfully capitalize on his invention, and Edison and Guy's system lacked sufficient electronic amplification.

Vitaphone, technically clumsy but capable of producing serviceable results, had the best corporate backing, and still—astonishingly—no other studio was interested in talkies. Sound films were seen as a novelty, if that, until *The Jazz Singer* opened on October 6, 1927, revolutionizing the film industry overnight (Silke 32). Suddenly, all the other studios were playing catch-up. Tragedy struck the brothers at almost the same moment, however: Sam Warner, exhausted from overwork and beset by illness, died of a cerebral hemorrhage on October 5, just a day before *The Jazz Singer*'s premiere (Silke 32). But the film's unexpected success soon put Warners out in front of the competition.

Jack pushed on, borrowing money (from Goldman, Sachs and the Hayden and S. Stone Company) to finance his purchase of both a chain of theaters and First National studios. First National, located in Burbank, controlled a glittering roster of stars, including Colleen Moore, Richard Barthelmess, Loretta Young, Edmund Love, Constance Bennett, Kay Francis, Basil Rathbone, and a young director named Mervyn LeRoy, who would soon become a major force within the company (Silke 32). Robert Lord and Hal Wallis were assigned the task of whipping the studio into shape. Production at First National had been leisurely, but now Jack Warner began running it like a proper dream factory.

Typical of this new "keep it moving" approach was Warner Bros.' follow-up to *The Jazz Singer*, Bryan Foy's gangster melodrama *The Lights of New York* (1928), the first real all-talking picture, which Foy shot as a supposed two-reel (twenty-minute) film, all the while intending to make a feature. He spent $18,000 on the film, infuriating Harry and Jack, but Albert thought it had possibilities, and so Jack let Foy continue shooting. When Foy was finished, Jack advertised the film as the "FIRST ALL TALKING PICTURE" in huge letters, opening it at the Strand Theater in

New York, where it took in $47,000 in its first week. The finished film was incredibly static, featuring lengthy dialogue scenes to the exclusion of almost anything else, but it was *indeed* "all talking," and the public was thrilled. Foy was in—he worked quickly and cheaply, and it was the start of a long and prolific career as a producer for WB and Fox (Silke 36).

Everything seemed to be clicking nicely; in 1929, Warner Bros. reported a net income of just under $14 million (Silke 36), but then, of course, came October 29, 1929, "Black Tuesday," as the stock market crashed, wiping out 40 percent of its value by November 11. The stock market continued to collapse, despite a few bear rallies, and by July 1932, the Dow Jones Industrial Average had lost a staggering 89 percent of its pre-crash value; the Great Depression was on. July 1932 marked the bottom of the stock market crash, but it would take nine more years, the dramatic intercession of Franklin Delano Roosevelt's New Deal programs, and the Second World War (and the resulting boom in the economy) to pull the country back from the brink of collapse.

Nor was Europe immune from the crisis; what had started in the United States soon spread around the globe. From 1930 to 1933, in stark contrast to the box office success of 1929, Warner Bros. had a three-year deficit of $113 million (Silke 37). Yet even in the midst of potential catastrophe, Jack Warner remained upbeat. The studio was now a major player in the industry, with 18,500 employees and an annual payroll of $36 million, boasting five complete studios, 93 film exchanges, and 812 theaters around the world, which served over 900 million viewers every year. As Albert Warner optimistically claimed that year, "There is not an instant during the 24 hours of the day that Warner Bros.' pictures are not being shown in some part of the world" (Silke 37–38).

It was during this period that Warners began making the crime films, social dramas, and exotic musicals for which it would become inextricably identified in the 1930s: William Wellman's *The Public Enemy* (1931), Mervyn LeRoy's *Little Caesar* (1931), LeRoy's *I Am a Fugitive from a Chain Gang* (1932), Wellman's explosive sex drama *Safe in Hell* (1931), LeRoy's equally controversial melodrama *Three on a Match* (1932), LeRoy and Busby Berkeley's *Gold Diggers of 1933* (1933), Lloyd Bacon's *42nd Street* (1933), Wellman's superb drama of dispossessed adolescents *Wild Boys of the Road* (1933), Robert Florey's scandalous Bette Davis vehicle *Ex-Lady* (1933), Bacon's James Cagney newspaper drama *Picture Snatcher* (1933), Ray Enright's crime thriller, with wide-eyed Joan Blondell as the head of a big-city crime syndicate, *Blondie Johnson* (1933), James Flood and Elliott Nugent's legal drama *The Mouthpiece* (1932), and numerous other hard-boiled films. Shot on a shoestring in rapid-fire fashion, Warner Bros.' films of the 1930s, perhaps more than those of any other studio, mirrored the desperation and uncertainty borne of the nation's financial collapse. Crooked lawyers, hardboiled gangsters, hardened chorines, big city slickers, and small-town rubes rubbed shoulders in a wave of films that captured the public's imagination, offering a potent mixture of escapism, realism, and even optimism in one of the darkest periods of the nation's history.

By late 1933, this "get tough" strategy was paying off—not handsomely, but the studio managed to eke out a marginal profit of $105,752 (Silke 39)—better than a loss in a deeply uncertain era. In this era before unions, the studio instituted a six-day work week, and many complete films were shot in a mere six days, from Monday morning through late Saturday night. Featured performers (bit players, second leads) were paid as little as $50 a week; everyone, no matter how high or how low, was required to sign the standard seven-year Warner Bros.' contract, with six-month options—if an actor, director, or any other contract employee refused an assignment, they were automatically put on suspension, and, as mentioned earlier, these unpaid suspensions were added to the seven-year time period. Thus, for performers like Bette Davis or James Cagney (and in the 1940s, Humphrey Bogart), who routinely refused inferior scripts, the "seven-year" contract could theoretically stretch into infinity with a series of prolonged suspensions, during which the actors were not permitted to work in any medium, including stage or radio appearances. Thus, at Warners, you did the studio's bidding, or you didn't eat. Extras earned from $3 to $7.50 a day (Silke 40).

Fed up with playing second fiddle to Harry and Jack Warner, Darryl Zanuck left the studio in 1934 and soon formed 20th Century Fox, which, following Jack Warner's example, he ran like an absolute dictator. Warners' studio executive Henry Blanke, a "production supervisor"—never called a "producer," an honor reserved for Jack Warner, Hal Wallis, and a few select others—recalled late in life Jack's style of running the studio, noting that "as much as I mislike [*sic*] what I'm saying now, Jack Warner was a genius. . . . His philosophy kept our egos down and made Warner Bros. rich. . . . It was the whole philosophy of the studio to never give anyone credit, or a percentage of stocks. . . . Jack was tough and we were tough as a studio. . . . If the other studios were tough, we'd be tougher, more realistic. The only theory we followed was that the characters had to talk like real people" (qtd. in Silke 119).

Bryan Foy, following his work directing *The Lights of New York*, now found his true calling as a producer of "B" films, averaging thirty films a year between 1935 and 1940, an astonishing figure by any standard. Foy did it by being ruthlessly pragmatic; "I never looked at sets, hair, or costumes, only the script . . . then Jack would say yes or no. Boom! Just like that. No man could run a studio better than Jack." Still, Foy had no illusions about Jack Warner's loyalty to anyone but himself, a harbinger of things to come in later years. "He won't stand up in a pinch. He'll shake your hand on Friday, and tell you that you're set for two years, then go to New York, call on Monday and fire you. . . . He has no guts. Warner would fire anybody. I was in and out seven times, but he was fearless about calling you up three months later and insisting you come back."

As for motion pictures as an art form, Foy and Warner both had little use for the concept. The bottom line was the bottom line: cash. As Foy noted, "It's not an art. Just look at any picture made twenty years ago, then look at Michelangelo. . . . Now *he* [original emphasis] seems to hold up. When Warners had a good picture, we would take the script and switch it around. We made [Howard Hawks's] *Tiger Shark* [1932] five times. I remember Howard Hawks when I told him I was 'switching' *Tiger Shark.* He said 'that's okay, I stole it from *They Knew What They Wanted,*' a Sidney Howard play that had been the hit of Broadway's 1924 season and had won a Pulitzer Prize. . . . As long as we were stealing, let's say adopting, we stole the best" (qtd. in Silke 119).

Warners' directors were every bit as tough as their boss. Lloyd Bacon had played villains in silent films, fought in the navy in World War I, and was, in general, one tough customer. Directors were relatively well paid, because, in a sense (as far as Jack Warner was concerned) they were the real supervisors of the films, along with the production managers (who made sure that sets, costumes, and cameras were ready and on schedule) and assistant directors (who kept one eye on the script, one eye on the clock, and kept things moving, no matter what). In the 1930s, Bacon directed no fewer than fourteen films with James Cagney, at a salary of $4,225 a week.

Michael Curtiz, a slave driver who was often paired with Errol Flynn (much to Flynn's displeasure), also worked feverishly throughout the 1930s, directing dozens of films at a weekly salary of $3,500; surprisingly, Busby "Buzz" Berkeley only rated $1,750 a week for directing his signature musical extravaganzas (Silke 144). William "Wild Bill" Wellman carried a gun on the set and was known to threaten actors with it if he didn't think they were performing up to par. And for all his reliance on directors to bring in films on time and on or under budget, Jack Warner didn't trust any of them, micromanaging their films by screening the dailies and then dictating scathing memos for them to read the next morning; he often walked on a set unannounced simply to watch—and usually criticize—a director's work.

John Huston, for one, thought Jack Warner's attitude was helpful, in a perverse sort of fashion. As he said later, "The resistance of the studio was good for you. Not only for the writers and the directors, but for all the talent. They were the establishment, you might say, and we were the criminals. It gave you something to fight" (qtd. in Silke 145). Actress and later director Ida Lupino concurred: "They were rough, tough men at Warner Bros.—go get your fanny out there and do it" (qtd. in Silke 148). Again, since there were no unions, many directors would work right through the day without even a lunch break. But all this would soon change; the craft unions and the actors' unions were beginning to form and take power away from Jack and his brothers, although—as we will see—the studio fought the nascent labor movement tooth and nail.

When Curtiz started filming *The Private Lives of Elizabeth and Essex* with Bette Davis, he blithely told her that "when you work with me, you don't need lunch. You just take aspirin." Curtiz's standard breakfast was four eggs, a big steak, and potatoes, washed down with large quantities of coffee, which he would inhale at great speed each morning before arriving on the set at 8 A.M. He would then work straight through until 9 or 10 at night, and if anyone didn't like it, well, there was the door (Silke 150).

Mervyn LeRoy, a journeyman director who did his best work in the early 1930s, married and then divorced Harry Warner's daughter, but through it all still managed to maintain good terms with brother Jack. A voluble man, LeRoy regularly called up assistants or even his superiors at three or four in the morning to ask a seemingly insignificant question, and he also had a volcanic temper, blowing up at the slightest provocation. But LeRoy had what Warners needed: the common touch. Edward G. Robinson pointed this out when he commented that "more than any director I know, Mervyn *is* [original emphasis] the audience. He is the man who goes to the box office and plunks down his 35 cents and loves or hates a picture" (qtd. in Silke 153). LeRoy was also an adept studio politician, who curried favor with all the right people, and, when the time was right, made the jump to MGM as a producer. At Warners, all directors were ultimately glorified hired guns. At MGM, LeRoy could stake out his own territory, for much better compensation. At Warner Bros., all the territory belonged to Jack—no interlopers were allowed.

As the 1930s gave way to the 1940s, the studio kept churning out hit after hit: Michael Curtiz's iconic *Casablanca* (1942); John Huston's *Across the Pacific* (1942, finished by Vincent Sherman when Huston was drafted); Raoul Walsh's *Objective Burma* (1945), a superior Errol Flynn war film; Huston's postwar *Key Largo* (1948), one of the last great gangster films of the studio era; Howard Hawks's superb noir *The Big Sleep* (1946), from a novel by Raymond Chandler, with a script by William Faulkner, Jules Furthman, and Leigh Brackett; Delmer Daves's bizarre Bogart and Bacall crime thriller *Dark Passage* (1947); and Raoul Walsh's violent crime drama *White Heat* (1949), one of James Cagney's finest performances as the psychopathic gangster Cody Jarrett.

In the mid-1940s, Jack Warner also received his first real taste of labor unrest, after running the studio like a medieval kingdom for more than two decades. On October 5, 1945, the Hollywood craft unions singled out Warner Bros. for using scab labor on its films, in defiance of its agreements with the various guilds. Harry and Jack Warner—now united by a common cause, their shared hatred of unions—fought back in typically brutal fashion. As one studio employee remembered, "The studio hired 'bully boys' and police dogs. . . . Large steel bolts from the machine shop were issued to the strikebreakers, and they threw them down on the strikers from the roofs of the soundstages. A hidden camera was placed next to the autogate to photograph striking employees" (qtd. in Silke 299).

The Burbank police sided with Harry and Jack, and used tire chains, high-powered fire hoses, and even guns to help the studio guards break through the picket lines. Many workers simply stayed on the lot, particularly the executives, waiting it out. For those who continued to work, Harry and Jack furnished free breakfasts of eggs, doughnuts, and coffee; people slept on cots and couches, and somehow production continued, albeit at a slower pace. Screenwriter Howard Koch was so appalled at the brothers' brutality that he bought out his contract for $10,000 and quit the studio.

In response, Jack Warner publicly decried the workers' action, saying pointedly that he would "no longer make pictures about the 'little man,'" since, in his eyes, he was a benevolent if despotic ruler, and the "little men" had betrayed his trust. It took eight months to settle the strike, with a 25 percent pay increase all around, and everyone went back to work (Silke 299). But the atmosphere had changed forever; the battle lines had been drawn, and, what was worse from Harry and Jack's viewpoint, their employees had prevailed. Who was running the studio, anyway? Harry and Jack Warner, or a ragtag group of malcontents?

In 1950, James Cagney left the studio, returning only once in a while for a one-picture deal; like almost everyone else in the business, Cagney was now a free agent. Bogart, Robinson, Flynn, Davis, and other topflight performers soon followed. Producer Jerry Wald's contract was sold to, of all people, Howard Hughes at RKO, but the two men soon parted ways. Henry Blanke's contract was cut from $5,500 a week to $3,500 a week. Warners' net profits in 1950 came to $10.3 million, yet most of this was the result of demotions, departures, and cutbacks (Schatz 437).

The year 1951 saw the same thing happening again; a $9.4 million profit, but only at the expense of cutting 6 percent of all Warner employees, this time in a single housecleaning in April of that year (Schatz 437). Like the other studio bosses, Jack fought dwindling audiences with gimmicks. André de Toth's *House of Wax* (1953), in Natural Vision 3-D, made a horror star out of Vincent Price and remains one of the more peculiar matches of director and program assignment; de Toth was blind in one eye and had no idea what 3D looked like, even in real life. Naturally, the film was a remake of an existing WB property, Michael Curtiz's *The Mystery of the Wax Museum* (1933), so the studio once again saved on story rights for the project.

Nevertheless, the film, shot in assembly-line fashion in narrative order for ease of assembly, the better to get it into the theaters faster, was a spectacular box-office success and the first major studio 3D film. But soon after, the 3D craze faded and Warner was at a loss as to what to do next. Howard Hawks, having long since left, came back to direct the indifferent and bloated historical spectacle *Land of the Pharaohs* in 1955; in 1956, John Huston checked back in to direct an equally ponderous version of Herman Melville's novel *Moby Dick*.

Both projects came to Warners as package deals, and the studio was simply becoming a financing production and distribution facility, as most modern studios now are (Schatz 439). Jack Warner had very little control over either project, and it showed. Warners still knew how to make effective entertainment, as it demonstrated when it signed up maverick director Nicholas Ray to helm *Rebel Without a Cause* (1955), starring the iconic rebel James Dean. Jack Warner had the sense to switch the film from a black-and-white cheapie, albeit shot in CinemaScope, to a much more lavish color and 'scope production after he saw how impressive the first few days of filming were while screening the daily rushes.

Or so the story goes; in his exhaustive study of *Rebel Without a Cause*, Douglas Rathgeb discounts the story of Warner's personal opinion, pointing to a clause in the studio's contract with Bausch and Lomb, makers of the CinemaScope lenses for both shooting and projection, that all CinemaScope projects had to be shot in color (111). Rathgeb's story sounds more convincing; Jack Warner, of course, spun it so that the decision was his alone and saw to it that reports trumpeting his faith in the film as the reason for the switch were leaked to the media.

Whatever the reason, *Rebel Without a Cause* was a massive hit and a brilliant piece of filmmaking, but Dean's death closed the door on any future collaborations. Faced with dwindling audiences and higher labor and operating expenses, Jack Warner took on negative pickup and co-production deals to cut production costs. He also relied increasingly on straightforward genre films such as Hawks's *Rio Bravo* (1959) and John Ford's *The Searchers* (1956), both now regarded as classics but at the time just routine westerns, albeit films that had a pre-sold audience, for both the genre and signature star John Wayne. Westerns had always been a safe bet, an industry staple since the days of Edwin S. Porter's *The Great Train Robbery* (1903). But their appeal was beginning to fade; science fiction was coming in, as were teen movies. Jack Warner's kingdom was slipping away fast, and he knew it. Television was making terrible inroads into the industry, and if the studio wanted to survive it would have to adapt.

As one example, Warner Bros. had been making cartoons since the late 1920s, and the animation staff—at first listed in the credits of each cartoon as "supervisors" rather than "directors," until the newly formed Cartoonists Guild forced Warner to relent—included such talented artists as Chuck Jones, Isidore "Friz" Freling, Tex Avery, Frank Tashlin, and Bob Clampett, to name just a few, each with their own distinctive visual style. In this, they were aided by the superb vocal artistry of Mel Blanc, who created nearly all the voices for the Warner Bros. Looney Tunes stable. Together, this group developed the most distinctive and popular roster of animated cartoon characters outside the Disney studio, with Bugs Bunny, Daffy Duck, Elmer Fudd, and Porky Pig leading the pack. But Jack Warner, convinced that (somehow) 3D would make cartoons obsolete, shut the animation unit down in 1953, then changed his mind and restarted production in 1955, moving the animators from the small outbuilding they had once occupied, known as Termite Terrace, to the main lot in Burbank, where Warner could keep a closer eye on their work. Sadly, the animation unit never really recovered its momentum after the shutdown and relocation (Schickel and Perry 263).

The 1950s represented a new crisis period for the studio. The real problem was television. How to deal with it? How to deal as well with the loss of the Warner theaters, the loss of the contract stars, the yearly overhead of the physical plant, and changing tastes in entertainment? Warner looked over to MCA/Revue and saw what was happening at Universal. Warners had to get into television production, quickly, but to do so it needed an infusion of cash. And so it was in March 1956 that Jack Warner made his second major miscalculation—he sold all rights to the studio's library of 750 features, 100 silent films, and 1,500 short subjects, including the Looney Tunes cartoon series for a paltry $21 million (of which taxes took $6 million) to Associated Artists Productions (AAP), an enormous tactical mistake by any standard (Anderson 221).

Rather than leasing the films, or setting up its own distribution system, or even renting them to television distributors but otherwise retaining all rights, Warner Bros., along with RKO and Paramount, took the easy way out, selling off their back catalogue outright (Anderson 221). With *I Love Lucy (1951–1957)*, Ann Sothern's sitcom *Private Secretary* (1953–1957), Dick Powell's *Four Star Playhouse* (1952–1956), and MCA's *General Electric Theater* (1953–1962) all profitably demonstrating that television programming could be run and rerun again to enormous profits, one would have to be extremely myopic not to see the financial and branding opportunities that well-managed television exposure could bring (Anderson 220). The studios were stuck in the past, still thinking of their films as a relatively disposable commodity; you ran them once on first release, then double-billed them at neighborhood theaters with a newer title, then put them in a vault, and if the film was particularly profitable in its first run you might rerelease it to theaters as a classic for a second go-round. But that was it.

Not everyone was so shortsighted. Walt Disney, for example, instantly realized that he could use television to solidify the Disney brand as family entertainment, and never once even dreamed of relinquishing ownership of any of his films, animated or live action. In the early television era, Disney's weekly TV show, *Disneyland*—which had an astonishing run from 1954 to 2008 under a variety of titles, including *Walt Disney Presents, Walt Disney's Wonderful World of Color, The Wonderful World of Disney,* and *The Magical World of Disney*—essentially functioned as an advertisement for the company's back catalogue, which would be rereleased every eight years or so for a new generation of youngsters. Even now, in the DVD era, Disney still sticks to their limited window, limited edition strategy for rerelease of their classic films on home video, which quickly sell out and become collector's items.

Warner Bros., however, was convinced that the past was dead, gone, and unprofitable; Jack Warner envisioned television solely as a market for new programming, tailored specifically to television's time and visual constraints. But more intriguingly, what Jack Warner waited to do was re-create the studio system of the golden age anew at Warner Bros., only this time exclusively for the small screen. He would still make feature films, of course, but with all this free agency business with actors, writers, and directors, and the unrelenting rise in production expense, television seemed like a much safer bet. It would be like making "B" movies all over again, and Jack Warner certainly knew how to do that. And so he set about to repeat the past, only this time for a brand-new audience.

Working with production executive William T. Orr, Jack Warner reorganized the studio's Sunset Productions, which had been making inroads but not a definitive impact in television under the guidance of producers Cedric Francis and Jack Warner Jr., and aimed at conquering the new medium. Jack Sr. shifted Sunset Productions into making television commercials, while Warner Bros.' television, with Orr firmly at the helm, handled all series production. Jack made it clear that Orr had total control over the new TV unit, telling Orr categorically that "I definitely want our TV division to be under your supervision. The making of pictures and the okaying of scripts is entirely in your hands. . . . I cannot make it plainer than this . . . [or] we will have turmoil in our TV department" (qtd in Anderson 226).

Orr took the challenge and ran with it. The studio soon had *Sugarfoot* (1957–1961), a TV western, up and running, as well as *Colt .45* (1957–1960) and the hugely successful *Maverick* (1957–1962), which made an overnight small-screen star out of actor James Garner. All debuted in 1957 on ABC, but *Maverick* was the runaway hit of the group, offering a wry, post-modern twist on the traditional western format, with the character of Maverick depicted as a distinct departure from the typical square-jawed genre hero. Maverick, as his name implies, was primarily a trickster, even a con man, who played outside the conventional rules of the game and would rather use his brains than his fists, much less a gun, to come out on top at the end of each episode. Garner took to the role with relish and would essentially reprise the same persona in his later hit series, *The Rockford Files* (1974–1980), as a private detective whose working methods are equally idiosyncratic.

Writer/producer Roy Huggins was the person chiefly responsible for the creation of the series, and in February 1958 Huggins refused to renew his contract unless he received better pay and recognition. In March 1958, Huggins signed a new deal at a still-modest $1,100 per week, echoing salary negotiations of an earlier era at the studio (Anderson 237). Huggins had also written the pilot for what would become a major hit for the studio, the detective series *77 Sunset Strip*, and so his services were clearly invaluable. Warners' contracts for its television performers, although not the seven-year straitjacket they had been in the 1930s and 1940s, were still extraordinarily strict.

As Christopher Anderson notes, "Under the terms of the studio's contracts, actors were required to work forty weeks per year in any vehicle selected for them by the studio—*whether it be television or feature films* [emphasis added]. . . . Some agents [for actors, directors and/or writers] countered the studio's policy by attempting to negotiate separate movie and TV contracts that would pay their clients a larger salary for feature film work," but Warners and Orr adamantly refused (238). As Orr put it, "Whatever the salary is, it encompasses all phases of film production. . . . TV is not a sideline with Warner Bros. but an important adjunct to the building of solid careers" (qtd. in Anderson 238). From the studio's public point of view, these "all-encompassing" contracts were actually a boon to actors, building up their reputations and careers much more quickly with continual exposure on television.

In truth, it was a sweeter deal for the studio than the actors, who received a minimal weekly salary, the Screen Actors Guild minimum for residual payments on reruns, and no profit-sharing in the series in which they appeared. Further, Warners' TV stars were obliged to make personal appearances to promote their shows, and when they did the studio collected half their salary from each engagement. As one executive put it, "If we clear $10,000 from appearances by actors when we pay $50,000 a year, the actor really only costs us $40,000" (qtd. in Anderson 239). Additionally, the stars' likenesses could be viewed in comic books, on lunch boxes, or in games and toys for nothing more than the SAG minimum royalty (Anderson 239). Additionally, all Warner Bros. TV stars were pushed into recording contracts for the company's musical recordings if they could sing even a little bit; one of the biggest hits was Edd "Kookie" Byrnes's (from *77 Sunset Strip*) "Kookie, Kookie, Lend Me Your Comb," with a vocal assist from Connie Stevens, which became a Top 40 pop sensation (Anderson 239).

Inevitably, performers began to rebel. Clint Walker of *Cheyenne*, noting that James Arness, among others, owned a percentage of the popular *Gunsmoke* series and kept all the money for his personal appearances, demanded the same for his services. Orr swiftly fired him (Anderson 239). If you worked for Warners, you did it their way, or you were out—never to return. *Cheyenne*, without Clint Walker—a replacement actor, Ty Hardin, was rushed into the series, and Walker's character, Cheyenne Bodie, was simply dropped from the series narrative—continued on as a hit series, and was even renewed for the 1958–59 season.

That season also saw the debut of *77 Sunset Strip* (1958–1964), the studio's first non-western series, and as a seriocomic detective thriller it soon became a model for future WB television productions. The ninety-minute pilot for the series (actually seventy-five minutes, plus commercials) was shot in just eleven days for a mere $130,000, and ABC snapped it up as a series immediately. Designed around a group of actors rather than just one performer—so anyone who proved hard to handle could easily be written out while the series continued without difficulty (a practice perfected many years later by producer Dick Wolf with *Law and Order* [1990–2010] and its many spinoffs, which routinely went through major cast changes without detriment to the series' ratings)—*77 Sunset Strip* soon became a staple of ABC's primetime lineup (Anderson 242–43).

As with the older Warner Bros. program pictures, continuity was never much of a concern for the new regime. When the pilot for *77 Sunset Strip* was test-screened for audiences, under the episode title "Girl on the Run" (Roy Huggins based the script on a short story he had written in

1952, published in *Esquire*, entitled "Death and the Skylark"), Edd Byrnes played a vicious serial killer who preyed on young women. But teens responded so enthusiastically to Byrnes's "cool cat" demeanor that the studio simply erased Byrnes's character in the pilot and blithely reintroduced him as a jive-talking parking lot attendant, a self-described "jalopy jockey" who worked at a restaurant next door to the detective agency.

Thus, at the start of the second episode of *77 Sunset Strip*, series star Efrem Zimbalist Jr. directly addressed the audience, telling them that "we previewed this show, and because Edd Byrnes was such a hit we decided that Kookie and his comb had to be in our series. So this week, we'll just forget that in the pilot he went off to prison to be executed." In fact, Byrnes soon eclipsed both Zimbalist and co-star Roger Smith in popularity and became one of the show's major drawing cards, even managing to renegotiate his contract midway through the second season, upping both his salary and his screen time—a first for a WB TV star.

The success of *77 Sunset Strip* soon led to a host of similar hour-long shows from the studio, including *Surfside Six* (1960–1962), *Bourbon Street Beat* (1959–1960), and *Hawaiian Eye* (1959–1963). By the end of 1958, Warner Bros. had no fewer than eight primetime ABC network series on the air, three of which had been sold without a pilot, and produced 127 hours of programming for the network; in 1959–60, with the addition of such series as *The Roaring Twenties* (1960–1962; a nod to WB's gangster past), the studio was faced with cranking out 260 hours of programming for ABC—equivalent, as Christopher Anderson points out, to making 170 feature films in a single year (247). So it seemed that the studio system, of a sort, was back, at least at Warner Bros., where in 1959 twenty-three soundstages were "devoted solely to TV series production, using 300 permanent personnel, ten producers, twenty-seven contract actors, and more than sixty-three freelance writers, as well as ninety film editors" (Anderson 247–48) to post-produce the torrent that the studio churned out week after week.

It was a return to the past. Every hour-long episode of each series was shot in six days, adhered to a strict budget and running time, with characters so paper-thin that scripts could be recycled from one series to another by simply changing the names of the characters and other minor details. Directors blasted through scripts at a blistering pace, concerned only with getting the requisite number of pages in the can. Orr limited directors to a maximum of three takes for any one shot—even if actors blew their lines—and mandated that camera coverage should be confined to master shots and close-ups only, to eliminate the need for reshooting and provide ample coverage for the editors. Scripts were shot in six days, edited in eight days immediately after shooting, and then fine-cut no less than two weeks later (Anderson 251).

Series television was profitable; in 1958, Warners grossed $70 million; by 1959, television production alone was bringing in $30 million (Anderson 252). Everything was shot in the studio, even exterior sequences, which were built on soundstages so that shooting could go on around the clock, in fair weather or foul. Stock footage was used to provide establishing shots of Hawaii (*Hawaiian Eye*), Miami (*Surfside Six*), New Orleans (*Bourbon Street*), and even Hollywood itself, only a few miles away (*77 Sunset Strip*). Though the offices of Stu Bailey and his cohorts on *77 Sunset Strip* were ostensibly located next to a real restaurant, Dean Martin's Dino's (Orr got permission from Martin to do this, to which the actor readily agreed—free publicity, why not?), the main units of the series never shot on location. Leaving the studio lot was just too risky. Second-unit crews were dispatched to shoot exterior establishing shots with only a camera and lights—no sound equipment—but this footage was minimal and was mercilessly recycled. It got to the point that the editing department formally petitioned Orr to shoot some new location material, noting that "we've used what stock is available until it is embarrassing to put it in shows" (Anderson 268).

Then the problems began in earnest, just as they did in the classical studio era. First the writers quit in droves, alienated not only by the killing production schedule but also the low pay—Warners paid $3,000 less per script than the going market rate at the time (Anderson 272). Then the overworked, underpaid actors started to flee, or at least to express their dissatisfaction with the new factory system in no uncertain terms. James Garner spoke for many WB television actors when he publicly commented that "I feel like a slab of meat hanging there. Every once in a while they cut off a piece." Jack Warner was unimpressed. "Naturally they want to get out of TV because the work is not easy. They want to get into features where they can have an easier occupation" (both qtd. in Anderson 273).

Finally, in 1960, Garner filed a lawsuit to escape his contract. Even though the studio capitulated to some of his demands, Garner successfully demonstrated that Warners had acted in bad faith when they suspended him and co-star Jack Kelly from *Maverick* at the end of the 1960 season, claiming that since the writers were striking, they had no scripts to shoot (Anderson 274). This was a standard *force majeure* tactic often used by the studios, stating that "extraordinary circumstances" beyond the studio's control made continued production impossible. The case wound up in court where, on the witness stand, Jack Warner undermined the studio's case by admitting that the studio simply used recycled scripts during the strike. Garner ended up winning his release from the studio (Anderson 275) and went on to a long career in feature films and TV.

Then writer/producer Roy Huggins jumped ship, fed up with low pay and the lack of a percentage of residuals from reruns; Warners was now the only studio that refused to give performers, producers, writers, or directors a cut of the lucrative rerun market (Anderson 276). Warners promised Huggins a low-budget feature film, *The Savage Streets*, to produce, starring Efrem Zimbalist Jr., but when actor Roger Smith was seriously injured in an accident, Zimbalist was recalled to duty on *77 Sunset Strip* and the film was never made. Jack Warner tried to reassign Huggins to television once more, but Huggins refused and went on suspension.

Huggins eventually produced one indifferent feature film for the studio, Vincent Sherman's *A Fever in the Blood* (1966), starring Zimbalist, Angie Dickinson, and Don Ameche in a tale of California political intrigue, but it was too little, much too late. Warners reluctantly released

Huggins from his contract, and almost immediately he was besieged with better offers for his services. In October 1960, Huggins accepted a position at 20th Century Fox as vice president in charge of television production (Anderson 278); it was he who would later create *The Rockford Files* at Universal. Thinking he could still operate with the same dictatorial control he had in the 1940s, Jack Warner made the fatal mistake of keeping his television personnel on too tight a leash. By treating his stars, producers, writers, and directors as if they were indentured servants rather than individuals, Warner essentially brought down the WB television division as rapidly as he had created it.

Further, by relying on ABC as their main distribution outlet—in retrospect, it's surprising they didn't more aggressively pitch their programming to NBC or CBS, simply as a fallback position—Warners limited the kinds of programming they could produce for television, as ABC's management wanted only westerns and crime dramas, moving Warner Bros.' story editor James Barnett to complain (with or without apologies to Joyce Kilmer) that "I think that I shall never see / A format new for ABC" (as qtd. in Anderson 280). The signs of decline were obvious. For the 1960–61 season, ABC cut their weekly programming demands to 6.5 hours per week (Anderson 280); further, the Warner Bros.' series were slipping in popularity, with only *77 Sunset Strip* placing in the top 25 TV series by 1961.

Responding to this trend, ABC cut their programming order to just four hours weekly for the 1962–63 season; by 1963–64, only *77 Sunset Strip*, now old and tired, was still limping along (Anderson 281). In short, Warner Bros. had gone from boom to bust in roughly eight years. In 1962, Warners and Orr axed 25 percent of the television production staff; in March of that year, Jack Warner announced that he was instituting a major overhaul of the television division, supposedly "guided by a spirit of imaginative exploration," actively seeking deals with ABC, NBC, or CBS, welcoming possible coproduction deals, independent producers— whatever it took to get the TV arm up and running again.

The results were disastrous. Jack Webb, famous for his monolith television crime drama *Dragnet*, came on the lot as an independent producer,
and at the same time former ABC executive Oliver Treyz was hired. The
two men jockeyed for power within the studio, but in February 1963 Warner
announced that Webb would oversee all television production, and Treyz
abruptly departed (Anderson 284). Webb's most conspicuous "accomplishment" was to completely redesign *77 Sunset Strip* into a foreign espi-
onage melodrama, working with actor-turned-director William Conrad.

Webb kicked off the new format of *77 Sunset Strip* with an ambitious
project entitled 5, a five-part, five-hour serial drama that followed Efrem
Zimbalist Jr., still playing investigator Stuart Bailey, in search of "art treasures stolen during World War II" (Anderson 285). Gone were the *77
Sunset Strip* offices and the rest of the supporting cast members; gone, too,
was the series' catchy theme music, as Zimbalist glumly worked his way
through a back-lot, stock-footage version of Europe and the Middle East,
supported by an enormous cast of guest stars, including Peter Lorre (an
old hand at Warners, to be sure), Tony Bennett, George Jessel, Brian
Keith, Herbert Marshall (a long way from Lubitsch's luminous 1932
romantic comedy *Trouble in Paradise*), Lloyd Nolan, Cesar Romero, Telly
Savalas, a young William Shatner, Ed *and* Keenan Wynn, and many
others. It was a complete reversal of what had made the series so initially
alluring, and viewers tuned out in droves. In December 1963, less than
year after being hired, Webb was fired, and the WB television unit was in
flux once more (Anderson 286).

At the same time Jack Warner fired Webb, he announced once again a
"complete reevaluation of all TV operations" to the public, but despite the
returning William T. Orr's best efforts, WB was only able to place three
new series, of which *F-Troop* (1965–1967) was the only real hit. At the same
time, ironically, independent producer Quinn Martin used Warner Bros.'
financing and production facilities to produce the highly successful series
The F.B.I., starring none other than Efrem Zimbalist Jr., which ran for
a solid nine seasons from 1965 to 1974 (Anderson 286).

Jack Warner began stepping back from hands-on management of the studio as the 1960s wore on, deferring much of his authority to Benjamin Kalmenson, who ran the company's New York offices. In late 1965, without warning, Kalmenson fired Orr and his entire staff, effectively shutting down television production at Warner Bros. once and for all; though he appointed former ABC executive Robert Lewine to replace Orr, it was merely in a caretaker position. Lewine wasn't given any resources to develop any new series, and he didn't; the new television factory at WB was a thing of the past (Anderson 281). While Universal continued with television production in the 1970s and 1980s, often working with NBC, Warners packed it in, and with it the assembly-line production system that had made it possible.

The studio's dwindling fortunes in film and television production over the preceding decade took place as Harry and Jack Warner's fraternal warfare continued to heat up over each brother's role within the company and their ownership thereof. On May 2, 1956, Toronto industrial magnate Lou Chester, along with Charles Allen, a stockbroker from New York, announced to the trade papers that they were on the verge of buying the studio. This deal, of course, had been put together by Jack without Harry's knowledge, and Harry was furious. "I'm not ready to be put out to pasture!" Harry yelled at Jack. The two brothers had been at odds for years— at one point Harry tried to kill Jack by bashing him over the head with a three-foot length of lead pipe (Sperling et al. 283–84)—and they had been fighting almost daily for years, with increasing intensity.

Harry was now seventy-five, an old man, tired of the day-to-day grind of the studio, tired of fighting with Jack. He still ran the financial end of the studio, but Jack was wearing him down. Warner Bros.' board of directors had total confidence in Harry's financial acumen; Harry had received a much-needed boost when the board reelected him president of the company, on February 24, 1956 (Sperling et al. 302). But Harry knew what Jack really wanted. Jack wanted to be president and ace out Harry. It had always been thus, a street fight all the way to the end.

Albert wanted out, too, but Harry refused to go along with the deal. As far as Harry was concerned, all the Warner brothers were going to sell out, retire, and leave the business permanently; there would be no back door through which Jack could sneak in. And so on May 3, 1956, Jack had to publicly disavow the Chester/Allen deal. Then on May 11, another group of investors, led by Boston banker Serge Semenenko, made an offer to buy out Harry, Jack, and Albert for $22 million, in return for 800,000 shares, or 90 percent, of their holdings; Harry, Jack, and Albert would remain on the board of directors (Sperling et al. 303).

This time Harry agreed, provided that all three sell out (Sperling et al. 303–04). And everyone, at least as far as Harry and Albert were concerned, was going to fade into the sunset. Louella Parsons wrote in her column on May 14 that "all three brothers dined together at Perino's [last night]. After selling the studio for $20 million, they could afford it" (qtd. in Sperling et al. 304). But Jack, of course, had his own scheme. He had made a prior arrangement with Semenenko to buy his shares back, keep his title, and keep running the studio, but without having to deal with Harry and Albert (Gabler 408; Sperling et al. 308). The coup was soon the talk of the town, and Jack Warner did nothing to calm the waters.

The very next day—subtlety was never Jack's strong suit—columnist Hedda Hopper wrote that "Jack Warner made Warners' studio employees very happy by calling a meeting of Warner department heads and announcing that the purchase of the studio . . . doesn't mean he is leaving as production head. . . . [Said Jack,] 'I'll be around as long as my feet hold out . . . and that should be many years. There's no truth in the rumor that I'm leaving in October and Jerry Wald is taking over as production head. Serge Semenenko has asked me to remain and I have every intention of continuing to head the studio'" (qtd. in Sperling et al. 304).

But worse news, at least for Harry and Albert, was still to come. On May 31, 1956, Harry was reading *Variety* and was surprised to read that "Jack Warner retains substantial stock holdings in the company," the 200,000 shares that Semenenko had sold back to Jack after the sale. Using that block of stock, Jack Warner had appointed himself the new president of Warner Bros., disingenuously telling *Variety* that "I am very happy that my brothers, the board of directors, and the distinguished financial group have placed under my direction the perpetuation of the company which our family has pioneered" (qtd. in Sperling et al. 306). Harry collapsed from what was later diagnosed as a minor heart attack and checked into Cedars of Lebanon Hospital for observation. There, Harry had a stroke, which made it necessary for him to use a cane for the remainder of his life (Sperling 307). Albert, in New York, was similarly appalled by the news of Jack's new position. Neither Harry nor Albert spoke to Jack for the rest of their lives.

Harry died on July 27, 1958, at the age of 76; Jack was vacationing at his villa on Cap d'Antibes and didn't come to the funeral (Sperling et al. 313). Instead, he sent a brief wire: "Unable to attend. Please pay my respects" (Sperling et al. 314). Four days later, on August 4, 1958, after winning two million francs at the Palm Beach Casino in Cannes during a six-hour game of baccarat, Jack Warner got into a 1947 Alfa-Romeo to drive to his home in Juan les Pins, but en route he fell asleep at the wheel. The car crashed head-on into a parked truck, the Alfa-Romeo flipped over, and Jack was thrown out the right door. He landed forty feet from the car, hitting the road head first, although at the last moment Jack apparently braced his arms to help absorb the impact (Sperling et al. 315).

Picked up by passing good Samaritans, Jack was taken to the local hospital. Miraculously, he began to recover. His son, Jack Jr., visited his bedside and was shocked by his father's appearance; afterward, Jack Jr. was misquoted by reporters as saying that he didn't think his father would recover, which enraged Jack Sr., and, if anything, redoubled his will to return to work (Sperling et al. 319). After four months in the hospital in France, at the end of 1958 Jack returned to the studio in Burbank and promptly fired Jack Jr., with six months' severance pay as the only compensation (Sperling et al. 321). When Jack Jr. tore up the resignation letter, Jack Sr. simply changed the locks on Jack Jr.'s office door and had him barred from the Warner Bros. lot. When Jack Jr. tried to get back into his office, the studio police refused to admit him.

Defeated, Jack Jr. drove off the lot for the last time, just as two workmen were putting up a huge banner reading "WELCOME BACK, JACK" (Sperling 323). Jack Jr. wrote his father several letters attempting reconciliation, but he never received a reply. In 1964, Jack Sr. published a self-serving autobiography, ghostwritten by Dean Jennings, which reinvented the past by omitting any mention of Harry Warner, their fights, the 1956 sale of the studio, his first wife, Irma, or Jack Jr.—in short, he made anyone who had opposed him disappear (Sperling et al. 324).

Though the television unit of Warner Bros. had collapsed, Jack Warner himself was, against all odds, returning to health, seemingly none the worse for his brush with death. Fred Zinnemann's *The Sundowners* (1960) and Morton DaCosta's *The Music Man* (1962) were nominated for Best Picture, and Robert Aldrich's gothic horror film *Whatever Happened to Baby Jane?* (1962), with Bette Davis and Joan Crawford, became one of the studio's biggest hits of the year. Jack Warner had initially passed on the latter film, famously telling Aldrich that "I wouldn't give you a dime for those two old broads." Aldrich ended up making the film as an independent but released it through Warner Bros.

Warner's initial misjudgment regarding the enduring star power of Davis and Crawford was echoed in his decision regarding the casting of *My Fair Lady* (1964), directed with an assured hand by George Cukor. Julie Andrews, who onstage had successfully created the musical role of Eliza Doolittle, the cockney gutter sparrow whom Rex Harrison's Professor Henry Higgins transforms into a lady of society, wanted to reprise her performance in the film version, but Jack Warner nixed the idea, seeing Andrews as a poor box office draw. Instead he went with the more popular Audrey Hepburn, whose singing in the finished film was dubbed by Marni Nixon. Andrews's rejection, however, freed her to accept the lead in Robert Stevenson's *Mary Poppins* (1964) for Disney. Though *My Fair Lady* won Best Picture at the Oscars that year (the studio's first Best

Picture award since *Casablanca* twenty-one years earlier), it was Andrews, not Hepburn, who won the Best Actress nod. Accepting her statuette, Andrews looked directly at Warner, sitting in one of the front rows of the auditorium, and serenely announced, "I want to express my gratitude to Jack Warner for making all this possible" (Sperling et al. 325).

In 1966 Mike Nichols's famously controversial production of *Who's Afraid of Virginia Woolf?*, based on Edward Albee's play, engendered a host of censorship problems and was instrumental in the creation of the Motion Picture Association of America's ratings code as we know it today; the new system was devised by MPAA president Jack Valenti (Sperling et al. 325) as a workable replacement for the old Production Code. It was another sign that the classical studio era was over; the artificial, back-lot world of Hollywood in the 1930s and 1940s was finally coming to an end. And by the mid-1960s, the great studio moguls themselves were a dying breed. Harry Cohn was dead. Louis B. Mayer was dead. Sam Goldwyn had retired. Darryl Zanuck was in self-imposed exile in Europe.

Finally, on November 14, 1966, Jack Warner sold out his interests—for $32 million—to Elliot and Kenneth Hyman, two Canadian investors, who promptly renamed the company Warner Bros./7 Arts (Thomas, *Clown Prince* 279). There were still a few final productions for Jack, who remained on the board of directors of the company: Arthur Penn's landmark *Bonnie and Clyde* (1967), which Jack opposed at every turn; Terence Young's suspense thriller *Wait until Dark* (1967); and Joshua Logan's extravagant adaptation of the musical *Camelot* (1967), which was a critical and commercial disaster, despite a $15 million budget.

With the failure of *Camelot* at the box office, the Hymans became fed up with Jack's autocratic crustiness, and though they stuck with the company through *Bonnie and Clyde*, they made plans to get out, unable to deal with the fact that Jack was still on the board of directors. In 1969, the Hymans sold out to Kinney National Company for $64 million (Thomas, *Clown Prince* 288), an odd arrangement because Kinney's most visible business was as an operator of a large chain of parking lots in major metropolitan areas, as well as a chain of funeral homes.

Sensing that this was truly the end of his reign at the studio, Jack drove off the Warner Bros. lot for the last time in October 1969 and never returned. Then came a surprise; unable to stay away entirely from the business that had made him such a wealthy man, Jack struck a deal with Columbia Pictures to produce Peter Hunt's film version of the Broadway musical *1776*, as well as Stan Dragoti's offbeat western *Dirty Little Billy*, a revisionist history of Billy the Kid starring Michael J. Pollard in the title role, with the odd tagline "Billy the Kid was a punk." Both films were released in 1972, and neither did well at the box office.

In 1973, Warner took a nasty spill while playing tennis, from which he never fully recovered. In 1977, he suffered a stroke and was forced to use a wheelchair; he died on September 9, 1978, at the age of 86, leaving an estate of roughly $15 million (Sperling et al. 334). Albert Warner, meanwhile, had died on November 26, 1967, at his home in Miami Beach at the age of 83. Jack Warner Jr. became an independent film producer and in 1982 wrote a thinly disguised fictional portrait of his father in the novel *Bijou Dream*; the novel was reissued in 1988 as a mass-market paperback under the much more marketable title of *The Dream Factory*, an ideal description of Warner Bros. and the other studios (Sperling et al. 338).

Meanwhile, Warner Bros. was going through a maze of corporate takeovers and buyouts. With Kinney in control, the Warner Bros.' logo had a line of text added beneath it in all promotional materials, identifying the studio as "A Kinney Leisure Services Company." Kinney also owned a talent agency, Ashley Famous, and with Jack Warner finally out of the picture for good, Ted Ashley became the new head of the studio (Thomas, *Clown Prince* 288). Shrewdly teaming with DC Comics and signing up such stars as Robert Redford, Barbra Streisand, and Clint Eastwood—a triple threat as actor, producer, and director (sometimes even composer)—Kinney gradually got out of the parking lot and funeral home business and renamed itself Warner Communications. In 1989, Time Inc. surprised many by acquiring control of the studio for $14.9 billion.

In 2000, America Online, then a huge name in the Internet service industry, bought out Time Warner, which became AOL Time Warner. But with the financial implosion of AOL, the company took a massive financial hit and reverted to the Time Warner name. In 1995, Warners launched the WB television network, where it could air its own programming and bypass the three major networks. *Dawson's Creek*, *Buffy the Vampire Slayer*, *Charmed*, and *7th Heaven* all emerged as hits, but it wasn't enough to sustain the fledgling operation. In 2006, CBS, Paramount, and Warners combined the WB and CBS's struggling UPN networks into a new hybrid, the CW, which has, of this writing, yet to prove out.

During this time, Robert Daly and Terry Semels ran the company and pushed through a series of box office hits, but they quit in 1999; since then, the studio has prospered with the Batman franchise, under the direction of Christopher Nolan, to say nothing of the Harry Potter films. In the meantime Warners bought out Turner Broadcasting in 1996, in the process reacquiring much of the motion picture and cartoon library they had so foolishly sold off to AAP in 1956; the AAP library had already passed through many hands, winding up at MGM and then Turner Broadcasting when Ted Turner bought the MGM/UA film library to launch his TNT channel and later Turner Classic Movies. It's all mind-numbingly complex, but at least there's an upside to all this; Warner Bros.' films are now a staple of the Turner Classic Movies' film library, along with the MGM library and many of United Artists' best films, and are screened at all hours of the day commercial free on cable systems nationwide, which is a nice legacy for any film company—to have your carefully manufactured dreams live forever, constantly being screened for new audiences.

———

Yet as with all the great Hollywood studios, the new corporate version of Warner Bros., as well as of the new Paramount, MGM, 20th Century Fox,

Columbia, and other studios, has lost the individual identity that each had
when they were run by one or two men who made all the decisions, were
the final judge and jury of every new project, and created not only a look
but also a philosophy that they incorporated into all their films. So what if
Zanuck's production of *Wilson* was a flop in 1944, or was even indifferent
filmmaking? It was the result of an individual's creative passion, rather
than a calculated risk taken by a group of businessmen and women who
are constantly searching for the next big package, the next new trend, the
next film to imitate, because they have no ideas of their own. As actor
Gregory Peck, a distinguished survivor of the classical Hollywood studio
system, noted of the corporate heirs of Hollywood in 1977, "They are not
used to making pictures with any real content. . . . I suppose they enjoy
scanning stock reports, counting grosses. They grind out mindless drivel
for T.V. They must watch the stuff in their home projection rooms. They
all have Henry Moore [sculptures] in the garden. I don't understand
them" (as qtd. in Freedland 241). These are the people who run
Hollywood today; not filmmakers, but rather executives, who view the
entire enterprise of movie making as strictly a profit or loss business,
and nothing more.

For all their personal flaws, and there were many, the moguls of the
classical Hollywood studio era were individuals who believed in what they
were doing as a business, but also as merchants of dreams, even artists,
though they would have brushed aside such claims in an instant. Yet,
with film budgets routinely climbing in 2012 to $150 million for even the
smallest mainstream film, due to star salaries, high-priced scripts,
directors, producers, and special effects personnel (this is the digital era,
after all), one ultimately can't blame today's studio executives if they're
reluctant to take creative risks. The entire system has changed.

The early moguls took those risks, which is what made their empires
grow, but they also banked on vast reservoirs of talent to make their
dreams come to life on the screen. In the process, they exploited nearly
everyone who worked for them. As inherently commercial as the movies

are, they are also potentially an escape, an enchantment, a shared dream that audiences can enter along with the filmmakers, for film is, above all, a mass medium. That dream is as potent today as it was in the early 1910s when the film industry first moved west to the raw space of Hollywood and staked its claim on our imagination.

What kinds of films will be made next? They'll probably be blockbusters, which will open everywhere, while the more thoughtful films will wind up in the "On Demand" tier of your cable box, or as streaming downloads from Amazon. It's a whole new world out there now, and the rules of the game have changed. What will happen as new delivery systems proliferate and new methods of filmmaking appear is anyone's guess. But as long as there are audiences waiting to be entertained and/or enlightened, the movies will be with us, in one form or another, drawing us inexorably into their phantom domain.

Works Cited and Consulted

Anderson, Christopher. *Hollywood TV: The Studio System in the Fifties.* Austin: U of Texas P, 1994. Print.

Anger, Kenneth. *Hollywood Babylon II.* New York: E. P. Dutton, 1984. Print.

Arnold, Jeremy. "*If You Could Only Cook.*" *TCM.com.* Web.

Behlmer, Rudy. *Behind the Scenes.* Hollywood: Samuel French, 1989. Print.

———. *Inside Warner Bros. (1935–1951).* New York: Viking, 1985. Print.

———. *Memo from Darryl F. Zanuck: The Golden Years at 20th Century Fox.* New York: Grove, 1993. Print.

———, ed. *Memo from David O. Selznick.* New York: Viking, 1972. Print.

Berg, A. Scott. *Goldwyn: A Biography.* New York: Knopf, 1989. Print.

Bogdanovich, Peter. *Who the Devil Made It.* New York: Knopf, 1997. Print.

Brand, Paul. "'Nice Town. I'll Take It': Howard Hughes and Hollywood." *Bright Lights Film Journal* 47 (February 2005). Web.

Bruck, Connie. *When Hollywood Had a King: The Reign of Lew Wasserman, Who Leveraged Talent into Power and Influence.* New York: Random House, 2003. Print.

Carringer, Robert L. *The Magnificent Ambersons: A Reconstruction.* Berkeley: U of California P, 1993. Print.

"Comcast and GE Complete Transaction to Form NBC Universal, LLC." Press Release, *Comcast,* January 29, 2011. Web.

Costello, John. *Virtue under Fire: How World War II Changed Our Social and Sexual Attitudes.* Boston: Little, Brown, 1985. Print.

Crowther, Bosley. *Hollywood Rajah: The Life and Times of Louis B. Mayer.* New York: Henry Holt, 1960. Print.

Custen, George F. *Twentieth Century's Fox: Darryl F. Zanuck and the Culture of Hollywood.* New York: Basic Books, 1997. Print.

Davis, Ronald L. *The Glamour Factory: Inside Hollywood's Big Studio System.* Dallas: Southern Methodist UP, 1993. Print.

DeMille, Cecil B. *Autobiography.* Englewood Cliffs, N.J.: Prentice-Hall, 1959.

Dick, Bernard F. *Hal Wallis: Producer to the Stars.* Lexington: UP of Kentucky, 2004. Print.

———. *The Merchant Prince of Poverty Row: Harry Cohn of Columbia Pictures.* Lexington: UP of Kentucky, 1993. Print.

———, ed. *Columbia Pictures: Portrait of a Studio.* Lexington: UP of Kentucky, 1992. Print.

Dixon, Wheeler Winston. *The Early Film Criticism of François Truffaut.* Bloomington: Indiana UP, 1993. Print.

———. "Fast Worker: The Films of Sam Newfield." *Senses of Cinema* 45 (2007). Web.

———. "Interview with Budd Boetticher." *Film Talk: Directors at Work.* Ed. Wheeler Winston Dixon. New Brunswick, N.J.: Rutgers UP, 2007. 38–57. Print.

———. *Lost in the Fifties: Recovering Phantom Hollywood.* Carbondale: Southern Illinois UP, 2005. Print.

Dixon, Wheeler Winston, and Gwendolyn Audrey Foster. *A Short History of Film.* New Brunswick, N.J.: Rutgers UP, 2008. Print.

Doherty, Thomas. *Cold War, Cool Medium: Television, McCarthyism and American Culture.* New York: Columbia UP, 2003. Print.

Donati, William. *Ida Lupino: A Biography.* Lexington: UP of Kentucky, 1996. Print.

Eames, John Douglas. *The MGM Story.* New York: Crown, 1979. Print.

Eisner, Lotte. *Fritz Lang.* New York: Da Capo, 1986. Print.

Eliot, Marc. *Walt Disney: Hollywood's Dark Prince.* Secaucus, N.J.: Carol Publishing, 1993. Print.

Evans, Robert. *The Kid Stays in the Picture.* New York: Hyperion, 1994. Print.

Eyman, Scott. *Lion of Hollywood: The Life and Legend of Louis B. Mayer.* New York: Simon and Schuster, 2005. Print.

Fabrikant, Geraldine. "The MCA Sale: The Deal: Seagram Puts the Finishing Touches on Its $5.7 Billion Acquisition of MCA." *New York Times* April 10, 1995. Web.

Fernett, Gene. *Hollywood's Poverty Row.* Satellite Beach, Fla.: Coral Reef, 1973. Print.

Finler, Joel W. *The Hollywood Story.* New York: Crown, 1988. Print.

Fleming, Michael. *From Amalgamated Morons to American Icons: The Three Stooges—An Illustrated History.* New York: Doubleday, 1999. Print.

Freedland, Michael. *Gregory Peck.* New York: William Morrow, 1980. Print.

Friedman, David F., with Don DeNevi. *A Youth in Babylon: Confessions of a Trash-Film King.* Buffalo: Prometheus, 1990. Print.

Friedrich, Otto. *City of Nets: A Portrait of Hollywood in the 1940s.* New York: Harper and Row, 1986. Print.

Gabler, Neal. *An Empire of Their Own: How the Jews Invented Hollywood.* New York: Crown, 1988. Print.

———. *Walt Disney: The Triumph of the American Imagination.* New York: Knopf, 2006. Print.

Gomery, Douglas. "Hollywood's Business." *Wilson Quarterly* 10.3 (Summer 1986): 42–57. Print.

———. *The Hollywood Studio System.* New York: St. Martin's, 1986. Print.

———. "Who Killed Hollywood?" *Wilson Quarterly* 15.3 (Summer 1991): 106–12. Print.

Gordon, William A. *The Ultimate Hollywood Tour Book.* Lake Forest, Calif.: North Ridge Books, 2010. Print.

Griffith, Richard, and Arthur Mayer. *The Movies.* Rev. ed. New York: Simon and Schuster, 1970. Print.

Guild, Leo. *Zanuck, Hollywood's Last Tycoon.* New York: Holloway House, 1970. Print.

Hallowell, John. "Hollywood Still Is Her Town But No One Knows She's There." *St. Petersburg Times* June 23, 1968: 5D. Web.

Harmetz, Aljean. *Round Up the Usual Suspects: The Making of Casablanca—Bogart, Bergman, and World War II.* New York: Hyperion, 1992. Print.

Harrison, Ian. *The Book of Lasts.* London: Cassell, 2005. Print.

Haver, Ronald. *David O. Selznick's Hollywood.* New York: Random House, 1980. Print.

Heimann, Jim. *50s All-American Ads.* Koln, Germany: Taschen, 2001. Print.

Higham, Charles. *Merchant of Dreams: Louis B. Mayer, MGM, and the Secret Hollywood.* New York: Donald I. Fine, 1993. Print.

Hirschhorn, Clive. *The Universal Story.* New York: Crown, 1983. Print.

Hoberman, Jim. *An Army of Phantoms: American Movies and the Making of the Cold War.* New York: New Press, 2011. Print.

Hodgins, Eric. "Amid Ruins of Empire, a New Hollywood Arises." *Life* June 10, 1957: 146–66. Print.

Howard, Moe. *Moe Howard and the Three Stooges.* New York: Citadel, 1977. Print.

Hurst, Richard Maurice. *Republic Studios: Between Poverty Row and the Majors.* Updated ed. Metuchen, N.J.: Scarecrow, 2007. Print.

Jewell, Richard B., and Vernon Harbin. *The RKO Story.* New York: Crown, 1982. Print.

Jones, G. William. *Black Cinema Treasures: Lost and Found.* Denton: U of North Texas P, 1991. Print.

Kashner, Sam, and Jennifer MacNair. *The Bad and the Beautiful: Hollywood in the Fifties*. New York: Norton, 2002. Print.

Katz, Ephraim. *The Film Encyclopedia*. 4th ed., rev. Fred Klein and Ronald Dean Nolan. New York: Harper Resource, 2001. Print.

Kobal, John. *Rita Hayworth: Portrait of a Love Goddess*. New York: Berkley, 1977. Print.

Krebs, Albin. "Adolph Zukor Is Dead at 103: Built Paramount Movie Empire." *New York Times* June 11, 1976. Web.

Lasky, Jesse L., with Don Weldon. *I Blow My Own Horn*. Garden City, N.Y.: Doubleday, 1957. Print.

Leibovitz, Liel. "Gentlemen Prefer Blondes: Why Jewish Producers Kept Jewish Women Off Stage and Screen." *Tablet* October 20, 2009. Web.

LeRoy, Mervyn, with Dick Kleiner. *Mervyn LeRoy: Take One*. New York: Hawthorn, 1974. Print.

Levy, Emanuel. *Vincente Minnelli: Hollywood's Dark Dreamer*. New York: St. Martin's, 2009. Print.

Linet, Beverly. *Star Crossed: The Story of Robert Walker and Jennifer Jones*. New York: G. P. Putnam's Sons, 1985. Print.

Lyons, Arthur. *Death on the Cheap: The Lost B Movies of Film Noir*. New York: Da Capo, 2000. Print.

Macnab, Geoffrey. *J. Arthur Rank and the British Film Industry*. London: Routledge, 1993. Print.

Mallory, Michael. *Universal Studios Monsters: A Legacy of Horror*. New York: Universe, 2009. Print.

Marshall, Wendy L. *William Beaudine: From Silents to Television*. Lanham, Md.: Scarecrow, 2005. Print.

Martin, Len D. *The Allied Artists Checklist: The Feature Films and Short Subjects, 1947–1978*. Jefferson, N.C.: McFarland, 1993. Print.

McCarthy, Todd, and Charles Flynn, eds. *Kings of the Bs: Working within the Hollywood System*. New York: Dutton, 1975. Print.

McDougal, Dennis. *The Last Mogul: Lew Wasserman, MCA, and the Hidden History of Hollywood*. New York: Crown, 1998. Print.

McLafferty, Gerry. *Elvis Presley in Hollywood: Celluloid Sell Out*. London: Robert Hale, 1989. Print.

Mills, Michael. "Blacklist: A Different Look at the 1947 HUAC Hearings." *Moderntimes*.com. Web.

Moldea, Dan E. *Dark Victory: Ronald Reagan, MCA, and the Mob*. New York: Viking, 1986. Print.

Mordden, Ethan. *The Hollywood Studios: House-Style in the Golden Age of the Movies*. New York: Knopf, 1988. Print.

Mosley, Leonard. *Zanuck: The Rise and Fall of Hollywood's Last Tycoon.* Boston: Little, Brown, 1984. Print.

"NBC and Vivendi Universal Entertainment Unite to Create NBC Universal." *CNBC Europe,* April 10, 2007. Web.

Parish, James Robert. *The Hollywood Book of Death.* New York: McGraw-Hill, 2002. Print.

———. *The Hollywood Book of Scandals.* New York: McGraw-Hill, 2004. Print.

Peri, Don. *Working with Walt: Interviews with Disney Artists.* Jackson: UP of Mississippi, 2008. Print.

Rathgeb, Douglas L. *The Making of Rebel without a Cause.* Jefferson, N.C.: McFarland, 2004. Print.

Rebello, Stephen. *Alfred Hitchcock and the Making of Psycho.* New York: Dembner Books, 1990. Print.

"Robert Walker's Wife Is Granted Divorce." *Washington Post,* December 17, 1948: 26. Print.

Rocco, Serge. "The Decline of the Hollywood Studio System or the End of a Magic Concept." *Los Angeles Examiner* April 26, 2011. Web.

Ross, Lillian. *Picture.* New York: Modern Library, 1997. Print.

Rothman, William. "Hats Off for George Cukor!" In *Hollywood's Chosen People: The Jewish Experience in American Cinema,* ed. Daniel Bernardi, Murray Pomerance, and Hava Tirosh-Samuelson. Detroit: Wayne State UP, 2012. Print.

Sayre, Nora. *Running Time: Films of the Cold War.* New York: Dial, 1982. Print.

Schatz, Thomas. *The Genius of the System: Hollywood Filmmaking in the Studio Era.* New York: Pantheon, 1988. Print.

Schickel, Richard, and George Perry. *You Must Remember This: The Warner Bros. Story.* Philadelphia: Running Press, 2008. Print.

Shepherd, Donald, Robert Slatzer, and David Grayson. *Duke: The Life and Times of John Wayne.* New York: Citadel, 2002. Print.

Shorris, Sylvia, and Marion Abbott Bundy. *Talking Pictures with the People Who Made Them.* New York: New Press, 1994. Print.

Silke, James R. *Here's Looking at You, Kid: 50 Years of Fighting, Working, and Dreaming at Warner Bros.* Boston, Little, Brown, 1976. Print.

Sklar, Robert. *Movie-Made America.* New York: Vintage, 1989. Print.

Sperling, Cass Warner, Cork Millner, and Jack Warner Jr. *The Brothers Warner: The Intimate Story of a Hollywood Studio Family Dynasty.* Burbank, Calif.: Warner Bros., 2008. Print.

Spoto, Donald. *The Dark Side of Genius: The Life of Alfred Hitchcock.* Boston: Little, Brown, 1983. Print.

Sullivan, George. *Quotable Hollywood: The Lowdown from America's Film Capital.* New York: Barnes and Noble, 2001. Print.

Thomas, Bob. *Clown Prince of Hollywood: The Antic Life and Times of Jack L. Warner.* New York: McGraw-Hill, 1990. Print.

———. *King Cohn: The Life and Times of Harry Cohn.* New York: G. P. Putnam's, 1967. Print.

Thomson, David. *Showman: The Life of David O. Selznick.* New York: Knopf, 1992. Print.

Usai, Paolo Cherchi. *The Death of Cinema: History, Culture Memory, and the Digital Dark Age.* London: BFI, 2001. Print.

Vaughn, Robert. *Only Victims: A Study of Show Business Blacklisting.* New York: G. P. Putnam's, 1972. Print.

"Vivendi Sells $2 Billion Stake in NBC to G. E." *New York Times,* September 27, 2010. Web.

Warner, Jack Jr. "Foreword." In *The Brothers Warner: The Intimate Story of a Hollywood Studio Family Dynasty* by Cass Warner Sperling, Cork Millner, and Jack Warner Jr. Burbank, Calif.: Warner Bros., 2008. x–xii. Print.

Wasson, Sam. *Fifth Avenue, 5 A.M.: Audrey Hepburn, Breakfast at Tiffany's, and the Dawn of the Modern Woman.* New York: Harper, 2010. Print.

Wayne, Gary. "Universal Studios Hollywood Studio Tour and Theme Park." *Seeing Stars: The Ultimate Guide to Celebrities and Hollywood.* May 30, 2011. Web.

Wiseman, John B. "Darryl F. Zanuck and the Failure of *One World,* 1943–1949." *Historical Journal of Film, Radio, and Television* 7.3 (1987): 279–87. Print.

Wu, Tim. *The Master Switch: The Rise and Fall of Information Empires.* New York: Knopf, 2010. Print.

Zukor, Adolph, with Dale Kramer. *The Public Is Never Wrong: The Autobiography of Adolph Zukor.* New York: G. P. Putnam's Sons, 1953. Print.

INDEX

About the Author

Wheeler Winston Dixon is the Ryan Professor of Film Studies, coordinator of the Film Studies Program, and professor of English at the University of Nebraska, Lincoln. With Gwendolyn Audrey Foster he is editor in chief of the *Quarterly Review and Film and Video.* His newest books are *A History of Horror* (Rutgers University Press, 2010), *Film Noir and the Cinema of Paranoia* (Rutgers University Press, 2009), and *A Short History of Film* (with Gwendolyn Audrey Foster; Rutgers University Press, 2008).